PUBLICATIONS OF THE NEWTON INSTITUTE

Real-time Computer Vision

Publications of the Newton Institute

Edited by P. Goddard
Deputy Director, Isaac Newton Institute for Mathematical Sciences

The Isaac Newton Institute of Mathematical Sciences of the University of Cambridge exists to stimulate research in all branches of the mathematical sciences, including pure mathematics, statistics, applied mathematics, theoretical physics, theoretical computer science, mathematical biology and economics. The four six-month long research programmes it runs each year bring together leading mathematical scientists from all over the world to exchange ideas through seminars, teaching and informal interaction.

Associated with the programmes are two types of publication. The first contains lecture courses, aimed at making the latest developments accessible to a wider audience and providing an entry to the area. The second contains proceedings of workshops and conferences focusing on the most topical aspects of the subjects.

REAL-TIME COMPUTER VISION

edited by
Christopher M. Brown
University of Rochester

and

Demetri Terzopoulos
University of Toronto

CAMBRIDGE
UNIVERSITY PRESS

CAMBRIDGE
UNIVERSITY PRESS

University Printing House, Cambridge CB2 8BS, United Kingdom

Cambridge University Press is part of the University of Cambridge.

It furthers the University's mission by disseminating knowledge in the pursuit of education, learning and research at the highest international levels of excellence.

www.cambridge.org
Information on this title: www.cambridge.org/9780521472784

© Cambridge University Press 1994

First published 1994

A catalogue record for this publication is available from the British Library

ISBN 978-0-521-47278-4 Hardback

Contents

Preface

From July to December 1993, the recently-founded Isaac Newton Institute for Mathematical Sciences in Cambridge, England, sponsored a programme on *Computer Vision*. Computer vision is a rapidly evolving field concerned with the study of vision using the ideas and methods of computation. Throughout most of its near three-decade history, the field has maintained strong ties to applied mathematics. The organization of the six month programme under the auspices of the Institute reflects the enthusiasm in the vision community for a larger infusion of mathematical ideas and methods leading ultimately to feasible vision algorithms.

The programme on Computer Vision was organized by Andrew Blake and Brian Ripley of Oxford University and David Mumford of Harvard University. Two weeks of lectures on real-time vision were organized by Andrew Blake, Demetri Terzopoulos, Roger Brockett (Harvard), and Christopher Brown. The chapters in this volume are based on selected lectures delivered during those two weeks in July 1993.

The Isaac Newton Institute was conceived with the aim of providing an environment for maximal interaction with minimal distraction for visiting scientists. The Institute's staff, headed by Peter Goddard, FRS, indeed provided a welcoming and supportive environment for the succession of vision researchers who stayed for varying amounts of time during the six months.

This volume would not have been possible without the active support of the Isaac Newton Institute. We thank Andrew Blake for encouraging us to edit the volume and all the authors, whose names are listed at the end of the book, for contributing chapters. George Ferguson and Liudvikas Bukys of the University of Rochester provided assistance with typesetting issues, as did Cambridge University Press.

CB gratefully acknowledges the financial support of the United States National Science Foundation (IRI-9202816) and Advanced Research Projects Agency (contract MDA972-92-J-1012).

DT gratefully acknowledges the financial support of the Canadian Institute for Advanced Research, the Natural Sciences and Engineering Research Council of Canada, the Institute for Robotics and Intelligent Systems, and the ARK (Autonomous Robot for a Known environment) Project, which receives its funding from PRECARN Associates Inc., Industry Canada, the National Research Council of Canada, Technology Ontario, Ontario Hydro Technologies, and Atomic Energy of Canada Limited.

Introduction

Real time computer vision (RTCV) refers to the computer analysis of dynamic scenes at rates sufficiently high to effect practical visually-guided control or decision-making in everyday situations. This means that the relevant visual information must be extracted several times a second, say from 10 to 30 Hz. RTCV has recently become possible because of technical advances, primarily in raw processor speed and secondarily through special-purpose vision hardware such as frame grabbers and pipelined low-level image analysis systems, microcontrollers and small powerful motors, and miniature cameras. This book is mostly devoted to the algorithmic side of RTCV, with occasional references to the underlying technology and ideology substrate.

The Real-Time Revolution

The real-time computer vision revolution has been nearly universal; it is hard to find a computer vision laboratory today without a multi-ocular computer-controlled "head" (Chapter 5), vision-guided autonomous roving vehicle (Chapters 8 and 9), or hand-eye system (Chapter 7). While the underlying technology supporting RTCV is worthy of study in its own right and continues to evolve at a rapid rate, equally fascinating is the wide range of philosophical positions and analytic techniques that have been inspired and enabled by the real-time technology. RTCV is neutral about the various ideological divisions [35] between reconstructionist vision (e.g. [22, 19, 44]) animate or purposive vision (e.g. [16, 4, 1, 5, 6]), and behaviourist vision [11]. RTCV can support reflexive behaviours (Chapter 8), active exploration (Chapter 5), or three-dimensional reconstruction (Chapter 6) equally well. Obviously, RTCV is crucial to the thriving "active vision" paradigm, which has inspired international workshops, special issues, and books [25, 9, 29, 2, 3, 32, 33].

Several basic techniques, some well known for decades in other contexts, and some relatively new, are needed for RTCV. Important topics for the RTCV researcher to master are *estimation, affine geometry, dynamic modeling*, and *control*. The traditional computer vision topics of *clustering, feature-finding*, and *recovery of three-dimensional scene parameters* all remain important, but RTCV inspires new approaches. Each chapter in this volume integrates a number of these topics, and others as well, into a coherent story. Table 0.1 lists those topics that are most emphasized in the chapters to follow, although it does not do justice to the range of topics covered in each chapter.

The organization of the volume does not reflect the underlying techniques at the low level represented by Table 0.1, many of which are shared over several chapters. Rather the chapters are divided into three parts according to common characteristics. The chapters in the *Visual Tracking* part (Chapters 1,2,3) have in common the ability to track image objects in a manner that is not critically dependent on the domain of the scene. In Chapter 1 the goal is the tracking itself, while in Chapters 2 and 3 higher-level applica-

Topic / Chapter	1	2	3	4	5	6	7	8	9
Estimation	×	×	×	×		×			
Affine Geometry	×	×			×		×		
Dynamic Models	×				×	×	×	×	
Control			×			×	×	×	×
Hybrid Systems					×			×	×
Clusters, Features	×	×	×	×	×				
3-D Recovery		×			×	×	×		

Table 0.1
Chapter emphases.

tions are subserved by the tracking capability. The *Model-Based Vision and Exploration* part (Chapters 4,5,6) presents techniques that take advantage more of the characteristics of particular scene domains. Finally, the *Visual Control* part (Chapters 7,8,9) explores various aspects of visually guided motor control.

The remainder of the introduction is a brief discussion about estimation, affine geometry, and dynamic models.

Estimation

By its nature real-time computer vision deals with the incremental acquisition, processing, and fusion of information. The extensive literature on estimation, filtering, and prediction for the on-line processing of time series (e.g. [15, 7]) was immediately recognized as foundational for RTCV techniques, both for purely visual processing and in control applications. Off-line processing of visual information (e.g. least-squares estimation) gave way to various forms of recursive processing (e.g. recursive least-squares), most notably to the family of *Kalman filtering* techniques based on linear dynamic system and observation models and to stochastic error models. Almost every paper in this volume uses Kalman filtering or a related technique, and familiarity with these methods is now a *sine qua non* for RTCV.

A recursive estimation technique receives observations sequentially, and can maintain a current estimate that can be used to predict the next observation and state. The Kalman filter extends recursive least-squares estimation to *time-varying* quantities, and has the advantage of computing an ongoing measure of its confidence in the estimate. The Kalman filter can be used to estimate the current state (filtering) given past observations, or improve earlier estimates (smoothing) (Chapter 6), or can be used to estimate future states (prediction). It can provide a principled choice of temporal and spatial processing scales (Chapter 1). Variants of the Kalman filter exist for continuous and discrete, linear and nonlinear dynamic systems. In its simplest form, the Kalman filter's dynamic model is "steady"; constant-velocity and constant-acceleration models are common, with actual deviations from these conditions being accommodated by the noise model. If the noise properties of the observed system and the observer are also unchanging, Kalman filtering simplifies further; with a constant-velocity assumption, the result is an $\alpha - \beta$ filter. If the system to be estimated has a nonlinear model, the Kalman filter equations can be applied to a linearized model around the estimated state, yielding the "extended Kalman filter". Both continuous and discrete Kalman filter equations are computationally realizable, and several practical computational issues, such as numerical stability and computational efficiency, have been treated in the literature.

Although they are not represented in this book, auto-regressive and moving average (ARMA) filters have been used successfully in predictive roles in computer vision [45]. These estimators (for instance, the lattice filters) do not have prior explicit system or noise models, but they are adaptive in the sense that they can "learn" coefficients for a simple tapped delay line filter implementation [18, 41, 17]. These coefficients encode information equivalent to (and convertible into) the power spectrum or autocorrelation of the signal-generating process, so these filters are based in the mathematics of stochastic, stationary signal-generating processes. Like Kalman filtering, their predictions are optimal in that the residuals (or innovations) are uncorrelated. Such an estimator, unlike a constant-velocity or constant-acceleration Kalman filter, can predict nonlocal signal variations such as periodicity.

Affine Geometry

The computational realities and time constraints of RTCV have been influential in reversing a previous trend of ever-increasing mathematical sophistication and generality in modeling the imaging process. In much influential early work (e.g. [19]), orthographic projection was assumed for mathematical tractability — the relation between image properties and physical properties did not vary over the image. Gradually several aspects of the imaging model became generalized. First, affine models ("weak perspective" and "paraperspective"), were used to capture the effects of object size diminution with distance and shearing due to off-axis lines of sight; not captured was true perspective distortion that turns planar parallelograms into trapezoids in the image. Full perspective (and projective) models are still a topic of intense investigation; a recent example is work on projective invariants [24].

In a RTCV context, *affine models* of projection are currently the most popular, and weak perspective has been reinstated as a model of necessary and sufficient power and computational properties. As with Kalman filtering, familiarity with affine models and their attendant geometric aspects and constraints is necessary for the RTCV researcher (Chapters 1, 2, 5, and 7).

Dynamic Models

Dynamic Models of one sort or another are a natural companion to RTCV, which necessarily deals with dynamic domains. First, the earlier, static 2-

D and 3-D models developed for off-line computer vision applications had
to be extended to accommodate time-varying behaviour. Physicists have,
of course, formulated mathematical models for this purpose. Techniques
for synthesizing realistic renditions of the shapes and motions of physical
objects according to physical laws are under development in related areas
such as computer graphics (e.g. [36]), and so it is natural to incorporate
similar physical models into RTCV systems.

Dynamic 3D models of objects that exhibit physical laws of continuity,
inertia, dissipation, etc., as formalized by theories such as Lagrangian mechanics, have been used for visual estimation of object shape and motion
[39, 37, 26, 37, 23], and this is especially useful for nonrigid motion analysis.
Further, the projection of a physically meaningful object is likely to obey
similar laws. Consequently, it makes sense to attribute physical models to
time-varying image boundaries of coherent scene objects. Physical models
such as elastic splines under tension and have been used in the guise of
dynamic contours, or *snakes* [20, 9].

A key formalism that paves the road towards practical RTCV applications
is the notion that physical models may be used as system models in recursive
estimators, including Kalman filters, for on-line visual data analysis [34, 38,
23]. Filtering, control, and affine techniques all come into play in algorithms
that manipulate these simulated physical systems. Dynamic models have
been extended in many ways to give them memory, render them more stable,
and so on (Chapters 1 and 7), and this area will continue to be a central
one in RTCV.

Control

RTCV provides a rich input stream for *control* of mechanisms. and many
contributions in RTCV are in the areas of control. Tracking ability (Chapters 1, 2, 3, 4, 5, 9) is necessary in other applications, such as manipulator
control (Chapter 7). Vision researchers have had to confront control issues
such as delay [13, 12, 28] and proper mode selection (Chapter 8), and have
designed controllers using traditional and highly nonlinear, hybrid techniques (Chapters 8 and 9).

"Classical" behaviourist architectures eschew any internal representation
of the outside world, and thus make do with independent simple sensors,
each associated with a single reflex [10, 11]. The idea of a flexible vision
capability that can support several different activities does not fit well into
such a scheme. For example, it seems natural for an autonomous system to
use the same input image sequence, in parallel, to dodge an obstacle, locate
itself via a landmark, and gauge its speed by optic flow. RTCV with more
sophisticated representation-generating capabilities naturally lends itself to
more complex *hybrid* control schemes (Chapters 8 and 9).

The systems in which RTCV is ultimately to be embedded continue to
increase in complexity and sophistication. Applications in intelligent high-
ways, autonomous vehicles, cooperating groups of vehicles, automated mon-

itoring and surveillance are not far off. Systems implementing such applications have high-level goals — vision (say object recognition or 3-D reconstruction) for them is a means to an end, not an end in itself. The
application system must control its resources, deciding where to point the
camera, what visual operation to use, what spatial resolution to use, where
to move, how much computational resource to allocate to what parallel sub-
task, in short, *what to do next*. The necessary planning, decision-making,
and resource allocation issues bring in other branches of computer science
and artificial intelligence, including real time operating systems, operations
research, scheduling and cost-benefit analysis, plausible and inexact reasoning, AI planning and knowledge representation [27, 14, 42, 43, 30, 31, 8].
Optimal solutions are not computationally feasible, and formalisms for analyzing the more realistic *satisficing* systems are not well developed. Certainly the topic of organizing and regulating a system of interacting reflex
behaviours is current and wide open (Chapter 8) [21]: how does one guard
against deadlocks, instabilities, singularities, etc.? The techniques for hybrid control will become increasingly important as the demand increases for
RTCV as a component of complex, parallel, decision-making sensori-motor
systems.

References

[1] Y. Aloimonos, A. Bandyopadhyay, and I. Weiss. Active vision. *International Journal of Computer Vision*, 1(4):333-356, 1988.

[2] Y. Aloimonos. Special issue on active perception. *Computer Vision, Graphics, and Image Processing*, 56(1), July 1992.

[3] Y. Aloimonos, editor. *Active Perception*. Lawrence Erlbaum, 1993.

[4] R. Bajcsy. Active perception. *IEEE Proceedings*, 76(8):996–1005, August 1988.

[5] D. H. Ballard. Animate vision. *Artificial Intelligence Journal*, 48:57–86, 1991.

[6] D. H. Ballard and C. M. Brown. Principles of animate vision. *Computer Vision, Graphics, and Image Processing*, 56(1):3–21, July 1992.

[7] Y. Bar-Shalom and T. E. Fortmann. *Tracking and Data Association*. Academic Press, 1988.

[8] T. E. Bihari and K. Schwan. Dynamic adaption of real-time software. *ACM Transactions on Computer Systems*, 9(2):143–174, May 1991.

[9] A. Blake and A. Yuille, editors. *Active Vision*. MIT Press, 1992.

[10] V. Braitenberg. *Vehicles: Experiments in synthetic psychology*. MIT Press, 1974.

[11] R. Brooks. Intelligence without reason. In *Proceedings: International Joint Conference on Artificial Intelligence*, 1991.

[12] C. M. Brown. Gaze controls with interactions and delays. *IEEE Transactions on Systems, Man, and Cybernetics, in press,* IEEE-TSMC20(2):518–527, May 1990.

[13] C. M. Brown. Prediction and cooperation in gaze control. *Biological Cybernetics,* 63:61–70, 1990.

[14] T. L. Dean and M. P. Wellman. *Planning and Control.* Morgan Kaufmann, 1991.

[15] A. C. Gelb. *Applied Optimal Estimation.* The MIT Press, 1974.

[16] J. J. Gibson. *The Ecological Approach to Visual Perception.* Houghton-Mifflin, Boston, 1979.

[17] G. C. Goodwin and K. S. Sin. *Adaptive Filtering, Prediction and Control.* Prentice-Hall, 1984.

[18] S. Haykin. *Modern Filters.* MacMillan, 1989.

[19] B. K. P. Horn. *Robot Vision.* MIT-Press, McGraw-Hill, 1986.

[20] M. Kass, A. Witkin, and D. Terzopoulos. Snakes: Active contour models. *International Journal of Computer Vision,* 1:321–331, 1988.

[21] R. A. McCallum. Short-term memory in visual routines. In *Working Notes of AAAI Spring Symposium Series, "Toward Physical Interaction and Manipulation",* March 1994.

[22] D. Marr. *Vision.* W.H. Freeman, San Francisco, 1982.

[23] D. Metaxas and D. Terzopoulos. Shape and nonrigid motion estimation through physics-based synthesis. *IEEE Transactions on Pattern Analysis and Machine Intelligence,* 15(6):580–591, 1993.

[24] J.L. Mundy and A. Zisserman, editors. *Geometric Invariants in Computer Vision.* MIT Press, 1992.

[25] R. C. Nelson. Vision as intelligent behavior – an introduction to special issue on machine vision research at the University of Rochester. *International Journal of Computer Vision,* 7(1):5–9, November 1991.

[26] A. Pentland and B. Horowitz. Recovery of Non-rigid Motion and Structure. *IEEE Trans. Pattern Analysis and Machine Intelligence,* 13(7):730–742, 1991.

[27] R. D. Rimey and C. M. Brown. Control of selective perception using bayes nets and decision theory. *International Journal of Computer Vision,* 12(2,3):173–208, April 1994.

[28] P. M. Sharkey, D. W. Murray, S. Vandevelde, I. D. Reid, and P. F. McLauchlan. A modular head/eye platform for real-time reactive vision. *Mechatronics,* 3(4):517–535, 1993. To appear.

[29] A. K. Sood and H. Wechsler, editors. *Active Perception and Robot Vision.* Springer Verlag, 1992.

[30] J. Stankovic and K. Ramamritham. The design of the spring kernel. *Proceedings of the Real–Time Systems Symposium*, pages 146–157, December 1987.

[31] J. A. Stankovic. Real-time operating systems: What's wrong with today's systems and research issues. *Real-Time Systems Newsletter*, 8(1):1–9, 1992.

[32] M. J. Swain. Special issue on active vision: I. *International Journal of Computer Vision*, 11(2), October 1993.

[33] M. J. Swain and M. A. Stricker. Promising directions in active vision. *International Journal of Computer Vision*, 11(2):109–126, October 1993.

[34] R. Szeliski and D. Terzopoulos. Physically-Based and Probabilistic Modeling for Computer Vision. In *SPIE Vol. 1570 Geometric Methods in Computer Vision*, pages 140–152, San Diego, July 1991. Society of Photo-Optical Instrumentation Engineers.

[35] M. J. Tarr and M. J. Black. A computational and evolutionary perspective on the role of representation in vision (discourse). *Computer Vision, Graphics, and Image Processing*, 59(3), May 1994.

[36] D. Terzopoulos and K. Fleischer. Deformable models. *The Visual Computer*, 4(6):306–331, 1988.

[37] D. Terzopoulos and D. Metaxas. Dynamic 3D models with local and global deformations: Deformable superquadrics. *IEEE Transactions on Pattern Analysis and Machine Intelligence*, 13(7).:703–714, 1991.

[38] D. Terzopoulos and R. Szeliski. Tracking with Kalman snakes. In *Active Vision*, pages 3–20. MIT Press, Cambridge, MA, 1992.

[39] D. Terzopoulos, A. Witkin, and M. Kass. Constraints on deformable models: Recovering 3D shape and nonrigid motion. *Artificial Intelligence*, 36:91–123, 1988.

[40] Y.F. Wang and J.-F. Wang. Surface Reconstruction using Deformable Models with Interior and Boundary Constraints. *IEEE Trans. Pattern Analysis and Machine Intelligence*, 14(5):572–579, May 1992.

[41] B. Widrow and S. D. Stearns. *Adaptive Signal Processing*. Prentice-Hall, 1985.

[42] R. W. Wisniewski and C. M. Brown. Ephor, a run-time environment for parallel intelligent applications. In *Proceedings of The IEEE Workshop on Parallel and Distributed Real-Time Systems*, pages 51–60, Newport Beach, California, April 13-15, 1993.

[43] R. W. Wisniewski and C. M. Brown. An argument for a runtime layer in sparta design. In *Proceedings of The IEEE Workshop on Real-Time Operating Systems and Software*, page to appear, Seattle Wahington, May 18-19 1994.

[44] L. B. Wolff, S. A. Shafer, and G. E. Healey, editors. *Radiometry, Color, Shape Recovery (3 Vols.)*. Jones and Bartlett, 1992.

[45] Y. Zheng, J. E. W. Mayhew, S. A. Billings, and J. P. Frisby. Lattice predictor for 3-d vision and intelligent tracking. Technical report, University of Sheffield, 1991.

I Visual Tracking

1 A Framework for Spatio-Temporal Control in the Tracking of Visual Contours

Andrew Blake, Rupert Curwen, and Andrew Zisserman

1.1 Introduction

This chapter is concerned with the principles of tracking curves in motion, at video rate. This has many potential applications, for instance in biomedical image-analysis (e.g. [1]) in surveillance (e.g. [32]) and in autonomous vehicle navigation (e.g. [14]). Earlier versions of our tracker have been used in the control of a robot arm, supporting closed-loop tracking [5] and various aspects of hand-eye coordination [12, 6, 8, 2, 5]. A review of existing methods in curve-tracking can be found in [7]. Our aim here is to set out a framework for contour tracking as a relatively autonomous process, in which tracking behaviour is determined as a mathematical consequence of some natural assumptions about geometry and uncertainty.

The framework has evolved from the principles of the snake of Kass et al. (1987), which is an elastic model for shapes in motion that can be coupled to image features. The elastic framework has been shown to be approximately equivalent to a Kalman filter that can be derived from statistical assumptions about curves and their motion [33]. In fact such an elastic system can be equivalent to the steady state of a Kalman filter. Here, the Kalman filter formalism will be developed further.

It is efficient to represent curves parametrically with a low-dimensional basis rather than using a pixel-based representation, or a fine polygonal chain. Such a basis has been used for tracking solid models [34] and for image curves using B-splines [28, 12] and other parameterisations [31]. The B-spline representation is used in this chapter, though most of the results apply to any reasonable curve basis.

Another theme that is related to the snakes idea has been the representation of geometric prior information that can be incorporated into the tracker by means of a template. Templates — parametrised shapes — have been used effectively in non-dynamic shape-fitting processes [16, 18, 25, 4, 38]. Some include statistical learning of shape variations [18, 4]. Bookstein (1988) derives one method of elastic matching, with thin-plate splines, that allows affine transformations freely whilst allowing other deformations with some "reluctance".

On a practical note it has been shown recently that curve-trackers can run at video rate without special hardware. Although it was originally thought that convolution hardware was needed for low level image processing to support tracking, this has proven not to be the case. It has been demonstrated [22, 35, 14, 19, 5, 26, 37] by several researchers that tracking of rigid or deforming bodies is possible, often at frame-rate and with modest hardware.

Several significant advances are reported in this chapter. First templates are coupled into the dynamics of a real-time tracker with allowance for spatio-temporal uncertainty — both elastic deformability and temporal noise. Secondly, the statistical basis of the tracker is used to control spatio-temporal scale automatically and in a way that fits the progress of the tracking task. This is a considerable advance on previous approaches in which the spatial scale for feature search was set by hand. Mathematical analysis elucidates the operation of the spatio-temporal scaling mechanism and establishes that the tracker behaves stably. Thirdly, the coupling of template to tracker is made invariant to affine transformations of the template. This allows both for 3D rigid motion of a planar shape and for uncertainty in camera calibration. Fourthly, the template mechanism is extended, representing the template by a *subspace* of the tracker's state-space. It is shown that this mechanism subsumes the affine-invariant 2D template and generalises it to full 3D rigid motion of a non-planar shape. Variations on the structure of the subspace allow for constrained tracking — for example panning — and surprisingly for exploring, simultaneously and dynamically, more than one object-hypothesis.

1.2   State space representation

The tracking model assumes that the moving feature is a contour $(X(s,t), Y(s,t))$ which can be expressed parametrically in terms of time-varying control points $(X_n(t), Y_n(t))$, $n = 1, ..M$. State vectors are defined in terms of $\mathbf{X}, \mathbf{Y}$ where $\mathbf{X} = (X_1, .., X_M)^T$ and similarly for $\mathbf{Y}$. (Note that the notation will omit explicit reference to s, t where appropriate.) The aim of the chapter is to develop a tracker that is an estimate $(\hat{X}(s,t), \hat{Y}(s,t))$, expressed in terms of estimated state vectors $\hat{\mathbf{X}}(t), \hat{\mathbf{Y}}(t)$. The estimate is updated continually by reference to a visual feature $(X_f(s,t), Y_f(s,t))$ that is measured by searching in the vicinity of $(\hat{X}(s,t), \hat{Y}(s,t))$ as in Fig. 1.1.

1.2.1   B-spline

The mathematical framework of this chapter largely applies to any parametric representation for curves. Specifically we will refer to the parametric B-spline representation, of which quadratic and cubic are particularly useful. A B-spline curve $(X(s), Y(s))$ of degree d is defined parametrically for $0 \le s \le N$, where $M = N$ for closed curves and $M = N + d$ for open ones (with appropriate variations where multiple knots are used to vary curve

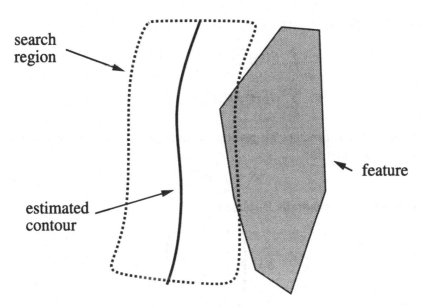

Figure 1.1
The basic tracker is an estimated contour updated continuously using features that
fall within its search region.

continuity):

$$X(s) = H(s)\mathbf{X}, \tag{1.1}$$

where

$$H(s+n) = \mathbf{s}^T B_{n+1} G_{n+1}, \quad 0 \leq s \leq 1, \; 0 \leq n < N \tag{1.2}$$

$\mathbf{s}^T = (1, s, .., s^d)$, B_n is a standard B-spline matrix [15, 3] and G_n is a $d \times M$
matrix that simply selects d consecutive control points:

$$G_n\mathbf{X} = (X_n, .., X_{n+d})^T, 1 \leq n \leq N.$$

Note that, for a closed curve, control point indices are evaluated modulo
M. The definition for $Y(s)$ is similar.

1.2.2   State space metric

Uncertainty in state space will be treated in terms of "Mahalanobis distance" [30] which is a norm $\|..\|$ on $\mathbf{X}, \mathbf{Y}$ compatible with true distance
measure in the image plane. We therefore define the norm so that:

$$\|\mathbf{X}\|^2 = \int_{s=0}^{N} X(s)^2 \, ds$$

or, equivalently:

$$\|\mathbf{X}\|^2 = \mathbf{X}^T \mathcal{H} \mathbf{X}, \tag{1.3}$$

where the "metric" matrix $\mathcal{H}$ is

$$\mathcal{H} = \int_0^N H(s)^T H(s)\, ds \quad \text{which, from (1.2)},\tag{1.4}$$

$$= \sum_{n=1}^N G_n^T B_n^T S B_n G_n,\tag{1.5}$$

a form that is convenient for practical computation of $\mathcal{H}$, and where S is the invertible matrix

$$S = \int_0^1 \mathbf{s}\mathbf{s}^T\, ds.\tag{1.6}$$

For instance, for quadratic B-splines:

$$S = \begin{pmatrix} 1 & \frac{1}{2} & \frac{1}{3} \\ \frac{1}{2} & \frac{1}{3} & \frac{1}{4} \\ \frac{1}{3} & \frac{1}{4} & \frac{1}{5} \end{pmatrix}.$$

The $\mathcal{H}$-matrices are sparse, becoming more so as the number N of spans increases. For closed contours the $\mathcal{H}$-matrix is a sparse circulant, for instance, for a quadratic spline with $N = 8$:

$$\mathcal{H} = \begin{pmatrix} 0.55 & 0.217 & 0.008 & 0. & 0. & 0. & 0.008 & 0.217 \\ 0.217 & 0.55 & 0.217 & 0.008 & 0. & 0. & 0. & 0.008 \\ 0.008 & 0.217 & 0.55 & 0.217 & 0.008 & 0. & 0. & 0. \\ 0. & 0.008 & 0.217 & 0.55 & 0.217 & 0.008 & 0. & 0. \\ 0. & 0. & 0.008 & 0.217 & 0.55 & 0.217 & 0.008 & 0. \\ 0. & 0. & 0. & 0.008 & 0.217 & 0.55 & 0.217 & 0.008 \\ 0.008 & 0. & 0. & 0. & 0.008 & 0.217 & 0.55 & 0.217 \\ 0.217 & 0.008 & 0. & 0. & 0. & 0.008 & 0.217 & 0.55 \end{pmatrix}\tag{1.7}$$

For an open curve, $\mathcal{H}$ is banded, pentadiagonal for quadratic splines, as shown here for the case $N = 4$:

$$\mathcal{H} = \begin{pmatrix} 0.2 & 0.117 & 0.017 & 0. & 0. & 0. \\ 0.117 & 0.333 & 0.208 & 0.008 & 0. & 0. \\ 0.017 & 0.208 & 0.55 & 0.217 & 0.008 & 0. \\ 0. & 0.008 & 0.217 & 0.55 & 0.208 & 0.017 \\ 0. & 0. & 0.008 & 0.208 & 0.333 & 0.117 \\ 0. & 0. & 0. & 0.017 & 0.117 & 0.2 \end{pmatrix}\tag{1.8}$$

and heptadiagonal for cubic splines.

Lastly, given the norm $\|..\|$ it is natural also to define a compatible inner product $< .. >$ such that:

$$< \mathbf{X}, \mathbf{X}' > = \mathbf{X}^T \mathcal{H} \mathbf{X}'.\tag{1.9}$$

1.3   Visual features

The feature $((X_f(s,t), Y_f(s,t))$ is defined by searching along fixed lines radiating from the current estimate $(\hat{X}(s,t), \hat{Y}(s,t))$. The lines may be unit normal vectors to the curve or, if a constrained tracker is required, along fixed parallel lines. Search occurs on a specified spatial scale (Fig. 1.1) defined by a search window, selecting a point of maximum contrast or other visual measure, as appropriate for the underlying object model. In our implementations, contrast is used. In practice, of course, $(X_f(s,t), Y_f(s,t))$ is not observed in its entirety but at sampled points s_i along the contour. Furthermore, in the interests of computational speed, contrast is examined at only three different points on each normal: on the curve and at the two extremes of an interval that is initially close to the full width of the search window. If one of the extremes has the highest contrast it is retained as the current $(X_f(s,t), Y_f(s,t))$. Otherwise the interval is halved in length and the process is repeated.

If the sampling is dense and uniform in s, it is a reasonable abstraction to model the measurement continuously and this will allow sufficient analysis to give some insight into the operation of our estimator as a control system. Similarly, although measurements are made at discrete times, they can usefully be regarded as continuous-time for the purposes of analysis. Then, assuming that sensor error is unbiased, homogeneous, isotropic and Gaussian, we have the following conditional p.d.f. (probability density function) for the measurement process:

$$p((X_f(s), Y_f(s))|(X(s), Y(s))) \propto$$

$$\exp -\frac{1}{2r} \int_0^N (X(s) - X_f(s))^2 + (Y(s) - Y_f(s))^2) \, ds \quad (1.10)$$

where r is a measurement variance constant (strictly, covariance spectral density — see [18]). As before, $(X(s), Y(s))$ is the *true* underlying position of the curve, as distinct from the *estimated* position $(\hat{X}(s), \hat{Y}(s))$.

Now the square error integral above can be re-expressed, using the fact that $X(s) = H(s)\mathbf{X}$, and completing the square:

$$\int_0^N (X(s) - X_f(s))^2 \, ds = ||\mathbf{X} - \mathbf{X}_f||^2 - ||\mathbf{X}_f||^2 + \int X_f(s)^2 \, ds \quad (1.11)$$

where $\mathbf{X}_f$ is the least-squares B-spline approximation to the feature:

$$\mathbf{X}_f = \mathcal{H}^{-1} \int_0^N H(s)^T X_f(s) \, ds, \quad (1.12)$$

and similarly for Y-terms. Now since the only term on the right of (1.11) that depends on $\mathbf{X}$ is $||\mathbf{X} - \mathbf{X}_f||^2$, the other terms being effectively constant, the conditional p.d.f. (1.10) can be expressed directly in terms of Mahalanobis distances:

$$p((X_f(s), Y_f(s))|(X(s), Y(s))) \propto \exp{-\frac{1}{2r}(||\mathbf{X}_f - \mathbf{X}||^2 + ||\mathbf{Y}_f - \mathbf{Y}||^2)} \quad (1.13)$$

and this depends on the feature $(X_f(s), Y_f(s))$ only via its B-spline approximation $(\mathbf{X}_f, \mathbf{Y}_f)$.

We can now regard a feature as a time varying measurement $(\mathbf{X}_f, \mathbf{Y}_f)$ in the joint state-space for the $\mathbf{X}, \mathbf{Y}$ processes. From (1.13) and (1.3), each of $\mathbf{X}_f$ and $\mathbf{Y}_f$ has covariance matrix

$$R = r\mathcal{H}^{-1}. \quad (1.14)$$

This abstraction of the sensor will be used for now to obtain analytic insights into performance. Later the modifications will be outlined that are required for real discrete measurements and due to the "aperture problem" [21] which allows only the normal component of displacement of $(X_f(s), Y_f(s))$ to be measured.

1.4   Stochastic dynamical model

A simple dynamical model is based on the assumption of uniform 2D motion with an additive Gaussian noise process representing randomly varying force applied continuously over time. In an augmented state-space of vectors $(\mathbf{X}, \dot{\mathbf{X}})^T$ this is expressed as a stochastic differential equation [18]

$$\frac{\mathrm{d}}{\mathrm{d}t} \begin{pmatrix} \mathbf{X} \\ \dot{\mathbf{X}} \end{pmatrix} = \begin{pmatrix} \dot{\mathbf{X}} \\ \mathbf{0} \end{pmatrix} + \begin{pmatrix} \mathbf{0} \\ \mathbf{w} \end{pmatrix} \quad (1.15)$$

where $\mathbf{w}(t)$ is a zero-mean, temporally uncorrelated Gaussian noise process. A similar equation applies for $\mathbf{Y}$, independently of the $\mathbf{X}$ process provided the noise process is assumed to be isotropic. Assuming an isotropic and homogeneous Gaussian distribution, and following similar reasoning to that used above for the measurement process, the covariance spectral density matrix for $\mathbf{w}$ is simply $q\mathcal{H}^{-1}$ where q is a variance (spectral density) constant.

1.4.1   Tracking filter

Under this simple model, one can build a standard continuous Kalman filter for the estimated contour $(\hat{\mathbf{X}}, \hat{\mathbf{Y}})$ of the form

$$\frac{\mathrm{d}}{\mathrm{d}t} \begin{pmatrix} \hat{\mathbf{X}} \\ \dot{\hat{\mathbf{X}}} \end{pmatrix} = \begin{pmatrix} \dot{\hat{\mathbf{X}}} \\ \mathbf{0} \end{pmatrix} + K(\mathbf{X}_f - \hat{\mathbf{X}}), \quad (1.16)$$

where $K(t)$ is the Kalman gain matrix, defined in terms of the covariance of the measurement process and the covariance $P(t) = E[(\mathbf{X} - \hat{\mathbf{X}})(\mathbf{X} - \hat{\mathbf{X}})^T]$ of the current state estimate:

$$K = PH^T R^{-1} \qquad (1.17)$$

and H is a measurement matrix:

$$H = (\ \mathbf{I} \quad \mathbf{0}\ ) \qquad (1.18)$$

representing the fact that the contour position $\mathbf{X}$ is measured, but not the velocity $\dot{\mathbf{X}}$.

1.4.2 Shape template

It remains to specify initial conditions for the filter. This is done by initialising the estimator to some fixed shape template which is defined to be a B-spline expressed as control point vectors $(\overline{\mathbf{X}}, \overline{\mathbf{Y}})$. Assuming, similarly to the measurement model, a spatially homogeneous and isotropic Gaussian prior distribution for the state $\mathbf{X}, \mathbf{Y}$ then, by similar reasoning, the prior distribution in the augmented state-space has covariance

$$P(0) = \begin{pmatrix} \alpha_1 \mathcal{H}^{-1} & 0 \\ 0 & \alpha_2 \mathcal{H}^{-1} \end{pmatrix}.$$

which serves as an initial condition for the Riccati equation [18] that specifies the evolution of $P(t)$ in a Kalman filter:

$$\frac{\mathrm{d}P}{\mathrm{d}t} = FP + PF^T + Q - KRK^T \qquad (1.19)$$

where, for constant velocity dynamics, the matrix F is

$$F = \begin{pmatrix} 0 & I \\ 0 & 0 \end{pmatrix} \qquad (1.20)$$

and $I, 0$ are the $M \times M$ identity and zero matrices, and where

$$Q = \begin{pmatrix} 0 & 0 \\ 0 & q\mathcal{H}^{-1} \end{pmatrix} \qquad (1.21)$$

is the plant-noise covariance spectral density matrix.

Now substituting a solution for $P(t)$ of the form

$$P(t) = \begin{pmatrix} p_{11}\mathcal{H}^{-1} & p_{12}\mathcal{H}^{-1} \\ p_{21}\mathcal{H}^{-1} & p_{22}\mathcal{H}^{-1} \end{pmatrix} \qquad (1.22)$$

into (1.19) and using (1.17) and the definitions (1.14) and (1.18) gives:

$$\frac{\mathrm{d}}{\mathrm{d}t} \begin{pmatrix} p_{11} & p_{12} \\ p_{21} & p_{22} \end{pmatrix} = \begin{pmatrix} 2p_{21} - p_{11}^2/r & p_{22} - p_{11}p_{12}/r \\ p_{22} - p_{11}p_{21}/r & q - p_{12}^2/r \end{pmatrix} \qquad (1.23)$$

with initial conditions

$$p_{11}(0) = \alpha_1, \; p_{22}(0) = \alpha_2, \; p_{12}(0) = p_{21}(0) = 0.$$

The Kalman gain in (1.17) is simply (the $\mathcal{H}$ terms cancelling):

$$K = \begin{pmatrix} k_1 I \\ k_2 I \end{pmatrix} \quad \text{where} \quad \begin{pmatrix} k_1 \\ k_2 \end{pmatrix} = \frac{1}{r} \begin{pmatrix} p_{11} \\ p_{21} \end{pmatrix}. \tag{1.24}$$

1.4.3   Tracking performance

The diagonal form of the Kalman gain means that the second order dynamics in state space (1.16) degenerate into a set of identical, independent 2nd order systems on each control point. This simple case arises because of the homogeneity of the measurement model. Non-trivial modal structure is created when measurements are inhomogeneous, for instance when part of the contour fails to lock onto a visual feature. However, the homogeneous case is useful for analysis as a guide to the stability and accuracy properties of the tracker. In the steady state, for instance, from (1.24) and taking $d/dt \equiv 0$ in (1.23):

$$\begin{pmatrix} k_1 \\ k_2 \end{pmatrix} = \begin{pmatrix} \sqrt{2}(q/r)^{\frac{1}{4}} \\ (q/r)^{\frac{1}{2}} \end{pmatrix}. \tag{1.25}$$

Now, in the steady state, the 2nd order systems have damping constant $\beta = k_1/2$ and natural frequency $\omega = \sqrt{k_2}$ so that, from (1.25), $\omega = \sqrt{2}\beta$, just underdamped relative to the critical damping condition $\beta = \omega$.

This means that tracking behaviour is good — fast but stable — regardless of the setting of the covariance parameters q, r. Furthermore, tracking is also accurate in the steady state. In fact tracking error is zero, in the steady state, for a constant velocity target, since

$$\hat{\mathbf{X}} = \mathbf{X}_f = \mathbf{V}t \text{ with } \mathbf{V} \text{ constant}$$

is a solution of (1.16).

1.5   Automatic control of spatiotemporal scale

Automatic control of spatial scale for search is achieved by applying a *validation gate* [2] in a spatially distributed fashion. In the isotropic case (isotropy is broken if measurements comprise only the normal component of displacement — see later), the filters for the $\mathbf{X}$ and $\mathbf{Y}$ processes are identical. A circular feature-search window (elliptical in the anisotropic case) of radius $2\rho(s,t)$ is constructed around each point on the curve where ρ^2 is

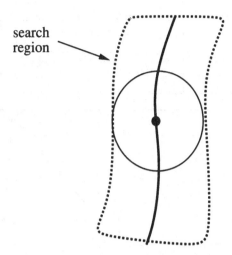

search
region

Figure 1.2
The search region is formed by sweeping an ellipse of uncertainty along the
estimated contour.

the positional variance of the current estimator at s:

$$\rho(s)^2 = H(s) \ P \ [H(s)]^T. \qquad (1.26)$$

Feature search is then performed along the normal to the estimated contour,
and within the window. The circle $\rho(s,t)$ can be pictured as sweeping along
the estimated contour to form an enclosing search region as in Fig. 1.2.

When P is also homogeneous, as in the previous section, its Riccati equation can be solved analytically to give some insight into the operation of
the scale control mechanism. The radius varies as $\rho(s)^2 \propto p_{11}(t)$ and $p_{11}(t)$
varies according to the differential equation (1.23) when a feature is present.
In fact it is also true that $\rho(s) \approx \sqrt{p_{11}}$, so the variation of ρ over time is
governed by the Riccati equation (1.23).

In the absence of a feature, when lock is lost (and assuming the whole
contour is unlocked), no measurements are made. This can be incorporated
into the Riccati equation (1.23) by regarding the measurement covariance
as infinite, and as $r \to \infty$, (1.23) becomes

$$\frac{d}{dt} \begin{pmatrix} p_{11} & p_{12} \\ p_{21} & p_{22} \end{pmatrix} = \begin{pmatrix} 2p_{21} & p_{22} \\ p_{22} & q \end{pmatrix}. \qquad (1.27)$$

which can be solved exactly to give

$$p_{11}(t) = p_{11}(0) + 2p_{12}(0)t + p_{22}(0)t^2 + \frac{1}{3}qt^3$$

so that asymptotically the search scale ρ grows as $t^{3/2}$. If at some time t,
assumed large so that (1.23) can be solved approximately, the whole feature

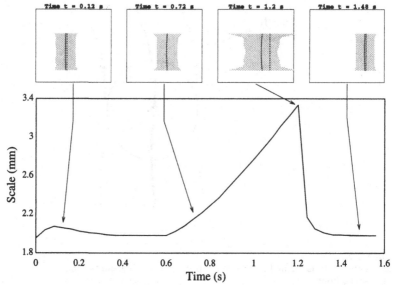

Figure 1.3
The time-course of spatial scale is illustrated here by applying the tracker to
simulated data. Spatial scale decays to a steady state value as tracking proceeds.
When the feature is lost, at $t = 0.6$s, spatial scale increases and theory predicts a
$t^{3/2}$ growth. Then the feature is recaptured at $t = 1.2$s and spatial scale decreases
again (theoretically inversely with t), once again reaching a steady state. Tracking
parameters for this simulation were $r = 2.0$deg^2.s and $q = 131$deg^2.s^{-3}, giving a
steady state scale of $\rho_\infty = 2.9$deg, in a total field of view of width 11.3deg.

locks on again, the search scale will contract again approximately as $\rho \propto 1/t$
until, asymptotically, it reaches the steady state scale of $\rho_\infty = 2^{1/4}(qr^3)^{1/8}$.
This behaviour is illustrated for a tracking contour with simulated data in
Fig. 1.3 and with real data in Fig. 1.4.

1.5.1   Automatic control of temporal scale

The Riccati mechanism takes care automatically also of temporal scale, the
effective memory of the tracker. The Kalman gain K has the dimensions
of inverse time and, in a multivariate system, governs the duration of the
negative exponential memory of each mode of the tracker. In the simple case
we are using for analysis, modes are degenerate and all have time constant
$\tau = 1/\beta$, where β is the damping constant defined above. Taking τ as the
characteristic time of the Kalman filter's negative exponential memory and,
using the definitions of β, k_1 above,

$$\tau = \frac{2r}{p_{11}} \approx \frac{2r}{\rho^2}$$

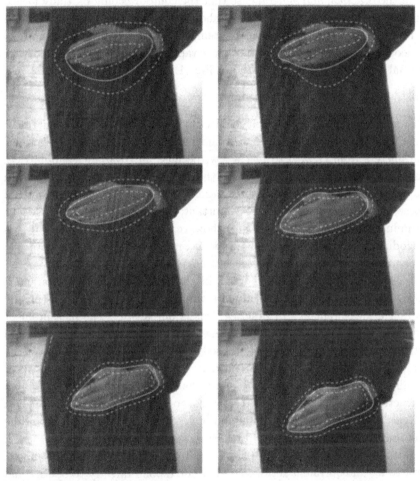

Figure 1.4
Frames are shown here at times $t = 0, 0.04, 0.08, 0.32, 0.56, 0.8$ seconds (raster order) in the tracking of a moving hand. The solid white line shows the estimated contour and the dotted line is the boundary of the search region. Initially, the lower edge of the hand is not locked on; the search region expands locally until the contour does lock on. Over time the search region reaches a steady state and the continuing motion of the hand is successfully tracked.

so that temporal scale varies as the inverse square of spatial scale. In the absence of a feature, temporal scale shortens so that feature acquisition and locking can occur rapidly. Once locked, temporal scale lengthens, allowing motion coherence to be exploited.

In the practical and general case that the contour is only partially locked onto a feature, spatial scale will be inhomogeneous, being larger where the contour is not locked. Consequently temporal scale should also be inhomogeneous. The contour should react more rapidly over segments with greater spatial scale and this is illustrated in Fig. 1.5.

1.5.2   Setting of system parameters

The assumptions of homogeneity and isotropy in system and measurement uncertainties dramatically reduced the number of unspecified covariance parameters from $O(M^2)$ to just a few, because all covariance submatrices turned out to be multiples of $\mathcal{H}^{-1}$, the inverse of the metric matrix. In fact there are just four covariance parameters to specify: r, q, α_1, α_2. Of these, α_1, α_2 will prove to be less important; they govern the initial strength of influence of the template. Later, however, the "persistent template" is introduced that has a continuing influence, not just an initial one, governed by an additional parameter $\bar{r}$ (see section 1.7).

Measurement covariance r is fixed, in principle, by the sensor characteristics, and might reflect a typical noise variance of a fraction of one (pixel)^2 in image measurement. In practice, this is unrealistic. The measurement process outlined earlier, searching along normals from the current estimated curve, is crude in the interests of speed and its error is of the order of the width of the search window, which may be much greater than one pixel. Ideally, then, we should set $r \propto \rho^2$ so that r is time-varying. This is an attractive idea, but it remains to solve the covariance equation (no longer a Riccati equation since R is a function of P) for this case. In the meantime the simpler case is considered in which r is constant.

Rather than setting the four parameters explicitly, it is actually more natural to fix an equivalent set of four that correspond directly to operational characteristics of the tracker. Initial and steady state values of the spatial scale ρ for search are set by q, α_1 as follows:

$$\rho_0 = \sqrt{\alpha_1} \quad \text{and} \quad \rho_\infty = 2^{1/4}(qr^3)^{1/8}. \tag{1.28}$$

The variation of temporal scale with spatial scale

$$\tau = 2\frac{r}{\rho^2} \tag{1.29}$$

is fixed by the choice of r and it is most natural to choose r for the desired

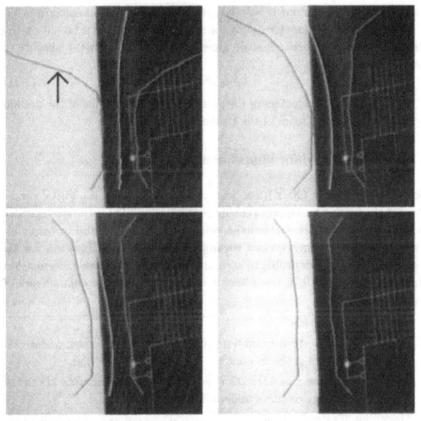

Figure 1.5
This simulation demonstrates that portions of a snake with greater spatial
uncertainty have shorter temporal memory, as predicted theoretically. The
estimated contour (white line) is initially close to a feature; the search region
(bounded by grey lines, arrowed in the first frame) is initialised to be larger at the
top than the bottom. Temporal scale should therefore be shorter at the top and in
the second frame the contour is indeed attracted to the feature more rapidly near
the top. Subsequently the remainder of the snake locks on. (Frames are
approximately at times $t = 0, 0.04, 0.08, 2.0$ seconds.)

steady state temporal scale

$$\tau_\infty = 2\frac{r}{\rho_\infty^2} \qquad (1.30)$$

which governs the degree to which coherence of motion is exploited once the contour is fully locked. (Of course, if a manoeuvre causes lock to be lost, τ rapidly becomes very short as ρ increases; the coherence assumption is cancelled and the contour is reactive, ready to follow the manoeuvre.)

The remaining parameter α_2 can be shown to determine a bound on the rate at which spatial search scale grows, at time $t = 0$, in the absence of any features to track:

$$\dot{\rho} < \sqrt{\alpha_2}. \qquad (1.31)$$

So all four free parameters of the system are fixed in terms of the desired operational characteristics of the tracker.

1.6   Affine invariant shape memory

So far, the template $(\overline{\mathbf{X}}, \overline{\mathbf{Y}})$ has been set up to influence the initial conditions of the tracker by a direct probabilistic coupling. The estimated contour is initialised to the template shape, with a homogeneous and isotropic allowance for uncertainty via the covariance matrix $P(0)$. However, for 3D tracking it is highly desirable to accommodate specially those deformations that occur as a result of projective effects. This could be done at any of several levels.

1. Allowing 2D rotation.
2. Allowing 2D affine transformations; this is sufficient to accommodate 3D transformations of a planar contour, under affine projection.
3. Allowing 3D affine transformation, sufficient to accommodate 3D transformations of a space curve under affine projection.
4. Modelling 3D rigid transformations of a 3D model and perspective projection [19].
5. Allowing full planar projective transformation.
6. Allowing 3D projective transformations

The last three of these are most general but require an extended Kalman filter to cope with nonlinearity. The first is least general but most tightly constrained, and is also nonlinear. The 2nd and 3rd are covered by the approach to be described here. An affine approximation is made to the camera projection (Horn 1986) with the benefit that the Kalman filter turns out to be linear and so to enjoy well understood convergence properties. Error in the approximation is absorbed by the general mechanism for uncertainty incorporated in the filter.

1.6.1   Affine invariance

Let us first consider case 2 above, of general 2D affine invariance. It is in some respects appealing to try to develop some affinely invariant shape-measure $I(\mathbf{X}, \mathbf{Y})$ that could then be used in an error-measure of the form

$$\|I(\hat{\mathbf{X}}, \hat{\mathbf{Y}}) - I(\overline{\mathbf{X}}, \overline{\mathbf{Y}})\|_I \qquad (1.32)$$

with some suitable norm $\|..\|_I$. Suitable candidates for I might be found, for instance, in [11]. This would have the desired effect of making the template $(\overline{\mathbf{X}}, \overline{\mathbf{Y}})$ an affinely invariant shape model because it was accessed only via $I(..)$.

There are disadvantages, though, in relying entirely on an affine invariant $I(..)$. Firstly affine invariants are non-linear functions and that introduces nonlinearity into the tracking filter, whereas a linear filter is attainable (see below). Secondly it may be difficult to construct an $I(..)$ that is not only invariant but also *complete*, in the sense that the error measure (1.32) should be sensitive to *all* non-affine differences between curve and template. Thirdly, the overwhelming disadvantage relates to the modelling of sensor error. Use of the error measure (1.32) would appear to have the advantage of allowing the (affine) camera to be uncalibrated, because $(\hat{\mathbf{X}}, \hat{\mathbf{Y}})$ is also accessed via $I(..)$. Our tracking framework rests firmly on modelling of sensor noise for which the *true* X, Y sensing frame is required to compute the Mahalanobis distance (1.13), not just some frame that is affinely related to (X, Y). This means that $(\hat{\mathbf{X}}, \hat{\mathbf{Y}})$ must be available explicitly, not just via $I(..)$ and the camera must be calibrated, at least approximately.

Aiming for an error measure that is invariant to affine transformations both in curve and template is therefore not only needlessly ambitious but actually undesirable. Instead we should aim for a measure that is affinely invariant only to the template $(\overline{\mathbf{X}}, \overline{\mathbf{Y}})$ but not to the estimated curve $\hat{\mathbf{X}}, \hat{\mathbf{Y}}$. Such a measure is derived next.

1.6.2   Invariant template

Continuing to consider the 2D affine case 2 above, we will exploit the fact that, instead of representing the template $(\overline{\mathbf{X}}, \overline{\mathbf{Y}})$ and an affine transformation A *explicitly*, the space of all possible transformations of the template can be represented as a subspace $\mathcal{V}$ of the state-space. This is mathematically efficient in the 2D case. Later, it will prove also to be a highly effective generalisation to regard this vector subspace $\mathcal{V}$ itself as the model, in place of the template.

Given a template obtained as one training view $(\overline{\mathbf{X}}_1, \overline{\mathbf{Y}}_1)$, and since A has 6 degrees of freedom as in Fig. 1.6, the set $\{A(\overline{\mathbf{X}}_1, \overline{\mathbf{Y}}_1)\}$ is a 6-dimensional vector subspace. The subspace can conveniently be expressed as a direct product of subspaces for the $\mathbf{X}, \mathbf{Y}$ processes respectively:

$$\mathcal{V} = \mathcal{V}_X \otimes \mathcal{V}_Y$$

so that the typical element of $\mathcal{V}$ is $v = (v_X, v_Y)$ where $v_X \in \mathcal{V}_X$ and $v_Y \in \mathcal{V}_Y$. The bases B_X, B_Y for $\mathcal{V}_X, \mathcal{V}_Y$ are:

$$B_X = B_Y = \{\mathbf{1}, \overline{\mathbf{X}}_1, \overline{\mathbf{Y}}_1\} \tag{1.33}$$

where $\mathbf{1}$ is the M-vector

$$\mathbf{1} = \frac{1}{\sqrt{M}}(1, 1, .., 1)^T.$$

Each basis contains the vector $\mathbf{1}$ to allow translation and the vectors $\overline{\mathbf{X}}_1, \overline{\mathbf{Y}}_1$ to allow arbitrary linear functions of the template, including planar rotation, scaling and foreshortening. We will assume, in general, that the bases are orthonormal with respect to the earlier defined inner product $< .. >$. This is achieved in the 2D affine case by normalising the position, size and orientation of the template $(\overline{\mathbf{X}}_1, \overline{\mathbf{Y}}_1)$ via the following steps

1. Translate it so that its centroid is at the origin. This achieves $< \mathbf{1}, \overline{\mathbf{X}}_1 >= < \mathbf{1}, \overline{\mathbf{Y}}_1 >= 0$.

2. Rotate the template through an angle θ given by

$$\tan 2\theta = 2 \frac{< \overline{\mathbf{X}}_1, \overline{\mathbf{Y}}_1 >}{||\overline{\mathbf{Y}}_1||^2 - ||\overline{\mathbf{X}}_1||^2}$$

and this achieves $< \overline{\mathbf{X}}_1, \overline{\mathbf{Y}}_1 >= 0$.

3. Scale the template vertically by a factor $1/||\overline{\mathbf{Y}}_1||$ and horizontally by $1/||\overline{\mathbf{X}}_1||$ to achieve $||\overline{\mathbf{X}}_1|| = ||\overline{\mathbf{Y}}_1|| = 1$.

Now, since already $||\mathbf{1}|| = 1$, $\{\mathbf{1}, \overline{\mathbf{X}}_1, \overline{\mathbf{Y}}_1\}$ forms an orthonormal set as required.

1.6.3   Prior p.d.f.

The next task is to show how the subspace model for shape amounts to incorporating affine invariance of the template into a distance measure and hence into the error measure prior p.d.f. for the curve. Consider the prior p.d.f. for positional uncertainty, whose covariance is the upper left submatrix $P_{11}(0)$ of $P(0)$. (The situation for the other non-zero submatrix, representing motion-uncertainty, is very similar.)

Now $(\overline{\mathbf{X}}, \overline{\mathbf{Y}})$ is no longer a fixed template, but ranges over the subspace $\mathcal{V}$ of affine transformations of the template $(\overline{\mathbf{X}}_1, \overline{\mathbf{Y}}_1)$. Previously, the positional covariance $P_{11}(0)$ implied a fixed prior p.d.f.

$$p(\mathbf{X}, \mathbf{Y}) \propto \exp -\frac{1}{2\alpha_1} \left(||\mathbf{X} - \overline{\mathbf{X}}||^2 + ||\mathbf{Y} - \overline{\mathbf{Y}}||^2 \right).$$

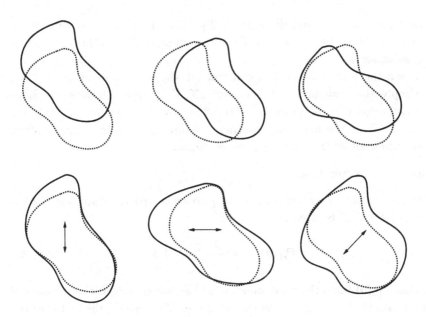

Figure 1.6
The six degrees of freedom of a 2D affine transformation are illustrated here: translation vertically and horizontally, rotation and scaling vertically, horizontally and diagonally.

Now that same expression is interpreted as a conditional p.d.f. $p(\mathbf{X}, \mathbf{Y}|\overline{\mathbf{X}}, \overline{\mathbf{Y}})$. From this conditional p.d.f., the prior p.d.f. $p(\mathbf{X}, \mathbf{Y})$ is computed by obtaining a maximum likelihood estimate (m.l.e.) [30] for $(\overline{\mathbf{X}}, \overline{\mathbf{Y}})$ as a function of $(\mathbf{X}, \mathbf{Y})$. This is done by maximising $p(..|..)$ above with respect to $(\overline{\mathbf{X}}, \overline{\mathbf{Y}})$, as it ranges over the subspace $\mathcal{V}$. The m.l.e. for the template is therefore the $(\overline{\mathbf{X}}, \overline{\mathbf{Y}}) \in \mathcal{V}$ which minimises the Mahalanobis distance

$$||\mathbf{X} - \overline{\mathbf{X}}||^2 + ||\mathbf{Y} - \overline{\mathbf{Y}}||^2.$$

The solution is

$$\overline{\mathbf{X}} = E'_X \mathbf{X}, \quad \text{where} \quad E'_X = \left(\sum_{\mathbf{v} \in B_X} \mathbf{v}\mathbf{v}^T \right) \mathcal{H} \qquad (1.34)$$

and similarly for $\overline{\mathbf{Y}}$ — simply the *projection* of the current state $(\mathbf{X}, \mathbf{Y})$ onto the subspace $\mathcal{V}$.

The prior p.d.f. for the contour can now be written as

$$p(\mathbf{X}, \mathbf{Y}) \propto \exp -\frac{1}{2\alpha_1} \left(||E_X \mathbf{X}||^2 + ||E_Y \mathbf{Y}||^2 \right) \qquad (1.35)$$

where $E_X = I - E'_X$ and similarly for E_Y. This means that the prior p.d.f. depends only on the component of the current state $(\mathbf{X}, \mathbf{Y})$ that lies *outside* the subspace $\mathcal{V}$.

Given the way in which $\mathcal{V}$ is constructed, the term in brackets in (1.35) is simply the minimum distance from $(\mathbf{X}, \mathbf{Y})$ to the subspace $\mathcal{V}$. Since the definition of $\mathcal{V}$ is invariant to an affine transformation of the training view $(\overline{\mathbf{X}}_1, \overline{\mathbf{Y}}_1)$, the minimum-distance measure is, itself, invariant to affine transformation of the training view, as required.

1.6.4 Invariant filter

The implication of the prior p.d.f. $p(..)$ above is that the positional covariance $P_{11}(t)$ of $\mathbf{X}$ is given initially by

$$(P_{11}(0))^{-1} = \frac{1}{\alpha_1}(E_X)^T \mathcal{H} E_X \tag{1.36}$$

so that $P_{11}(0)$ takes the same value $\alpha_1 \mathcal{H}^{-1}$ as before *outside* the subspace $\mathcal{V}$ but is effectively infinite inside the subspace. This reflects the fact that the template determines initially only the non-affine component of the estimated curve. In a continuous Kalman filter this would create a singularity problem, in that the initial Kalman gain is unbounded. In the discrete filter, described later, the problem does not arise because the Kalman gain is bounded even though (1.36) is rank deficient. Provided a feature $(\mathbf{X}_f, \mathbf{Y}_f)$ is observable at time $t = 0$ it will be absorbed via the Kalman gain into the estimate $(\hat{\mathbf{X}}(0), \hat{\mathbf{Y}}(0))$. Within the affine subspace, the initial estimate is simply a copy of the feature:

$$E'_X \hat{\mathbf{X}}(0) = E'_X \mathbf{X}_f$$

whereas outside the subspace it is a linear mixture of template and feature[1]. The initial conditions for the estimate are now determined both inside and outside the subspace and this is reflected in the fact that P_{11} becomes nonsingular.

1.7 Persistent template

So far, the template or training views have had an influence on the tracker that continually decreased over time so that, in the steady-state, no shape memory remains. However, in practice, it is crucial that a shape-specific tracker should continue, throughout its lifetime, to retain some shape memory. It is essential to stability that it should do so, otherwise there is undue disturbance when features are temporarily obscured and the tracker is

---

[1] The Kalman filter is in fact acting, in this initialisation step, as a Wiener filter [18].

Figure 1.7
The persistent template is essential to the stability of the contour tracker,
especially with more complex shapes. The figure shows a contour without a
persistent template. Over the portion of the contour that has lost lock, it has
become too tangled to be able to recover lock subsequently.

bumped out of its steady state. The more complex the shape to be tracked,
the worse is the instability when lock is lost, and this is illustrated in Fig.
1.7. With persistence however, the tracker remains stable with or without
features and retains its ability to track across a cluttered background as
Fig. 1.8 shows.

The persistent template has the effect of building additional smoothness
into the estimate $\hat{X}$, beyond the implicit smoothness of the B-spline. Prob-
abilistically, it can be regarded as a prior distribution, for the stochastic
component of the dynamical model, specified by its mean $(\overline{X}, \overline{Y})$ and by
the covariance implicit in the Kalman gain $\overline{K}$ defined below.

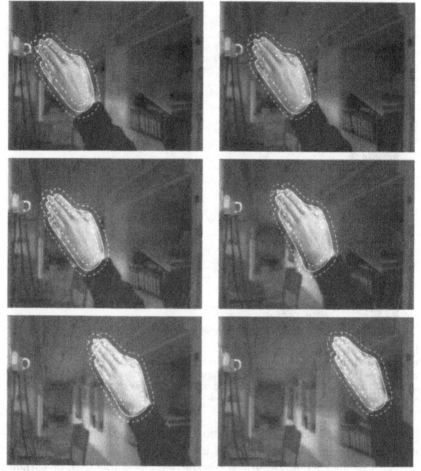

Figure 1.8
A hand, accelerating from left to right, sweeps across a cluttered background (total
elapsed time: 1.1s). The template imposes shape specificity without total rigidity.
Note that in the fourth frame the lower left corner of the contour is momentarily
distracted by the chair but the disturbance is successfully filtered out over time.

1.7.1   Mechanism

The mechanism for persistence of the template is as follows. In addition to the feature $(\mathbf{X}_f, \mathbf{Y}_f)$, a *virtual* input of $\mathbf{0}$ is applied to the filter, but coupled only *outside* the subspace $\mathcal{V}$. In the 2D planar case, for instance, this tends to extinguish those components of shape that are not related by affine transformation to the template. Now the Kalman filter becomes

$$\frac{d}{dt}\begin{pmatrix} \hat{\mathbf{X}} \\ \hat{\mathbf{X}} \end{pmatrix} = \begin{pmatrix} \dot{\hat{\mathbf{X}}} \\ \mathbf{0} \end{pmatrix} + K(\mathbf{X}_f - \hat{\mathbf{X}}) - \overline{K}E_X\hat{\mathbf{X}}. \tag{1.37}$$

The extra, final term is the virtual input and its associated Kalman gain is $\overline{K} = PH\overline{R}^{-1}$ where the covariance (spectral density) $\overline{R}$ associated with the persistent template is

$$\overline{R}^{-1} = \frac{1}{\overline{r}}(E_X)^T\mathcal{H}E_X \tag{1.38}$$

and $\overline{r}$ is a covariance (spectral density). Typically we choose $\overline{r} < r$ so that the real input to the tracker dominates the virtual one.

1.7.2   Results

The effectiveness of the affine tracker with persistent template is demonstrated by the tracking of a moving hand. The four affine degrees of freedom are independently exercised in Fig. 1.9 and successfully tracked. The transformation of the hand outline is not *precisely* affine because the hand is not perfectly planar, has extremal boundaries and may flex a little during motion. However the stochastic allowance for shape uncertainty in the filter ensures that such deviations can be accommodated. When a non-affine distortion of significant magnitude occurs, however, the tracker correctly ignores it, preferring to maintain its memorised shape (Fig. 1.10).

1.8   Subspaces as shape models

As claimed earlier, the subspace $\mathcal{V}$ can itself be regarded as a rather general form of prior model for shape. Varying the structure of the subspaces $\mathcal{V}_X, \mathcal{V}_Y$ allows different modelling assumptions to be applied to the tracker.

Camera rotation

A simple case of a restricted subspace occurs if motion is restricted to pan and tilt of the camera. In that case, image motion is approximately a rigid 2D translation and the appropriate subspaces are given by the bases

$$B_X = B_Y = \{\mathbf{1}\}$$

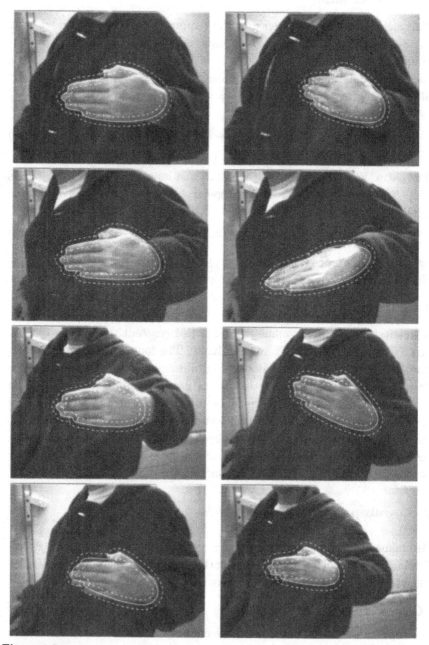

Figure 1.9
Hand tracking. Exercising 4 affine degrees of freedom, in raster order: home — slant horizontal — home — slant vertical — home — rotate — home — distance scaling. (The remaining 2 affine degrees of freedom are horizontal and vertical translation.)

Figure 1.10
Hand-tracking. A non-affine distortion, extending the thumb, is correctly ignored
by the tracker.

so that $\mathcal{V}$ has dimension $1 + 1 = 2$ as appropriate for the two degrees of
freedom of image-plane translation.

Space curve

A larger subspace than the six-dimensional one used in the planar, affine
case is needed for space-curve motion. Affine transformations of a 3D space-
curve under rigid transformations can be modelled by a subspace $\mathcal{V}$, defined
as follows. Given views $(\overline{\mathbf{X}}_i, \overline{\mathbf{Y}}_i)$, $i = 1, 2, ..$, B_X and B_Y can be constructed from three views, corresponding to the observation of Ullman and
Basri (1991) that, under affine projection, any view of an object is a linear
combination of three prototype views, so that

$$B_X = \{\mathbf{1}, \overline{\mathbf{X}}_1, \overline{\mathbf{X}}_2, \overline{\mathbf{X}}_3\}, \quad B_Y = \{\mathbf{1}, \overline{\mathbf{Y}}_1, \overline{\mathbf{Y}}_2, \overline{\mathbf{Y}}_3\}.$$

An alternative version, requiring only $1\frac{1}{2}$ views, constructs the bases as

$$B_X = B_Y = \{\mathbf{1}, \overline{\mathbf{X}}_1, \overline{\mathbf{Y}}_1, \overline{\mathbf{X}}_2\}.$$

The use of $1\frac{1}{2}$ views here is effectively a form of affine stereo [9]. It can
be regarded as a single view $(\overline{\mathbf{X}}_1, \overline{\mathbf{Y}}_1)$ together with horizontal stereoscopic
disparities $\overline{\mathbf{X}}_2 - \overline{\mathbf{X}}_1$ which together imply the underlying 3D structure. Thus
the bases B_X, B_Y each, independently, span the space of affine $\mathcal{R}^3 \to \mathcal{R}$
transformations or, jointly, the affine transformations $\mathcal{R}^3 \to \mathcal{R}^2$, as required.

Multiple space curves

A further, more ambitious, development of the mechanism would be to
include views of more than one shape into the tracker, and then the its
shape memory would span both shapes, linearly, and with affine invariance.
In that case the tracker could track either of two objects without the initial
knowledge of which one might appear. Alternatively the views might be

from different states of a deformable object in which case, to the extent
that the deformation could be approximated by a 3D affine transformation,
the tracker would follow the deforming object.

It is assumed throughout that $\mathcal{V}$ is orthonormal, which was true in 2D if
the template was normalised. In 3D, when several training views are used, $\mathcal{V}$
needs to be orthonormalised, for instance by the Gram-Schmidt procedure.
Trackers for each of the subspace models are generated using exactly the
same structures as for the planar affine case, simply by redefining E_X, E_Y
in (1.34) in terms of the new subspace $\mathcal{V}$. The 2D result about the prior
p.d.f. for $(\mathbf{X}, \mathbf{Y})$ being invariant to affine transformations of the training
view also extends to the 3D rigid body case, now with respect to 3D affine
transformations.

1.9   Discrete filter

The continuous Kalman filter model used so far is good for analysis, deriving
the scale-behaviour over time and the steady state performance. However,
in practice, measurements are discrete, synchronised with video-frames. It
is crucial to the maintenance of real-time performance, that no video-frame
should be missed. This means that it may not be possible to sample all
curve points within a single frame-period Δt. Instead it is better to process as many points, chosen randomly with a uniform spatial distribution
over the curve, as the frame-period allows. Then, as soon as a new video
frame is available, $P(t)$ and $K(t)$ are updated to allow for the elapsed time
Δt and the filter continues with the new frame using randomly sampled
measurements to update the estimated curve.

1.9.1   Measurements

In this practical framework, it is convenient to regard a unit measurement
not as a set of time-varying B-spline coefficients $(\mathbf{X}_f, \mathbf{Y}_f)$ but as a single
(X, Y) point observation at the curve parameter s, taken at a discrete time
t. This observation has an associated discrete Kalman gain matrix $K(s, t)$
defined by

$$K(s, t) = \mathbf{P}(t)H^T(s)\frac{1}{\sigma^2}, \tag{1.39}$$

where $H(s)$ is the point-wise measurement matrix defined in (1.2) and

$$\frac{1}{\sigma^2}\begin{pmatrix} 1 & 0 \\ 0 & 1 \end{pmatrix} \tag{1.40}$$

is the inverse covariance for the measured point, assumed isotropic. Then
$K(s, t)$ is used twice, once in the $\mathbf{X}$ process and once in the $\mathbf{Y}$ process.

For the purpose of setting parameters to obtain desired tracking performance, the standard deviation σ of individual measurements must be related to the measurement variance spectral density r in the continuous filter. Assuming that L measurements are made in each span — that is NL measurements in total per video frame — and that they are evenly distributed over the curve parameter s, then it can be shown that:

$$\sigma^2 = \frac{Lr}{\Delta t}. \tag{1.41}$$

Once r is fixed to achieve desired filter properties, as earlier in section 1.5, σ for the discrete filter is therefore also fixed.

It is also highly desirable to take into account the aperture problem [20]. In practice, if the point-measurement model is used, the estimated curve does not rotate freely, because the parametrisation of the estimated curve is projected along normals onto the feature curve, and this discourages motion orthogonal to the normals. The problem is cured when displacement only along the normal $\mathbf{n}(s)$ is used. In that case the Kalman gain $K(s,t)$ is applied once to a coupled $\mathbf{X}$ and $\mathbf{Y}$ process, the coupling arising because the measurement model is no longer isotropic. In place of the isotropic matrix in (1.40) the inverse covariance for the normal measurement is:

$$\frac{1}{\sigma^2}\mathbf{n}(s)\mathbf{n}(s)^T,$$

and this can be used to define the Kalman gain for the measurement. However, for the remainder of this section on the discrete filter we will, for simplicity of notation, treat the point-measurement model. The above modifications required to take account of the aperture problem are then quite straightforward to apply.

1.9.2   Filter

The discrete-time measurement model assumes that observations are made at times $t_k = t_0 + k\Delta t$, where Δt is the interval between video-frames. Our notation will use suffix k to refer to a discrete-time quantity at time t_k. The continuous filter described earlier can be transformed into a discrete one, following the treatment given by Gelb (1974).

First, during the interval $t_{k-1} \leq t < t_k$ during which no observations are made, the filter (1.16) becomes simply

$$\frac{d}{dt}\begin{pmatrix} \hat{\mathbf{X}} \\ \hat{\dot{\mathbf{X}}} \end{pmatrix} = \begin{pmatrix} \hat{\dot{\mathbf{X}}} \\ 0 \end{pmatrix} \tag{1.42}$$

which can be integrated directly. Approximating to $O(\Delta t)$, this gives the discrete prediction $\hat{\mathbf{X}}_k$ immediately prior to the time $t = t_k$:

$$\begin{pmatrix} \hat{\mathbf{X}}_k \\ \dot{\hat{\mathbf{X}}}_k \end{pmatrix} = \begin{bmatrix} \mathbf{I} & (\Delta t)\mathbf{I} \\ \mathbf{0} & \mathbf{I} \end{bmatrix} \begin{pmatrix} \hat{\mathbf{X}}_{k-1} \\ \dot{\hat{\mathbf{X}}}_{k-1} \end{pmatrix}. \tag{1.43}$$

The Riccati equation (1.19) is also simplified, in the absence of measurements, to

$$\frac{\mathrm{d}P}{\mathrm{d}t} = FP + PF^T + Q$$

which, being linear, can also be integrated directly to give:

$$\hat{P}_k = \begin{bmatrix} \mathbf{I} & (\Delta t)\mathbf{I} \\ \mathbf{0} & \mathbf{I} \end{bmatrix} \hat{P}_{k-1} \begin{bmatrix} \mathbf{I} & \mathbf{0} \\ (\Delta t)\mathbf{I} & \mathbf{I} \end{bmatrix} + (\Delta t)Q \tag{1.44}$$

and again this has been approximated[2] to $O(\Delta t)$.

Secondly, discrete measurements for time t_k are applied sequentially. A given observation of a point-feature $(X_f(s), Y_f(s))$ is applied via the Kalman gain

$$K_k(s) \equiv K(s, t_k) = \hat{P}_k \begin{pmatrix} H(s)^T \\ \mathbf{0} \end{pmatrix} \left[\begin{pmatrix} H(s) & \mathbf{0} \end{pmatrix} \hat{P}_k \begin{pmatrix} H(s)^T \\ \mathbf{0} \end{pmatrix} + \sigma^2 \right]^{-1} \tag{1.45}$$

where $\hat{P}_k$ is the covariance of the state as it was immediately before application of the current measurement — that is, taking into account all measurements for $t = t_k$ up to, but not including, the current measurement. The current measurement is applied to the state by:

$$\begin{pmatrix} \hat{\mathbf{X}}_k \\ \dot{\hat{\mathbf{X}}}_k \end{pmatrix} \rightarrow \begin{pmatrix} \hat{\mathbf{X}}_k \\ \dot{\hat{\mathbf{X}}}_k \end{pmatrix} + K_k(s) \left(X_f(s, t_k) - H(s)\hat{\mathbf{X}}_k \right). \tag{1.46}$$

The state covariance is updated by a discrete Riccati equation

$$\hat{P}_k \rightarrow \left[\mathbf{I} - K_k(s) \begin{pmatrix} H(s) & \mathbf{0} \end{pmatrix} \right] \hat{P}_k \tag{1.47}$$

where $H(s)$ is the point-wise measurement matrix defined earlier in (1.2).

1.9.3 Persistent template

In an exact discretisation the persistent template (1.37) should be treated as a continuous measurement, integrated over the time interval $t_{k-1} \leq t \leq t_k$, as part of the prediction phase. When Δt is small this can be approximated by one discrete virtual observation per timestep. Allowing for invariance

---

[2] It is also possible to write an exact solution to the integral using exponentials.

over the subspace $\mathcal{V}$, as earlier, the virtual observation of the template is applied via the discrete Kalman gain

$$\overline{K}_k = \hat{P}_k H^T \left[H\hat{P}_k H^T + \overline{R}/\Delta t \right]^{-1},\tag{1.48}$$

where $\overline{r}$ is the variance spectral density (1.38) from the continuous filter and

$$H = (\ \mathbf{I}\quad \mathbf{0}\ ),$$

as in the continuous filter. The template update is

$$\begin{pmatrix} \hat{\mathbf{X}}_k \\ \hat{\dot{\mathbf{X}}}_k \end{pmatrix} \to \begin{pmatrix} \hat{\mathbf{X}}_k \\ \hat{\dot{\mathbf{X}}}_k \end{pmatrix} - \overline{K}_k \hat{\mathbf{X}}_k\tag{1.49}$$

with covariance updated by

$$\hat{P}_k \to \left[\mathbf{I} - \overline{K}_k H \right] \hat{P}_k.\tag{1.50}$$

1.9.4   Computational complexity

The implementation of this filter requires $O(M^2)$ floating point operations for the prediction step. Each observation takes $O(M^2)$ arithmetic operations, due to the $2M \times 2M$ matrix multiplication in (1.47) (note: $H(s)$ is sparse). Finally the virtual observation for the persistent template requires $O(M^3)$ operations. Alternatively, the equivalent *Information Filter* or *Inverse Kalman Filter* [27] makes prediction the expensive step, giving $O(M^3)$ for prediction and $O(M^2)$ for each observation, which may be preferable in the typical case that there are many (more than M) observations per timestep. It has the advantage of allowing an efficient parallel implementation because the observation updates can be applied in an arbitrary order. This contrasts with the Kalman filter described earlier in the section in which the covariance update for one measurement must be calculated before the next measurement can be applied.

1.9.5   Spatial search

The prediction step (1.43) is used to find the expected feature position in each frame of the image sequence, and the corresponding covariance is used to constrain the search for the features within that image. Search along the predicted contour normal is bounded within the uncertainty-ellipse, derived from the state-covariance, which will contain the feature with a 98% likelihood (2 standard deviations). Anisotropy arising from the aperture problem and the measurement of normal displacements only is taken into account in the construction of the uncertainty ellipse. Full details are given in [12].

Features are not necessarily found at all sample points. They may for example be obscured along a portion of the contour, or of insufficient contrast to be registered. In such a case no observation is applied so that no new information is introduced into the state and covariance for that sample point.

1.10   Conclusions

The value of the statistical basis for contour tracking has been established by elucidating and demonstrating the mechanism for automatic control of spatio-temporal scale. Despite the substantial size of the state space that is needed to deal with geometric complexity of the contour, some natural assumptions lead to a system that has few free parameters and those are fixed, via control-theoretic analysis, to obtain desired dynamic behaviour. The incorporation of the template mechanism with its affine invariance has proved to be crucial in procuring shape-selective tracking that is immune to background clutter. It remains for future work to experiment further with extensions of the subspace mechanism that is used here to represent affine degrees of freedom. This includes tracking of space curves, tracking with two or more models simultaneously, and integration of the learning of shapes and their associated spatio-temporal uncertainty into the tracking process.

Acknowledgements

The financial support of the SERC, the EEC and Oxford Metrics is gratefully acknowledged.   Discussions with M.Brady, N.Ferrier, A.Nairac, B.Ripley and C.Rothwell were most helpful.

References

[1] N. Ayache, I. Cohen, and I. Herlin. Medical image tracking. In Blake, A. and Yuille, A., editors, *Active Vision*, pages 285–302. MIT Press. 1992.

[2] Y. Bar-Shalom and T. Fortmann. *Tracking and Data Association*. Academic Press. 1988

[3] R. Bartels, J. Beatty, and B. Barsky. *An Introduction to Splines for use in Computer Graphics and Geometric Modeling*. Morgan Kaufmann. 1987.

[4] A. Bennett and I. Craw. Finding image features for deformable templates and detailed prior statistical knowledge. In Mowforth, P., editor, *Proc. British Machine Vision Conference*, pages 233–239, Glasgow. Springer-Verlag, London. 1991.

[5] A. Blake. Computational modelling of hand-eye coordination. *Proc. Roy. Soc. Lond. B.*, 337:351–360.

[6] A. Blake, M. Brady, R. Cipolla, Z. Xie, and A. Zisserman. Visual navigation around curved obstacles. In *Proc. IEEE Int. Conf. Robotics and Automation*, volume 3, pages 2490–2499. 1991.

[7] A. Blake and A. Yuille, editors. *Active Vision*. MIT Press. 1992.

[8] A. Blake, A. Zisserman, and R. Cipolla. Visual exploration of freespace. In Blake, A. and Yuille, A., editors, *Active Vision*, pages 175–188. MIT Press. 1992.

[9] F. L. Bookstein. Thin-plate splines and the decomposition of deformations. *IEEE Trans. Pattern Analysis and Machine Intell.* 1988.

[10] R. Cipolla and A. Blake. Motion planning using image divergence and deformation. In Blake, A. and Yuille, A., editors, *Active Vision*, pages 39–58. MIT Press. 1992.

[11] R. Cipolla and M. Yamamoto. Stereoscopic tracking of bodies in motion. *Image and Vision Computing*, 8(1):85–90. 1990.

[12] R. Curwen. *Dynamic and Adaptive Contours*. PhD thesis, University of Oxford. 1993.

[13] R. Curwen and A. Blake. Dynamic contours: real-time active splines. In Blake, A. and Yuille, A., editors, *Active Vision*, pages 39–58. MIT Press. 1992.

[14] E. Dickmanns and V. Graefe. Applications of dynamic monocular machine vision. *Machine Vision and Applications*, 1:241–261. 1988.

[15] I. Faux and M. Pratt. *Computational Geometry for Design and Manufacture*. Ellis-Horwood. 1979.

[16] M. A. Fischler and R. A. Elschlager. The representation and matching of pictorial structures. *IEEE. Trans. Computers*, C-22(1). 1973.

[17] A. Gelb, editor. *Applied Optimal Estimation*. MIT Press, Cambridge, MA. 1974.

[18] U. Grenander, Y. Chow, and D. M. Keenan. *HANDS. A Pattern Theoretical Study of Biological Shapes*. Springer-Verlag. New York. 1991.

[19] C. Harris. Tracking with rigid models. In Blake, A. and Yuille, A., editors, *Active Vision*, pages 59–74. MIT Press. 1992.

[20] C. Harris and C. Stennett. Rapid – a video-rate object tracker. In *Proc. 1st British Machine Vision Conference*, pages 73–78. 1990.

[21] B. Horn. *Robot Vision*. McGraw-Hill, NY. 1986.

[22] H. Inoue and H. Mizoguchi. A flexible multi window vision system for robots. In *Proc. 2nd Int. Symp. on Robotics Research*, pages 95–102. 1985.

[23] M. Kass, A. Witkin, and D. Terzopoulos. Snakes: Active contour models. In *Proc. 1st Int. Conf. on Computer Vision*, pages 259–268, London. 1987.

[24] J. Koenderink and A. Van Doorn. Affine structure from motion. *J. Optical Soc. America A.*, 8(2):337–385. 1991.

[25] P. Lipson, A. Yuille, D. Keeffe, J. Cavanaugh, J. Taaffe, and D. Rosenthal. Deformable templates for feature extraction from medical images. In Faugeras, O., editor, *Proc. 1st European Conference on Computer Vision*, pages 413–417. Springer–Verlag. 1990.

[26] D. Lowe. Robust model-based motion tracking through the integration of search and estimation. *Int. Journal of Computer Vision*, 8(2):113–122. 1992.

[27] P. Maybeck. *Stochastic Models, Estimation and Control, Vol. I*. Academic Press. 1979.

[28] S. Menet, P. Saint-Marc, and G. Medioni. B-snakes:implementation and application to stereo. In *Proceedings DARPA*, pages 720–726. 1990.

[29] J. Mundy and A. Zisserman. *Geometric invariance in computer vision*. MIT Press. 1992.

[30] C. Rao. *Linear Statistical Inference and Its Applications*. John Wiley and Sons, New York. 1973.

[31] G. Scott. The alternative snake – and other animals. In *Proc. 3rd Alvey Vision Conference*, pages 341–347. 1987.

[32] G. Sullivan. Visual interpretation of known objects in constrained scenes. *Phil. Trans. R. Soc. Lond. B.*, 337:109–118. 1992.

[33] R. Szeliski and D. Terzopoulos. Physically-based and probabilistic modeling for computer vision. In Vemuri, B. C., editor, *Proc. SPIE 1570, Geometric Methods in Computer Vision*, pages 140–152, San Diego, CA. Society of Photo-Optical Instrumentation Engineers. 1991.

[34] D. Terzopoulos and D. Metaxas. Dynamic 3D models with local and global deformations: deformable superquadrics. *IEEE Trans. Pattern Analysis and Machine Intell.*, 13(7). 1991.

[35] W. D. Thompson and J. L. Mundy. Three-dimensional model matching from an unconstrained viewpoint. In *Proceedings of IEEE Conference on Robotics and Automation.* 1987.

[36] S. Ullman and R. Basri. Recognition by linear combinations of models. *IEEE Trans. Pattern Analysis and Machine Intell.*, 13(10):992–1006. 1991.

[37] H. Wang and M. Brady. Vision for mobile robots. *Proc. Roy. Soc. Lond. B.*, 337. 1992.

[38] A.L. Yuille, P. W. Hallinan, and D. S. Cohen. Detecting facial features using deformable templates. *International Journal of Computer Vision.* To Appear. 1992.

2 Tracking Moving Heads

Larry S. Shapiro, Michael Brady, and Andrew Zisserman

2.1 Introduction

The world is constantly in motion, so it comes as no surprise that time-varying imagery reveals valuable information about the environment. Indeed, the analysis of image sequences to extract 3D motion and structure has been at the heart of computer vision research for the past decade. An important reason why motion analysis is such an active research field is its large number of practical applications, which include automatic vehicle driving ("road following"), aerial surveillance, medical inspection, mobile robot navigation and global model construction [23, 36, 49, 66]. The application we focus on is low bit-rate image communication, specifically videoconferencing and videophone systems [26, 61], which involve moving head-and-shoulder scenes. This chapter develops new algorithms to interpret visual motion using a single camera, and demonstrates the practical feasibility of recovering scene structure and motion in a data-driven (or "bottom-up") fashion.

There are two key obstacles to successful motion understanding. First, the useful content of an image sequence is intricately coded and implicit in an enormous volume of sensory data. Making the useful information *explicit* entails decoding the spatio-temporal correlations of the intensity values to eliminate redundancy. This notion that image pixels carry unequal information suggests a feature-based approach [6], and this has two advantages. First, feature extraction reduces the vast data throughput, without necessarily eliminating salient information [49]. Second, the observed image velocity field (*optic flow*) differs from the true image motion field (the theoretical projection of the 3D velocity field) except where image gradients are strong [57], e.g. at corner and edge locations. We use *corner features*, curvature extrema on the image intensity surface which are increasingly being used in vision applications [2, 10, 11, 13, 19, 35, 37, 49, 60].

The second obstacle is that information is lost in projecting the three spatial dimensions of the world onto the two dimensions of the image. Assumptions about camera models and imaging geometry are therefore required. We model the projection operation as an *affine camera* [11], a generalisation of the familiar orthographic and scaled orthographic camera models. This provides a good approximation to the perspective projection model when the field of view is small and the variation in scene depth along the line of sight is small compared to its average distance from the camera. The affine camera requires no camera calibration (see Section 3), thereby enabling the identification of quantities that can be computed *without* calibration, such as affine epipolar geometry [46] and new views of an object [45]. When calibration *is* needed, the precise stage at which it must be introduced into the computation can be determined, e.g. aspect ratio is required to compute rigid motion parameters (cf. Section 2.6).

Fig. 2.1 shows our system architecture. Images are processed as they enter sequentially, with three distinct layers of computation:

1. *Low-level vision*:   Corners are extracted from the incoming grey-level images and matched to the corners from previous images, generating an "image trajectory" for each feature. The feature extraction, tracking and prediction modules operate wholly within the image plane, and each feature is treated independently.

2. *Medium-level vision*:   The image trajectories are grouped into putative objects, representing the projections of rigid bodies in the world moving independently of one another and of the viewer. Each object's structure and motion parameters are then computed, and this knowledge is passed back to the low-level routines to assist the correspondence process. All modules in this layer use three-dimensional information, without needing object-specific data (e.g. prior object models).

3. *High-level vision*:   The final stage of processing depends on the goal of the computation, e.g. objects can be matched to a prior database for recognition, coded efficiently for bandwidth compression, and so on. The modules in this layer operate at the symbolic level, using high-level object knowledge.

The first two layers are entirely data-driven; they depend only on the input, and are guided by general organisational principles rather than object-specific knowledge. It is these first two layers that form the subject of this chapter. Space permits only a brief summary of the various modules, and the reader is referred to [47] for further details. Particulars of the feedback loop are also omitted here.

This system makes several important contributions. First, the algorithms use *all* available features. This overcomes a key limitation of many existing point-based structure and motion algorithms (e.g. [9]), which operate on the minimum amount of data required; such approaches are extremely sensitive to errors and noise, and often rely crucially on the selection of an appropriate "local coordinate frame". The advantages of our approach include improved noise immunity, the ability to identify outliers ("rogue observations") and avoidance of the computational burden of selecting a suitable frame.

Second, we consider the statistical performance of the algorithms, with noise models constructed to assess confidence in the computed parameters.

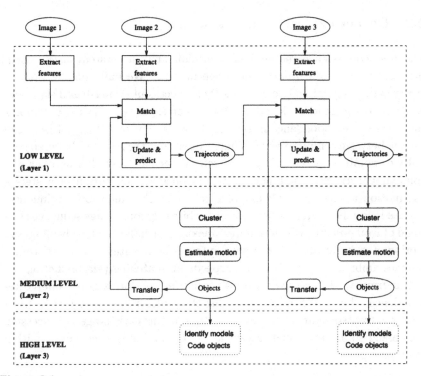

Figure 2.1
Three-layer architecture for a motion analysis system, designed to operate over long, monocular image sequences.

Least-squares minimisation is performed in the *image plane,* where the noise enters the system, rather than in the scene. Third, 3D information is introduced without computing explicit depth (or even Euclidean structure). This accords with recent trends to move away from the "vision as photogrammetry" approach. Finally, we emphasize the need for reliable algorithms; the system has been widely tested on both simulated and real data.

The chapter is organised as follows. Section 2.2 describes the first layer of the architecture, showing how corner features are extracted and tracked through the image sequence. Section 2.3 defines the affine camera model and Section 2.4 presents a novel local, parallel, clustering algorithm (based on graph theory) to group the trajectories into putative objects. Section 2.5 then derives the affine epipolar geometry, and Section 2.6 shows how to compute the rigid motion parameters (along with confidence estimates) *directly* from this epipolar geometry.

2.2   Corner extraction and tracking

The first competence required of a motion analysis system is the accurate and robust measurement of image motion. We build on the work of Wang and Brady [59, 60], extending their successful corner-based stereo algorithm to the motion domain. Motion correspondence is more complex than stereo correspondence in several respects. For one thing, objects can change between temporal viewpoints in ways that they cannot between spatial viewpoints, e.g. their shape and reflectance can alter. For another, the epipolar constraint is not hard-wired by once-off calibration of a stereo-rig; motion induces *variable* epipolar geometry that must be continuously updated. Furthermore, motion leads to arbitrarily long image sequences (instead of frame-pairs), which requires tracking machinery. The advantages of motion over stereo are that temporal integration facilitates noise resistance, resolves ambiguities over time, and speeds up matching (via prediction).

Our framework has two parts: the *matcher* performs two-frame correspondence while the *tracker* maintains the multi-frame trajectories. Each corner is treated as an *independent* feature at this early stage of processing (i.e. assigned an individual tracker as in [7]), and is tracked purely within the image plane.

2.2.1   Corner detection

"Corners" are distinctive point features that are loci of two-dimensional intensity change, i.e. *second-order features*. They include points of occlusion (e.g. T, Y and X junctions), structural discontinuities (e.g. L junctions) and various curvature maxima (e.g. texture flecks or surface markings). They have the advantage of being discrete and distinguishable (so they can be explicitly tracked over time), and they impose more constraint on the motion parameters than edges (because the *full* optic flow field μ is recoverable at a corner location).

Three important benefits accrue from using such low-level primitives, namely *generality, opportunism* and *graceful degradation*. Corners appear in almost every scene, and a system that doesn't need to know precisely what it is looking at (e.g. in the form of a model) will obviously work on a wider variety of scenes. Such a system can also take advantage of unanticipated scene features (e.g. earrings), and will degrade more gracefully than a model-based scheme that fails to locate and/or identify the object of interest.

To date, corner features have mainly been used in factory- or laboratory-type environments where physical corners abound (Fig. 2.2(a)). However, they are equally useful in more "natural" scenes. Figs. 2.2(b)–(d) show corners detected on images of a human face, which has no right-angles or sharp discontinuities; the facial features are rounded and the skin surface is smooth. Although (impressively) the detected corners do often correspond to salient facial features (e.g. nostrils, corners of eyes, tips of eyebrows, endpoints of mouth), it is more relevant that the corners are *stable, robust* beacons that are extracted automatically.

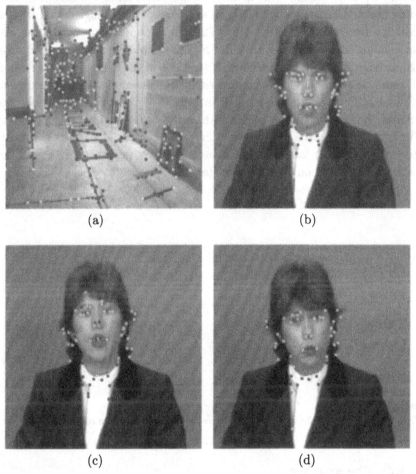

(a)   (b)

(c)   (d)

Figure 2.2
Corners (marker colour set for maximum contrast): (a) A typical laboratory scene; (b)(c)(d) Three frames in the standard CCITT sequence "Clair". Her eyes close in (c), and her mouth closes in (d). Notice that the eyes, mouth and nostrils remain well-localised.

Numerous strategies exist for extracting corner features [2, 10, 11, 13, 19, 27, 33, 35, 37, 49, 60]. We employ the Wang-Brady corner detector [60],

$$\begin{cases} \Gamma = D_{\mathbf{t}}^2 - S \, |\nabla I|^2 \longrightarrow \max \\ \Gamma > R \\ |\nabla I|^2 > E \end{cases} \qquad (2.1)$$

where $D_{\mathbf{t}}^2$ is the second order directional derivative along the edge tangential direction $\mathbf{t}$. Corners are thus defined at points of high image curvature that attain a local maximum (Fig. 2.3). The four parameters to specify are: S, a measure of image surface curvature; R, a threshold for the corner response; E, an edge strength measure; and M, the side of the square area over which Γ must be maximal. Experiments with these parameter settings and with Gaussian smoothing are described in [47]. Note that Γ doesn't only find corners lying along edges; points with sharp autocorrelations (e.g. texture flecks) also give strong responses. This is important since such points are potentially robust features, and because visually striking features may be isolated, not lying on continuous edges.

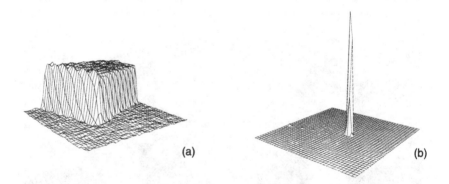

(a)   (b)

Figure 2.3
Corner detection: (a) Image intensity surface; (b) Corner response function Γ.

2.2.2   The matcher

The matcher receives as input two grey-scale images, I_1 and I_2, along with their respective corners, $\mathbf{x}_i$ and $\mathbf{x}_j'$ (where $i = 0 \ldots n-1$ and $j = 0 \ldots n'-1$). The task is to match $\mathbf{x}_i$ to $\mathbf{x}_j'$, and this well-known *correspondence problem* has a worst case enumeration of nn' possible matches. The following constraints are imposed to reduce the computational effort:

• Each corner pairs with only one other corner (uniqueness).

- Small search neighbourhoods are utilised since the high frame-rate ensures small inter-frame motion.

Local image patch correlation is employed to verify matches, resolve ambiguities and measure match confidences. The key idea is thus to base correspondence on similarity of local image structure *as well as* geometric proximity. The correlation measure used [58] is an adaptation of the standard *product moment coefficient*, which assumes a linear dependence between two N-point data sets $\{x_i\}$ and $\{y_i\}$,

$$c = \frac{S_{xy}}{S_x S_y} = \frac{\sum_{i=1}^{N}(x_i - \bar{x})(y_i - \bar{y})}{\sqrt{\sum_{i=1}^{N}(x_i - \bar{x})^2}\sqrt{\sum_{i=1}^{N}(y_i - \bar{y})^2}}, \quad -1 \leq c \leq 1,$$

where $\bar{x}$ and $\bar{y}$ are the sample means. Perfect correlation is indicated by $c = \pm 1$. The 1D analysis is extended to 2D by raster-scanning the pixels in the blocks of interest. Further algorithmic details can be found in [43].

Fig. 2.4 shows the results of two-frame matching. The vectors accurately convey the direction of motion, giving a clear indication of "what motion occurs where" in the image. The accuracy of the displacement vectors (despite the small motion) testifies to the temporal consistency of the corners and indicates that they are well localised. It is also apparent that corners are a sparse shape representation; additional information (e.g. edge motion) would obviously be a useful complement (especially when finding motion boundaries, as in [17, 49]). Finally, it is clear that there are some incorrect matches, highlighting the need for outlier rejection (see [44]).

2.2.3   The tracker

The tracker oversees the matcher: it supervises the initial startup (*boot mode*), secures the transition to normal operation (*run mode*), performs prediction and maintains an image trajectory for each feature. Simple linear predictors of the form

$$\mathbf{x}(k+1) = \sum_{i \geq 0} w_i \, \mathbf{x}(k-i) \tag{2.2}$$

are used, where w_i are fixed weighting factors and $i + 1$ is the number of frames needed for startup. For instance, a constant velocity model has $i = 1$. At best, these predictors are approximate since they operate purely in the *image plane,* without attempting to model three-dimensional motion or camera projection. Nonetheless, this prediction speeds up the matching process significantly [43].

Figs. 2.5 and 2.6 show equal-length trajectories for different image sequences obtained over several frames. Fig. 2.5 shows Richard (bespectacled) nodding his head downwards before a cluttered background, and

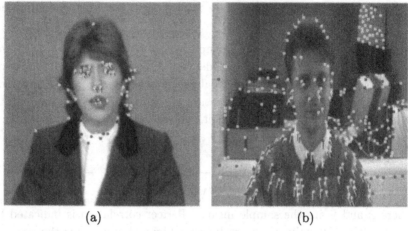

(a)   (b)

Figure 2.4
Two-frame matches (double-length vectors): (a) Clair nods her head downwards
and opens her mouth slightly (CCITT); (b) Ian looms towards the camera
(diverging flow pattern) amidst a cluttered background.

Larry and Phil nodding and shaking their heads (two independent motions). Fig. 2.6(a) shows Larry translating his upper body parallel to the
image plane. The trajectories clearly indicate the image motion.

For many applications involving stationary cameras (e.g. videophones), it
is useful to identify background corners. This entails analysing the corner's
velocity history, the criteria for classification as stationary being low speed
and low standard deviation in speed (Fig. 2.6(b)).

2.3   The affine camera

A camera model is needed in order to compute 3D information from the
image. Orthographic and scaled orthographic projection are widely used in
computer vision to model the imaging process [4, 4, 20, 24, 9, 53, 18, 56].
They provide a good approximation to the perspective projection model
when the field of view is small and the variation in depth of the scene
along the line of sight is small compared to its average distance from the
camera [52]. More importantly, they expose the ambiguities that arise when
perspective effects diminish. In such cases, it is not only *advantageous* to
use these simplified models but also *advisable* to do so, for by explicitly
incorporating these ambiguities, one avoids computing parameters that are
inherently ill-conditioned [20].

This section briefly describes the *affine camera*, a model introduced by
Mundy and Zisserman [11] to generalise the orthographic and scaled orthographic models. It is the natural projection of a 3D affine space to a 2D

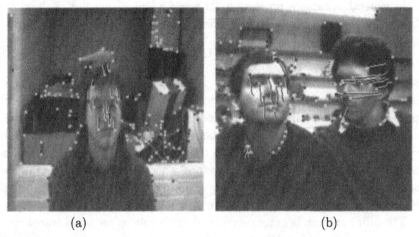

(a) (b)

Figure 2.5
Equal-length trajectories obtained over several frames (true length vectors
superimposed on final frame, markers show final corner positions): (a) "Richard";
(b) "Larry & Phil".

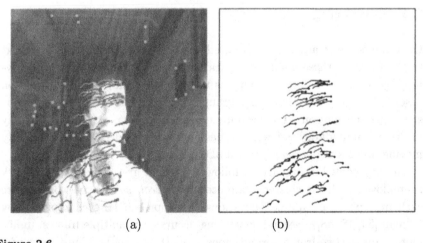

(a) (b)

Figure 2.6
Equal-length trajectories obtained over several frames (markers show final
positions): (a) "Trans"; (b) "Trans" with stationary points removed automatically.

affine image. For example, parallelism is preserved, so that parallel lines in the scene project to parallel lines in the image.

In general, a camera projects a 3D world point $\mathbf{X} = (X, Y, Z)^\top$ onto a 2D image point $\mathbf{x} = (x, y)^\top$. The *affine camera* takes the particular form

$$\mathbf{x} = \mathbf{MX} + \mathbf{t}, \qquad (2.3)$$

where $\mathbf{M}$ is a 2×3 matrix and $\mathbf{t}$ a 2-vector. This camera has eight degrees of freedom, and since its optical centre lies on the plane at infinity, all projection rays are parallel. The affine camera covers the composed effects of: (i) a 3D *affine* transformation between world and camera coordinate systems; (ii) parallel projection onto the image plane; and (iii) a 2D affine transformation of the image. It therefore generalises the orthographic and scaled orthographic models in two ways: *non-rigid* deformation of the object is permitted, and calibration is unnecessary.

The affine camera is extremely useful in its role as an *uncalibrated weak perspective camera,* for although Euclidean measurements (e.g. angles and distances) are only meaningful with a calibrated camera, various affine measurements (e.g. parallelism, ratios of lengths in parallel directions, ratios of areas on parallel planes [5]) are still well-defined without requiring arduous and often ill-conditioned calibration. Such properties are often sufficient for vision tasks. For instance, affine epipolar geometry can be determined without camera calibration (see Section 2.5).

2.4   Clustering

Once the corner tracker has generated a set of image trajectories, the next task is to group these points into putative objects. The practice of classifying objects into sensible groupings is termed "clustering", and this section describes a novel technique that groups points on the basis of their affine structure and motion. The system copes with sparse, noisy and partially incorrect input data, and with scenes containing multiple, independently moving objects undergoing general 3D motion.

The key contributions are as follows. First, a graph theory framework is employed with the clusters computed by a *local, parallel* network, where each unit performs simple operations (an approach long championed by Ullman [54, 18, 48]). Second, clustering occurs over multiple frames, unlike more familiar two-frame formulations (e.g. [1, 29, 49]). Third, a *graduated motion analysis scheme* extends the oft-used simplistic motion models; for instance, grouping on the basis of parallel and equal image velocity vectors [29, 49] is only valid for a fronto-parallel plane translating parallel to the image. Thus, while our layered complexity of models utilises *3D informa-*

tion where available, it doesn't use a more complex model than necessary. Finally, the termination criteria (to control cluster growth) are based on sound statistical noise models, in contrast to many heuristic measures and thresholds (e.g. [41, 49]).

We first consider the abstract problem of organising data according to perceived similarities: Section 2.4.1 formulates the problem in graph theory terms and Section 2.4.2 describes our clustering philosophy. We then tailor the algorithm to the structure and motion domain: Section 2.4.4 defines the relevant affinity measures and Section 2.4.5 explains how to halt cluster growth. Implementation details are provided in Section 2.4.7 along with results.

2.4.1   Maximum affinity spanning trees

Consider an image with N points, which form the universal point-set $\mathcal{U} = \{p_1, p_2, \ldots, p_N\}$. Each point p_i possesses a set of properties (e.g. colour, brightness, position) and "attractive forces" (or *affinities*) are computed between the points, based on some similarity function. The affinity[1] between p_i and p_j is denoted by a_{ij} or $a(\ell_{ij})$, and is transmitted via a "virtual" link ℓ_{ij} (Fig. 2.7(a)). The task is then, on the basis of these affinities, to partition $\mathcal{U}$ into Q disjoint non-empty sets (or *clusters*) $C_1, C_2, \ldots, C_Q$ $(Q \leq N)$, so that

$$\mathcal{U} = C_1 \cup C_2 \cup \cdots \cup C_Q, \quad C_i \neq \emptyset (i = 1 \ldots Q) \quad \text{and} \quad C_i \cap C_j = \emptyset (i \neq j),$$

where Q is not known *a priori*. The resulting clusters give a *partition* of $\mathcal{P}$.

We first give a brief review of the relevant graph theory, in whose terminology [38, 63] the above system of points, links and affinities is a *weighted graph* $\mathcal{G}$; the points are *vertices*, the links are *edges* and the affinity values are *edge weights*. The points are distinct, so $\mathcal{G}$ is said to be *labelled*, and the point-set associated with $\mathcal{G}$ is denoted $\mathcal{P}$, with finite cardinality $|\mathcal{P}| = N$.

The graph $\mathcal{G}$ is defined as a set of two-element sets $\{p_i, p_j\}$, each an unordered pair of distinct elements of $\mathcal{P}$ (i.e. $p_i \neq p_j$ if $i \neq j$). A link ℓ_{ij} is some element $\{p_i, p_j\} \in \mathcal{G}$ joining p_i to p_j (or equivalently p_j to p_i):

$$\ell_{ij} = \{p_i, p_j\}. \tag{2.4}$$

Points p_i and p_j are the *end-points* of ℓ_{ij}, and ℓ_{ij} is *incident* on these two points. A point in $\mathcal{P}$ lies in the *span* $\mathcal{S}$ of $\mathcal{G}$, denoted $\mathcal{S}(\mathcal{G})$, if at least one link is incident on it, i.e. if it is joined to at least one other point in $\mathcal{G}$. Formally, p_i is in $\mathcal{S}(\mathcal{G})$ if it participates in an element of $\mathcal{G}$:

$$\mathcal{S}(\mathcal{G}) = \{p \mid \exists \ell \in \mathcal{G}, p \in \ell\}. \tag{2.5}$$

---

[1] Here, the term "affinity" means "attraction"; it has no relation to the affine camera.

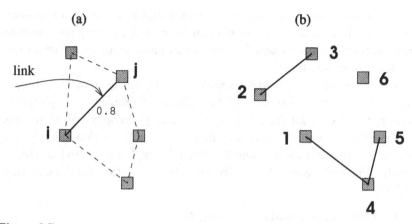

Figure 2.7
(a) The points p_i and p_j are connected by link ℓ_{ij} with affinity $a_{ij} = 0.8$; (b) The
graph $\mathcal{G}$ has 6 points and 3 links, with $\mathcal{G} = \{\ell_{14}, \ell_{23}, \ell_{45}\}$,
$\mathcal{P} = \{p_1, p_2, p_3, p_4, p_5, p_6\}$ and $\mathcal{S} = \{p_1, p_2, p_3, p_4, p_5\}$.

The span has cardinality $|\mathcal{S}|$ and we say that "$\mathcal{G}$ spans $\mathcal{S}$". The affinity
measure is a function $a : \mathcal{G} \rightarrow \mathcal{R}^1$ where a_{ij} (also written $a(\ell_{ij})$ is the affinity
of p_i for p_j. The *affinity score* is the sum of the affinities of $\mathcal{G}$'s links, viz.

$$\sum_{\ell \in \mathcal{G}} a(\ell). \tag{2.6}$$

Two points p_a and p_b in $\mathcal{G}$ are *connected* if some *path* (a sequence of links)
leads from p_a to p_b. That is, if p_a and p_b are points of $\mathcal{G}$, then p_a connects p_b
if and only if: (i) $\{p_a, p_b\} \in \mathcal{G}$; or (ii) $\exists p_c \in \mathcal{P}$ such that $\{p_a, p_c\} \in \mathcal{G}$ and p_c
connects p_b. If the path returns to the starting point (i.e. p connects p), it is
termed a *cycle*. Two connected points are said to be in the same *component*
of the graph, and when every point in $\mathcal{G}$ is connected to every other point,
the graph itself is connected. A *tree* T is a connected acyclic graph, and
a *spanning tree* T_s of $\mathcal{G}$ is a tree that spans the same point-set as $\mathcal{G}$. This
represents a minimal collection of links that preserves the connectedness of
the graph, yielding the important definition:

Definition 1 A **maximum affinity spanning tree** (MAST) $\mathcal{M}$ is a spanning tree for which the affinity score is maximum.

Such a MAST $\mathcal{M}$ provides a solution to the well-known *connector problem*:
given N vertices and the distances between them, find which edges to include
so that (a) there exists a path between every pair of vertices, and (b) the
total distance is a minimum. This problem can be posed in terms of road
construction, water mains, and so on. Other popular names for our MAST
include maximum weight spanning trees, maximal spanning trees, economy
trees and shortest connection networks.

There are many ways to construct a MAST and notable algorithms were proposed by Kruskal [30] and Prim [40]. One simple algorithm due to Kruskal [30] is as follows:

1. Sort the links in order of decreasing affinity.

2. Accept the maximum affinity link in the sorted list provided it doesn't form a closed loop with any previously chosen link. The spans of the connected subgraphs define the clusters.

3. Remove the accepted link from the list. Stop if all points are connected, else return to step 2.

Importantly, Prim [40] showed that an alternative way to construct the identical MAST is to start at *any point* $p_r \in \mathcal{P}$ (the *root* point) and successively add the *maximum affinity link* available to the evolving tree $\mathcal{T}$. Thus, by making the optimal decision at each step, an optimal tree eventually obtains, and this is the algorithm we employ.

There exists a wide range of clustering techniques [12, 18, 25, 41, 50, 65], differing greatly in the extent of their mathematical foundations. Indeed, many methods are defined only by an algorithm, without any established properties or specified optimisation criterion. A taxonomy of clustering algorithms [25] defines our method as a hierarchical agglomerative single-link algorithm. Existing algorithms are designed for a "single processor" possessing global information about the graph; the simplest technique builds on Kruskal's algorithm (Section 2.4.1), iteratively choosing the largest link that doesn't form a closed loop with any previously chosen link, and allowing the connected components to define the clusters (as in Fig. 2.8). We show that *identical* clusters can be obtained by distributing the computation, with each node performing local operations in parallel.

2.4.2 Clustering concepts

A *cluster* is a set of points $\mathcal{C} \subseteq \mathcal{P}$ that are grouped together on the basis of some clustering criterion. This section examines what constitutes a suitable clustering criterion and how to compute clusters that satisfy it. The clustering criterion will obviously be a function of the affinities, since these are the sole indicators of similarity between points. For instance, one simple criterion is a global threshold [25], i.e. delete all links whose affinities fall below a specified value a_0. The resulting "threshold graph" comprises isolated points and connected components, which define the clusters (Fig. 2.8). This scheme has the drawback of being very sensitive to the choice of a_0.

An "ideal" cluster $\mathcal{C}$ would be a group of points in which every point, of its own volition, selected the others in the group. The MAST paradigm provides a natural framework for defining and generating such clusters, since a

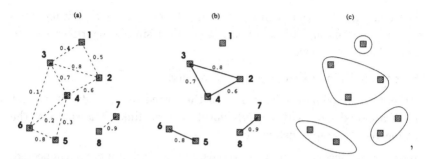

Figure 2.8
Threshold clustering: (a) Graph $\mathcal{G}$; (b) Links remaining after applying the
threshold $a_0 = 0.55$; (c) Resulting clusters.

MAST $\mathcal{M}_r$ grown from a root point p_r evolves by successively incorporating
the points to which it is most attracted. The resulting scheme is inherently
local and permits variable, automatically-chosen thresholds in different regions of the graph. We thus grow a MAST for *every point* in $\mathcal{P}$ and define
a cluster as follows:

Definition 2 The k points $\{p_1, p_2, \ldots, p_k\}$ are defined to be a cluster $\mathcal{C}$
if and only if all of their k evolving MAST's $\{\mathcal{M}_1, \mathcal{M}_2, \ldots, \mathcal{M}_k\}$ span the
same set of points.

The above cluster definition meshes elegantly with the MAST generation
process; once k points have satisfied the above criterion, the growth of their
k MAST's would be identical anyhow, since all have the same choices of
affinities. It is therefore logical to assign a single common MAST to the
cluster, effectively "shrinking" the group of points to a single point. The
hierarchy of partitions is thus generated as follows:

1. Initialise N singleton clusters $\mathcal{C}_i = \{p_i\}$ with MAST's $\mathcal{M}_i$ ($i = 1 \ldots N$).

2. Let each MAST $\mathcal{M}_i$ acquire the point p_{ni} for which it has the largest
   affinity, and update $\mathcal{M}_i$'s affinities for the points not yet acquired.

3. Check whether any MAST's share the same span. If so, the span becomes
   a new cluster, superseding the previous clusters of that span.

4. Stop when one global cluster remains (this will span $\mathcal{P}$, after $N - 1$
   iterations); otherwise, return to step 2 for another iteration.

Significantly, Theorem 1 in Shapiro [47] (Appendix A) proves that this parallel clustering algorithm gives *identical clusters to a single-link agglomerative method*. Local clusters of points thus form *simultaneously* in different
spatial regions of the graph, with clusters of cardinality k being discovered
on iteration $k - 1$.

A vital issue that remains is how to control the growth of these parallel MAST's; if they are permitted to grow fully, then a single global cluster will emerge after $N - 1$ iterations! A *termination condition* is therefore needed to decide when to halt the growth of a cluster (see Section 2.4.5). Once all MAST's have ceased growing, a graph with several connected components remains, and the clusters are the spans of these connected subgraphs.

2.4.3   The evolving MAST clustering algorithm

Although the clustering algorithm using parallel MAST's has been shown to generate the same clusters as the sequential single-link method, it clearly involves more computation. Indeed, it may seem strange to grow N MAST's in parallel when the same solution may be obtained by simply sorting the links once! Nonetheless, the new approach has important benefits.

First, when the affinity measure falls off with distance, distant points will have no direct affinity for one another, so each point need only be aware of its *local neighbourhood*. The parallel scheme can take advantage of this fact and use purely local operations to compute the desired clusters, without a single node having global knowledge. Naturally, as each MAST grows, its awareness of the global point-set gradually increases: it gains access to the neighbours of its neighbours, then to their neighbours and so on, until its growth is halted. In this way, each point obtains glimpses of the wider world purely on a "need-to-know" basis. Obviously, were all the MAST's to grow to full size, the benefits of this scheme would be lost, since each MAST would by then have global knowledge. In practice, MAST growth is halted by the termination condition so the MAST's are never globally aware.

Second, the computational cost can be greatly reduced by efficiently programming the local operations. The algorithm appears to have complexity $O(N^3)$, for there are N MAST's each with worst-case cost $O(N^2)$ (see Section 2.4.1). However, as we will show below, this cost can be greatly reduced by using the computations of neighbouring processors.

The clustering algorithm of Section 2.4.2 requires MAST's to be grown in parallel from every point in $\mathcal{G}$. This involves replicating Prim's algorithm for every point in the graph. Clearly, this "isolationist" approach (with each point oblivious to the other MAST's being grown simultaneously around it) is inefficient, and significant computational savings result from examining the MAST's of neighbouring points and utilising their decisions.

Importantly, Theorems 2 and 3 in [47] (Appendix A) prove for the general case that "trusting one's neighbours" gives the identical clusters to growing the N MAST's independently. That is, *a MAST fares no worse (in the affinity score sense) by trusting its neighbour's choices than if it grew in the normal way.* We term our algorithm the "grapevine algorithm" due to the "gossip" about desirable acquisitions that passes between the nodes.

2.4.4   The affinity measure

The choice of an appropriate affinity measure is crucial to the success of a clustering algorithm [12, 25]. Affinity measures are necessarily application-dependent; for example, shape and colour would obviously be important attributes when sorting apples, bananas and oranges. The properties most appropriate for our domain are those encoding structure and motion. Unfortunately, many existing structure/motion-based clustering schemes cope only with simple image motions (e.g., [29, 49]), which greatly restricts their applicability. We achieve greater generality by incorporating *3D* information in the affinity measure, employing the concepts of "affine structure" (3D structure defined up to an arbitrary 3D affine transformation). The intuition behind our approach is to extract groups of points that maintain their structural integrity over the m views. This requires examining the "shape" of the point-set in each frame, rather than individual trajectories.

There are, however, obstacles to grouping points on the basis of 3D scene structure. First, *four* points are needed to define 3D affine structure [9], making a point-to-point affinity measure impossible. Bootstrapping is thus problematic, since the combinatorics involved in initially generating all possible five-point groups[2] are prohibitively large. Second, the approach violates the "least exertion philosophy", namely "don't use a more complicated structure-motion model than necessary". After all, a full 3D affine model is unnecessary for an object undergoing, say, pure image translation; a simple 2D model suffices.

We therefore employ a *graduated clustering scheme,* starting with a simple motion interpretation and gradually increasing the complexity of the model as needed. There are many possible models: 2D translation, 2D Euclidean motion (translation, rotation and uniform scale), 2D affine motion, 3D fixed axis rotation, 3D Euclidean motion, 3D affine motion, 3D projective motion, and so on. We use a simple three-stage progression:

1. Rigid object undergoing fronto-parallel translation

   Each frame is formed by a 2D translation of the reference 2D shape (Fig. 2.9(a)),

   $$\mathbf{x}_i(k) = \mathbf{P}_i + \mathbf{d}(k),$$

   where $\mathbf{x}_i(k)$ is the image position of point i at time k, $\mathbf{P}_i$ is the reference position for point i, and $\mathbf{d}(k)$ is the displacement in frame k (a 2-vector).

---

[2] Four points define the affine frame; a fifth point is needed to form an invariant to assess the structure.

2. <u>Rigid plane undergoing 3D affine motion transformation</u>

Each frame is formed by a 2D affine transform of the reference 2D shape (Fig. 2.9(b)),

$$\mathbf{x}_i(k) = \mathbf{B}(k)\,\mathbf{P}_i + \mathbf{d}(k),$$

where $\mathbf{B}$ is a 2×2 matrix and $\{\mathbf{B}(k), \mathbf{d}(k)\}$ describes the 2D affine transform at time k of the points $\mathbf{P}_i$ (which lie on a plane).

3. <u>General rigid object undergoing 3D affine motion transformation</u>

Each frame is formed by an affine camera (projected linear combination of the reference 3D affine structure, as in Fig. 2.9(b) but with an extra point),

$$\mathbf{x}_i(k) = \mathbf{M}(k)\,\mathbf{X}_i + \mathbf{d}(k),$$

where $\mathbf{M}$ is a 3×2 matrix and $\mathbf{X}_i$ the 3D affine structure.

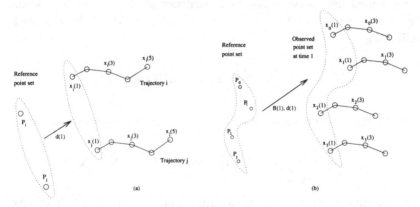

Figure 2.9
Affinity measures for the graduated clustering scheme: (a) Pure image translation (at least two points required); (b) Planar object undergoing general 3D affine motion (at least four points required).

2.4.4.1   The SVD-based affinity measure

The affinity measure encodes the attraction between two sets of trajectories, comprising N_a and N_b trajectories respectively ($N_a, N_b \geq 1$), where $N = N_a + N_b$ and each trajectory spans m views. The measure a must: (i) be *symmetric* (i.e. $a(\ell_{ij}) = a(\ell_{ji})$), since the algorithm uses undirected graphs; (ii) be *bounded* (i.e. $a_{min} \leq a \leq a_{max}$); and (iii) attain its maximum a_{max} when the attraction is *strongest* (i.e. the similarity is greatest). All of the above models can be formulated in terms of a noisy measurement matrix $\mathbf{V}$

of known rank (see later), whose best estimate $\hat{\mathbf{V}}$ is determined by singular value decomposition [51]. A suitable "goodness of fit" expression to assess the quality of this estimate $\hat{\mathbf{V}}$ is [42]

$$a = \frac{\mu_1^2 + \cdots + \mu_p^2}{\mu_1^2 + \cdots + \mu_r^2},$$

where r is the actual rank of $\mathbf{V}$, p is its theoretical (desired) rank ($p \le r$), and $\{\mu_1, \ldots, \mu_r\}$ are the r singular values in decreasing order. This function satisfies our requirements for an affinity measure, with a varying between 0 and 1 according to the quality of the SVD approximation ('1' representing a perfect match).

2.4.4.2   Example: Model 3 (projected 3D affine transform)

We provide the affinity measure for our 3D model; the other two models have similar measures, details of which can be found in [47]. The affinity measure used here is based on the consistency of the *3D* affine structure. The affine shape $\mathbf{X}_i$ and transformations $\{\mathbf{M}(k), \mathbf{d}(k)\}$ are determined by minimising

$$\epsilon_3(\mathbf{X}, \mathbf{M}, \mathbf{d}) = \sum_{k=1}^{m} \sum_{i=0}^{N-1} \mid \mathbf{x}_i(k) - \mathbf{M}(k)\,\mathbf{X}_i - \mathbf{d}(k) \mid^2,$$

which becomes (after registration with respect to the space-centroids[3])

$$\epsilon_3(\mathbf{X}, \mathbf{M}) = \sum_{k=1}^{m} \sum_{i=0}^{N-1} \mid [\mathbf{x}_i(k) - \bar{\mathbf{x}}(k)] - \mathbf{M}(k)\,[\mathbf{X}_i - \bar{\mathbf{X}}] \mid^2 .$$

The solution is given by the rank-3 approximation to the $2m \times N$ matrix

$$\mathbf{V} = \begin{bmatrix} \mathbf{x}_0(1) - \bar{\mathbf{x}}(1) & \mathbf{x}_1(1) - \bar{\mathbf{x}}(1) & \cdots & \mathbf{x}_{N-1}(1) - \bar{\mathbf{x}}(1) \\ \mathbf{x}_0(2) - \bar{\mathbf{x}}(2) & \mathbf{x}_1(2) - \bar{\mathbf{x}}(2) & \cdots & \mathbf{x}_{N-1}(2) - \bar{\mathbf{x}}(2) \\ \vdots & \vdots & & \vdots \\ \mathbf{x}_0(m) - \bar{\mathbf{x}}(m) & \mathbf{x}_1(m) - \bar{\mathbf{x}}(m) & \cdots & \mathbf{x}_{N-1}(m) - \bar{\mathbf{x}}(m) \end{bmatrix}, \quad (2.7)$$

computed by singular value decomposition into $2m \times 3$ and $3 \times N$ matrices:

$$\mathbf{V} \approx \mathbf{LS} = \begin{bmatrix} \mathbf{M}(1) \\ \mathbf{M}(2) \\ \vdots \\ \mathbf{M}(m) \end{bmatrix} \begin{bmatrix} \mathbf{X}_0 - \bar{\mathbf{X}} & \mathbf{X}_1 - \bar{\mathbf{X}} & \cdots & \mathbf{X}_{N-1} - \bar{\mathbf{X}} \end{bmatrix}.$$

---

[3] The *space-centroid* of the N-point cluster in a single frame is defined as $\bar{\mathbf{x}}(k) = \sum_{i=0}^{N-1} \mathbf{x}_i(k)/N$.

The columns of $\mathbf{L}$ are mutually orthogonal unit vectors, the rows of $\mathbf{S}$ are mutually orthogonal, and $\mathbf{V}$ and $\mathbf{L}$ have only $N - 1$ independent columns (due to the centering operation). Computing the rank-3 approximation requires $m \geq 2$ $(2m \geq 4)$ and $N \geq 5$ $(N - 1 \geq 4)$. The final affinity measure is

$$a_3(\mathcal{C}_a, \mathcal{C}_b) = \frac{\mu_1^2 + \mu_2^2 + \mu_3^2}{\mu_1^2 + \cdots + \mu_r^2} \ e^{-|\bar{\mathbf{x}}_a - \bar{\mathbf{x}}_b|^2 / \sigma_d^2}, \quad (2.8)$$

where σ_d is a Gaussian width. The affinity function is bounded ($a_{3,min} = 0$ and $a_{3,max} = 1$), and a poor value in any property (large centroid separation or poor shape correlation) decreases the affinity.

2.4.5 Termination criteria

As mentioned in Section 2.4.2, hierarchical agglomerative clustering schemes require a means of halting cluster growth, to prevent a single global cluster emerging. A *termination criterion* is therefore needed to assess the homogeneity of the grouped points. Thus, given the clusters $\mathcal{C}_a$ and $\mathcal{C}_b$, the task is to determine whether $\mathcal{C}_a \cup \mathcal{C}_b$ is a viable grouping, or whether the clusters have "grown too far".

A naive approach would be to simply threshold the affinity value; however, selecting a meaningful cut-off value is difficult. A more sophisticated approach is to use a *statistical noise model*, and if the variation in the joint cluster exceeds a specified confidence level (say 95%), the clusters are not merged. The noise model is assumed to be isotropic, additive, Gaussian image noise, making ϵ/σ^2 a χ^2 variable. If the χ^2 statistic for $\mathcal{C}_a \cup \mathcal{C}_b$ is excessively large, the merge is rejected and the growth of $\mathcal{C}_a$ and $\mathcal{C}_b$ halted. The degrees of freedom for the χ^2 tests quantify the redundancy present in the observations. We derive this below for the third motion model; similar derivations for the other two models can be found in [47].

2.4.6 Example: Model 3 (projected 3D affine transform)

The image positions are perturbed by noise $\mathbf{w}$,

$$\mathbf{x}_i(k) = \mathbf{M}(k)\,\mathbf{X}_i + \mathbf{d}(k) + \mathbf{w}_i(k),$$

where $\mathbf{w}$ is a zero-mean random variable ($E\{\mathbf{w}_i(k)\} = \mathbf{0}$), both temporally and spatially uncorrelated ($E\{\mathbf{w}_i(k)\mathbf{w}_j(k)\} = \delta_{ij}\sigma^2\mathbf{I}_2$ and $E\{\mathbf{w}_i(k)\mathbf{w}_i(\ell)\} = \delta_{k\ell}\,\sigma^2\,\mathbf{I}_2$). The samples fill a $2m \times N$ matrix, of which $2m(N - 1)$ elements are independent. The computed parameters fill $2m \times 3$ and $3 \times N$ matrices ($\mathbf{L}$ and $\mathbf{S}$ respectively); $\mathbf{L}$ has $2m(3) - 6$ independent elements and $\mathbf{S}$ has $3(N - 1) - 3$ independent elements[4]. The degrees of freedom in the χ^2

---

[4] The three mutually orthogonal columns of $\mathbf{L}$ give 6 constraints; the centred rows in $\mathbf{S}$ along with their mutual orthogonality contribute another 6 (cf. Section 2.4.4.2).

variable ϵ_3/σ^2 are thus

$$d_3 = [2m(N-1)] - [(6m-6) + (3N-6)] = 2mN - 8m - 3N + 12,$$

and d_3 must always exceed zero. For example, when $m = 2$ and $N = 5$, then $d_3 = 1$. If ϵ_3/σ^2 then exceeds $\chi^2_{d_3,95\%}$ (say), the merge is prohibited.

2.4.7 Implementation

The three stages in the graduated clustering scheme are performed in sequence, i.e. the network first finds clusters satisfying Model 1, then Model 2, and finally Model 3. Each stage completes its growth fully before the next stage begins, with the final clusters of one stage (including singleton points that haven't yet been grouped) serving as the starting nodes for the following stage. This strategy ensures that clusters are always disjoint. Each stage can therefore be considered a "pre-grouping step" for the next stage. The scheme is realised in a two-layer network (Fig. 2.10):

- the first layer contains simple nodes, each representing an m-frame image trajectory;

- the second layer contains compound nodes, which encode the MAST's (and eventually the final clusters).

Each node in the first layer (the *child*) has a corresponding *super-node* in the second layer (the *parent*) to maintain its personal MAST (Fig. 2.10). A *cluster-node* is a special super-node supervising more than one child, and is formed when two or more super-nodes merge (in which case the MAST's of the children coincide). Once the two-layer network has been created, each point p_i is assigned a set of neighbours to establish the initial graph $\mathcal{G}$ (from which links will be selected). These local neighbourhoods are formed by Delaunay triangulation of the point-set [39] (Fig. 2.11), with neighbours then defined as those points directly connected to p_i by a triangle side.

All three stages follow the same basic control strategy. First, each node sets up its affinity vector **a** by calculating its attraction for the nodes falling within its spatial neighbourhood. Then a grow-merge-update cycle iterates until the final clusters for that stage emerge:

1. *Grow*. Each compound node selects the best neighbour to acquire and updates its MAST. If no neighbours remain (i.e. there are no options for expansion), the node's growth terminates.

2. *Merge*. Each compound node checks its neighbours to see whether they can cluster; to do so, their MAST's must be identical and the termination criterion must approve the merge. If the merge is acceptable, one compound node (designated the "cluster-node") assumes responsibility

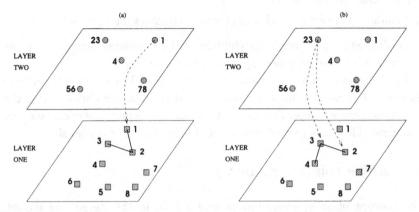

Figure 2.10
The two-layer architecture. Layer 1 contains simple nodes (squares) and layer 2
contains compound nodes (circles): (a) The super-node for p_1; (b) The cluster-node
for (p_2, p_3).

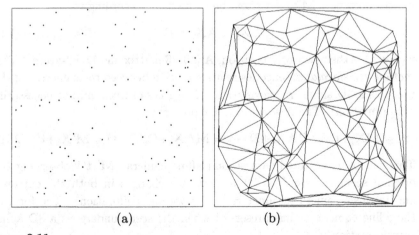

Figure 2.11
A point-set (defined by the time-centroids of the trajectories) and its Delaunay
triangulation.

for all the points in the cluster and the other compound nodes are destroyed; if the merge is unacceptable, the appropriate compound nodes have their growth halted.

3. *Update* : Various network maintenance counters are updated.

Once all growth has ceased, the children of the remaining compound nodes (super-nodes and cluster-nodes) are the final clusters.

Fig. 2.12 shows an example with two rotating heads, one nodding and one shaking. A moving 5-frame window is used to form the clusters, and the size of the groups change due to points disappearing and new points coming into view. The trajectory of the centroid of each cluster is also shown.

2.5 Affine epipolar geometry

The concept of an epipolar line is well known in the stereo and motion literature. For an affine stereo-pair, all projection rays are parallel (the optic centre lies at infinity). Since the affine camera preserves parallelism, the epipolar lines are also parallel and the epipoles are situated at infinity in the image planes. The following sections derive the equations of the epipolar line.

2.5.1 Affine motion equations

Consider a 3D world point $\mathbf{X}_i$ projected by an affine camera $\{\mathbf{M}, \mathbf{t}\}$ to an image point $\mathbf{x}_i = \mathbf{M}\mathbf{X}_i + \mathbf{t}$. Let the scene move according to

$$\mathbf{X}'_i = \mathbf{A}\mathbf{X}_i + \mathbf{D}, \qquad (2.9)$$

where $\mathbf{X}'_i$ is the new world position, $\mathbf{A}$ a 3×3 matrix and $\mathbf{D}$ a 3-vector. This *motion transformation* encodes relative motion between the camera and the world as a 3D affine transformation (12 degrees of freedom, not necessarily a rigid motion). The new world point projects to

$$\mathbf{x}'_i = \mathbf{M}\mathbf{X}'_i + \mathbf{t} = \mathbf{M}(\mathbf{A}\mathbf{X}_i + \mathbf{D}) + \mathbf{t} = \mathbf{M}\mathbf{A}\mathbf{X}_i + (\mathbf{M}\mathbf{D} + \mathbf{t}) = \mathbf{M}'\mathbf{X}_i + \mathbf{t}'. \quad (2.10)$$

This can be interpreted as a second affine camera $\{\mathbf{M}', \mathbf{t}'\}$ observing the original scene, where $\{\mathbf{M}', \mathbf{t}'\}$ account for changes in both the extrinsic and intrinsic camera parameters (i.e., pose and calibration). The form of the affine camera is thus preserved when the scene undergoes a 3D affine transformation.

An important advantage of the affine camera model is that *relative image coordinates* cancel out translation vectors; if $\mathbf{X}_0$ is a designated reference point (or *origin*), then registering the points gives

$$\Delta\mathbf{x} = \mathbf{x} - \mathbf{x}_0 = \mathbf{M}\Delta\mathbf{X} \quad \text{and} \quad \Delta\mathbf{x}' = \mathbf{x}' - \mathbf{x}'_0 = \mathbf{M}'\Delta\mathbf{X} = \mathbf{M}\mathbf{A}\Delta\mathbf{X}, \quad (2.11)$$

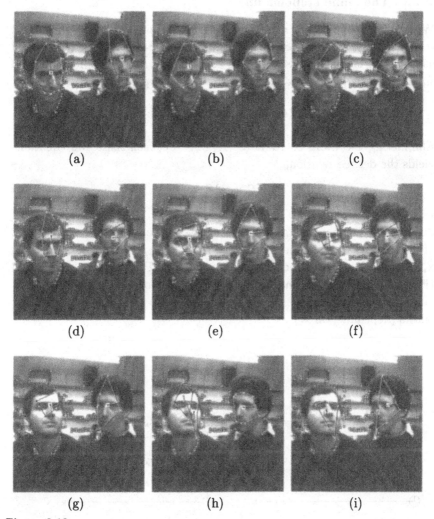

Figure 2.12
Sequence of two moving heads. The left head nods and the right head shakes.
Crosses indicate background points, and a convex hull is drawn around the moving
points. The centroid of these points (along with its trajectory) is also shown, with
the marker indicating the current centroid position.

which are clearly independent of $\mathbf{D}$ (and also of $\mathbf{t}$ and $\mathbf{t}'$). This cancellation relies crucially on linearity and is not possible in general under perspective projection. It will be used frequently in later sections.

2.5.2 The affine epipolar line

We can now relate a point in one image to its position in the other image and to the intrinsic and extrinsic camera parameters. Suppose $\mathbf{M}$ is partitioned as $(\mathbf{B} \mid \mathbf{b})$, where $\mathbf{B}$ is a (non-singular) 2×2 matrix and $\mathbf{b}$ a 2×1 vector, and similarly $\mathbf{M}'$ is partitioned into $(\mathbf{B}' \mid \mathbf{b}')$. Then Equations (2.3) and (2.10)

$$\mathbf{x}_i = \mathbf{B}\left[\begin{array}{c} X_i \\ Y_i \end{array}\right] + Z_i\,\mathbf{b} + \mathbf{t} \quad \text{and} \quad \mathbf{x}'_i = \mathbf{B}'\left[\begin{array}{c} X_i \\ Y_i \end{array}\right] + Z_i\,\mathbf{b}' + \mathbf{t}'. \quad (2.12)$$

Eliminating the world coordinates $(X_i, Y_i)^\top$ between these two equations yields the desired relation,

$$\mathbf{x}'_i = \boldsymbol{\Gamma}\,\mathbf{x}_i + Z_i\,\mathbf{d} + \boldsymbol{\varepsilon}, \quad (2.13)$$

with $\boldsymbol{\Gamma} = \mathbf{B}'\,\mathbf{B}^{-1}$, $\mathbf{d} = \mathbf{b}' - \boldsymbol{\Gamma}\mathbf{b}$ and $\boldsymbol{\varepsilon} = \mathbf{t}' - \boldsymbol{\Gamma}\mathbf{t}$. Quantities $\boldsymbol{\Gamma}$, $\mathbf{d}$ and $\boldsymbol{\varepsilon}$ depend only on the cameras and the relative motion; they are independent of scene structure. Equation (2.13) shows that the point $\mathbf{x}'_i$ associated with $\mathbf{x}_i$ lies on a line in the second image with offset $\boldsymbol{\Gamma}\,\mathbf{x}_i + \boldsymbol{\varepsilon}$ and direction $\mathbf{d}$ (Fig. 2.13). The unknown depth Z_i determines how far along this line $\mathbf{x}'_i$ lies. The epipolar lines are clearly parallel ($\hat{\mathbf{d}}$ is constant) and have different offsets (depending on $\mathbf{x}_i$).

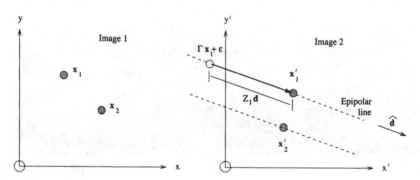

Figure 2.13
The affine epipolar line: $\mathbf{x}'_i = \boldsymbol{\Gamma}\,\mathbf{x}_i + \boldsymbol{\varepsilon} + Z_i\,\mathbf{d}$.

Taking difference vectors $\boldsymbol{\Delta}\mathbf{x}_i = \mathbf{x}_i - \mathbf{x}_0$ and $\boldsymbol{\Delta}\mathbf{x}'_i = \mathbf{x}'_i - \mathbf{x}'_0$ gives translation-invariant versions of these formulae, by eliminating $\boldsymbol{\varepsilon}$ (and hence $\mathbf{D}$, $\mathbf{t}$ and $\mathbf{t}'$):

$$\boldsymbol{\Delta}\mathbf{x}'_i = \mathbf{B}'\left[\begin{array}{c} \Delta X_i \\ \Delta Y_i \end{array}\right] + \Delta Z_i\,\mathbf{b}' = \boldsymbol{\Gamma}\,\boldsymbol{\Delta}\mathbf{x}_i + \Delta Z_i\,\mathbf{d} \quad (2.14)$$

Equation (2.13) defined the epipolar line in parametric form; an *explicit* form is obtained by eliminating the depths Z_i, giving a single equation in the *image measurables*,

$$(\mathbf{x}'_i - \mathbf{\Gamma}\mathbf{x}_i - \boldsymbol{\varepsilon}) \cdot \mathbf{d}^\perp = 0, \tag{2.15}$$

where $\mathbf{d}^\perp$ is the perpendicular to $\mathbf{d}$. Equation (2.15) can also be written

$$\boxed{a\,x'_i + b\,y'_i + c\,x_i + d\,y_i + e = 0} \tag{2.16}$$

with $(a,b)^\top = \mathbf{d}^\perp$, $(c,d)^\top = -\mathbf{\Gamma}^\top \mathbf{d}^\perp$ and $e = -\boldsymbol{\varepsilon}^\top \mathbf{d}^\perp$. This *affine epipolar constraint equation* [67] is a linear equation in the unknown constants $a \ldots e$, which depend only on the camera parameters and the relative motion. Only the *ratios* of the five parameters $a \ldots e$ can be computed, so Equation (2.16) has only *four* independent degrees of freedom. The difference vector form is

$$a\,\Delta x'_i + b\,\Delta y'_i + c\,\Delta x_i + d\,\Delta y_i = 0. \tag{2.17}$$

Since Equation (2.16) is defined up to a scale factor, only four point correspondences are needed to solve for the four independent degrees of freedom. When n correspondences are available ($n > 4$), it is advantageous to use *all* the points, since this improves the accuracy of the solution, allows detection of outliers, and obviates the need to select a minimal point set.

Least squares solutions, degeneracies and the relation to previous work were discussed in [46], along with the appropriate noise models. Fig. 2.14 shows an example with a head nodding relative to a stationary camera. The mean perpendicular distance between corner and epipolar line is 0.49 pixels, i.e. the epipolar lines are typically within a pixel accuracy (on 256×256 images), despite the lack of subpixel accuracy in the corner detection stage. These epipolar lines therefore provide effective constraints for correspondence.

2.6   Rigid motion estimation

We now tackle the *3D motion estimation* problem, using affine epipolar geometry as the tool. Given m distinct views of n points located on a rigid object, the task is to compute its 3D motion without prior 3D knowledge.

We relate affine epipolar geometry to the rigid motion parameters, and formalise Koenderink and van Doorn's motion representation [9]. The scale, cyclotorsion angle and projected axis of rotation are then computed *directly* from the epipolar geometry (i.e. using two views). The only camera calibration parameter needed here is aspect ratio. A suitable error model is derived along with a linear Kalman filter to determine optimal estimates over long

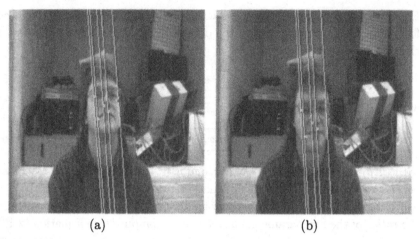

(a)   (b)

Figure 2.14
Affine epipolar lines: (a)(b) The head nods (every 2nd epipolar line shown).

sequences. Unlike some previous point-based structure and motion schemes (e.g. [7]), we do not assign an individual Kalman filter to each 3D feature; this liberates us from having to track individual 3D points through multiple views. Least squares formulations are employed to utilise *all* available points, not just a minimum set. This improves the accuracy of the motion solution and also obviates the need to *select* a local coordinate frame.

This chapter only considers the motion parameters computable from the two-view case; details on the three-view case can be found in [46]. It is well-known that two distinct views of four non-coplanar, rigid points generate a one-parameter family of structure and motion solutions under parallel projection [4, 24, 9]. Koenderink and van Doorn [9] showed further that from two views, the change in scale, the cyclorotation angle and the projections of the axes of rotation can be recovered. Their algorithm used the minimum set of points, required a perceptual frame and involved a succession of stages. These shortcomings are overcome by deriving this partial motion solution *directly from the affine epipolar geometry*. The resulting algorithm uses the full set of points and requires no local coordinate frame.

First, rigidity is imposed on the world motion parameters $\{\mathbf{A}, \mathbf{D}\}$ by requiring $\mathbf{A}$ to be a rotation matrix. A scale factor $s = Z_{ave}/Z'_{ave}$ is introduced ($s > 1$ for a "looming" object and $s < 1$ for a "receding" one), and scaled depth is defined as $\Delta z_i = f\Delta Z_i/Z_{ave} = f(Z_i - Z_{ave})/Z_{ave}$. Equation (2.14) then becomes

$$\Delta\mathbf{x}' = s \begin{bmatrix} R_{11} & R_{12} \\ R_{21} & R_{22} \end{bmatrix} \Delta\mathbf{x} + s\,\Delta z \begin{bmatrix} R_{13} \\ R_{23} \end{bmatrix} \qquad (2.18)$$

This is the rigid motion form of the epipolar line, with direction $(R_{13}, R_{23})^{\top}$. Taking the component of $\Delta\mathbf{x}'$ perpendicular to this direction and using standard cross product equalities for a rotation matrix gives the rigid motion form of the affine epipolar constraint equation (Equation (2.17)):

$$\boxed{R_{23}\Delta x' - R_{13}\Delta y' + sR_{32}\Delta x - sR_{31}\Delta y = 0} \tag{2.19}$$

Equations (2.18) and (2.19) generalise the pure orthographic forms ($s = 1$) derived by Huang and Lee [24] and used in [8, 22].

2.6.1   The KvD rotation representation

Koenderink and van Doorn [9] introduced a novel rotation representation (which we term *KvD* and show in [46] to be a variant of Euler angles), and presented a geometric analysis of it. We have formalised their representation algebraically to illustrate its advantages. In *KvD*, the rotation is decomposed into two parts. First, there is a rotation through angle θ in the image plane (i.e. about the line of sight). This is followed by a rotation through an angle ρ about a unit axis $\boldsymbol{\Phi}$ lying in a plane parallel to the image plane, with $\boldsymbol{\Phi}$ angled at ϕ to the positive X axis, i.e. a pure rotation *out of* the image plane.

KvD has three main advantages. First, rotation about the optic axis provides no new information about structure, so it makes sense to first remove this "useless" component. Second, *KvD* exposes the "bas-relief" (depth-turn) ambiguity in a way that the more popular angle-axis form doesn't—an advantage of Euler forms in general [20]. Third, *KvD* is elegant in that two views enable us to solve completely for two rotation angles (ϕ and θ), with the third (ρ) parameterising the remaining family of solutions. This contrasts with, say, the angle-axis form, for which only one angle can be solved from two views, the two remaining angles satisfying a non-linear constraint equation [4]. The disadvantage of *KvD* is that the physical interpretation of rotation occurring about a single 3D axis is lost.

2.6.2   Solving for s, ϕ and θ

It is now shown how to solve for the scale factor (s), the projection of the axis of rotation (ϕ) and the cyclotorsion angle (θ) directly from the affine epipolar geometry. Substituting the KvD expressions for the rotation matrix elements into the epipolar constraint (Equation (2.19)) gives

$$\boxed{\sin\rho\left[\cos\phi\,\Delta x'_i + \sin\phi\,\Delta y'_i - s\cos(\phi-\theta)\,\Delta x_i - s\sin(\phi-\theta)\,\Delta y_i\right] = 0}$$
$$\tag{2.20}$$

It is evident from Equation (2.20) that s, θ and ϕ can be computed directly from the affine epipolar geometry, because Section 2.5 solved

$$a\Delta x_i' + b\Delta y_i' + c\Delta x_i + d\Delta y_i = 0$$

for the ratios of a, b, c and d. A direct comparison with Equation (2.20) yields the central result,

$$\tan\phi = \frac{b}{a}, \quad \tan(\phi - \theta) = \frac{d}{c} \text{ and } s^2 = \frac{c^2 + d^2}{a^2 + b^2}, \qquad (2.21)$$

with $s > 0$ (by definition). We then compute a noise model for s, ϕ and θ (see [46]). Fig. 2.15(a) graphs successive two-frame estimates of s, θ and ϕ in a synthetic 30-frame sequence with additive Gaussian image noise. The object undergoes two different, constant motions separated by a step change: s is initially unity (no translation in depth) and then increases as the object approaches the camera at constant speed; θ changes from 4° to -2°; and ϕ changes from 82° to 50°. The true parameter values clearly lie within the computed 95% error bounds.

Now, physical objects have inertia and it is sensible to exploit this temporal continuity to improve the motion estimates. This is achieved by means of a linear discrete-time Kalman filter [3], a popular framework for weighting observations and predictions [7, 14, 66]. Fig. 2.15(b) shows the filtered results of the example, along with the 95% confidence intervals obtained from the Kalman filter variances. The solution is clearly smoother after filtering and the variances decrease as the filter becomes more confident in its predictions. Note the increase in variances at the motion discontinuity; at that stage, the filter detects that the observation falls outside the validation region and re-initialises itself.

Fig. 2.16 shows a second example with a subject shaking his head. Here the true axis is unknown, but it is approximately vertical and the results are qualitatively correct.

2.7 Conclusions

This chapter has developed a coherent framework for analysing image sequences based on the affine camera, and has demonstrated the practical feasibility of recovering 3D structure and motion in a bottom-up fashion, using "corner" features. New algorithms have been proposed to cluster points into 3D affine objects, and the theory of affine epipolar geometry has been derived and applied to rigid motion estimation. Due consideration has been paid to error and noise models, with a χ^2 test serving as a termination criterion for cluster growth and confidence limits in the motion parameters facilitating Kalman filtering. The algorithms have been implemented and

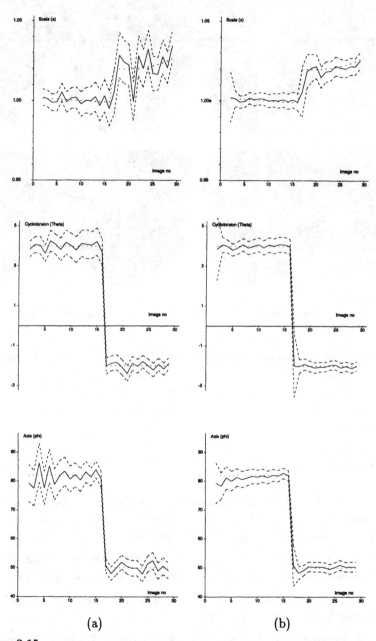

(a)   (b)

Figure 2.15
Estimates of s, θ and ϕ over a 30-frame synthetic sequence with $\sigma = 0.5$ pixels and
a discontinuity in constant motion. Solid lines show computed values, dotted lines
show true values, and dashed lines show 95% confidence intervals: (a) Raw 2-frame
estimates with associated error models (input to filter); (b) Kalman filtered
estimates with 95% confidence regions (within which the true values fall).

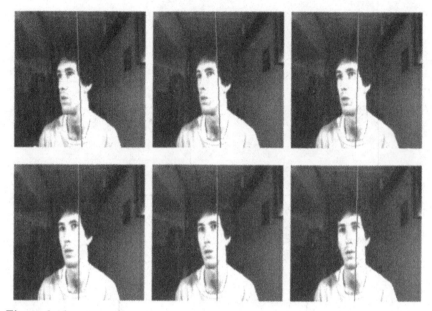

Figure 2.16
The subject shakes his head. The true axis is roughly vertical, giving qualitatively
correct results.

tested on a wide range of sequences, with focus on the problem of tracking
human heads. The use of n points and m frames has lead to enhanced
noise immunity and has also simplified the algorithms in important ways,
e.g. local coordinate frames are no longer needed to compute rigid motion
parameters.

References

[1] G. Adiv, "Determining 3D motion and structure from optical flow gen-
    erated by several moving objects", *IEEE Trans. Pattern Anal. Machine
    Intell.*, Vol. PAMI-7, July 1985, pp. 384–401.

[2] H. Asada and M. Brady, "The curvature primalsketch", *IEEE Trans.
    Pattern Anal. Machine Intell.*, Vol. PAMI-8, No. 1, Jan. 1986, pp. 2–14.

[3] Y. Bar–Shalom and T.E. Fortmann, *Tracking and data association*,
    Academic Press Inc., USA, 1988.

[4] B.M. Bennett, D.D. Hoffman, J.E. Nicola and C. Prakash, "Structure
    from two orthographic views of rigid motion", *Journal of Optical Soci-
    ety of America*, Vol. 6, No. 7, July 1989, pp. 1052–1069.

[5] M. Berger, *Geometry I*, Springer Verlag, 1980.

[6] J.M. Brady, "Seeds of perception", *Proceedings of the 3rd Alvey Vision Conference,* Cambridge University, Sept. 1987, pp. 259–265.

[7] D. Charnley, C. Harris, M. Pike, E. Sparks and M. Stephens, "The DROID 3D vision system: algorithms for geometric integration", Plessey Research, Roke Manor, Technical Note 72/88/N488U, Dec. 1988.

[8] H.C. Chen and T.S. Huang, "Using motion from orthographic views to verify 3D point matches", *IEEE Trans. Pattern Anal. Machine Intell.,* Vol. PAMI-13, No. 9, Sept. 1991, pp. 872–878.

[9] R. Cipolla, Y. Okamoto and Y. Kuno, "Robust structure from motion using motion parallax", *Proceedings International Conference on Computer Vision (ICCV-4),* Berlin, May 1993, pp. 374–382.

[10] J. Cooper, S. Venkatesh and L. Kitchen, "Early jump–out corner detectors", *IEEE Trans. Pattern Anal. Machine Intell.,* Vol. PAMI-15, No. 8, Aug. 1993, pp. 823–828.

[11] R. Deriche and G. Giraudon, "A computational approach for corner and vertex detection", *International Journal of Computer Vision,* Vol. 10, No. 2, Nov. 1993, pp. 101–124.

[12] R.O. Duda and P.E. Hart, *Pattern Classification and Scene Analysis,* John Wiley & Sons, USA, 1973.

[13] L. Dreschler and H. Nagel, "Volumetric model and 3D trajectory of a moving car derived from monocular TV–frame sequence of a street scene", *Computer Vision, Graphics and Image Processing,* Vol. 20, No. 3, Nov. 1982, pp. 199–228.

[14] O.D. Faugeras, F. Lustman and G. Toscani, "Motion and structure from motion from point and line matches", *Proceedings International Conference on Computer Vision (ICCV-1),* London, UK, May 1987, pp. 25–34.

[15] O.D. Faugeras, Q-T. Luong and S.J. Maybank, "Camera self-calibration: theory and experiments" in G. Sandini (ed.), *Proceedings European Conference on Computer Vision* (ECCV–92), 1992, pp. 321–334.

[16] O.D. Faugeras, "What can be seen in three dimensions with an uncalibrated stereo rig?" in G. Sandini (ed.), *Proceedings European Conference on Computer Vision* (ECCV–92), 1992, pp. 563–578.

[17] S. Gong and M. Brady, "Parallel computation of optic flow" in *Proceedings European Conference on Computer Vision* (ECCV–90), 1990, pp. 124–133.

[18] J.C. Gower and G.J.S. Ross, "Minimum spanning trees and single linkage cluster analysis", *Applied Statistics*, Vol. 18, No. 1, 1969, pp. 54–64.

[19] C.G. Harris and M. Stephens, "A combined corner and edge detector", *Proceedings 4th Alvey Vision Conference*, 1988, pp. 147–151.

[20] C. Harris, "Structure–from–motion under orthographic projection", *First European Conference on Computer Vision* (ECCV–90), 1990, pp. 118–123.

[21] R.I. Hartley, R. Gupta and T. Chang, "Stereo from uncalibrated cameras," *Proceedings CVPR'92*, 1992, pp. 761–764.

[22] X. Hu and N. Ahuja, "Motion estimation under orthographic projection", *IEEE Transactions on Robotics and Automation*, Vol. 7, No. 6, 1991, pp. 848–853.

[23] T.S. Huang (ed.), *Image Sequence Analysis*, Springer–Verlag, USA, 1981.

[24] T.S. Huang and C.H. Lee, "Motion and structure from orthographic projections", *IEEE Trans. Pattern Anal. Machine Intell.*, Vol. PAMI-11, No. 5, 1989, pp. 536–40.

[25] A.K. Jain and R.C. Dubes, *Algorithms for Clustering Data*, Prentice Hall, USA, 1988.

[26] N.D. Kenyon, "Videoconferencing", *British Telecom Technical Journal*, Vol. 2, No. 2, April 1984, pp. 5–18.

[27] L. Kitchen and A. Rosenfeld, "Gray level corner detection", *Pattern Recognition Letters*, Vol. 1, Dec. 1982, pp. 95–102.

[28] J.J. Koenderink and A.J. van Doorn, "Affine structure from motion", *Journal of Optical Society of America*, Vol. 8, No. 2, Feb. 1991, pp. 377-385.

[29] D. Koller, N. Heinze and H.H. Nagel, "Algorithmic characterisation of vehicle trajectories from image sequences by motion verbs" in *Proceeding CVPR'91*, Hawaii, June 1991, pp. 90–95.

[30] J.B. Kruskal, "On the shortest spanning subtree of a graph and the traveling salesman problem", *Proceedings American Mathematical Society*, Vol. 7, No. 1, 1956, pp. 48–50.

[31] C. Lee and T. Huang, "Finding point correspondences and determining motion of a rigid object from two weak perspective views", *Computer Vision, Graphics and Image Processing*, Vol. 52, 1990, pp. 309–327.

[32] H.C. Longuet–Higgins, "A computer algorithm for reconstructing a scene from two projections", *Nature*, Vol. 293, 1981, pp. 133–135.

[33] H.P. Moravec, "The Stanford cart and the CMU rover", *Proceedings of the IEEE,* Vol. 71, No. 7, 1983, pp. 872–884.

[34] J.L. Mundy and A. Zisserman (eds), *Geometric Invariance in Computer Vision,* MIT Press, USA, 1992.

[35] H–H. Nagel, "Displacement vectors derived from second–order intensity variations in image sequences", *Computer Vision, Graphics and Image Processing,* Vol. 21, 1983, pp. 85–117.

[36] H.H. Nagel, "Image sequences – ten (octal) years: from phenomenology towards a theoretical foundation" in *Proc. 8th International Conference on Pattern Recognition,* Paris, Oct. 1986, pp. 1174–1185.

[37] J.A. Noble, *Description of Image Surface,* D.Phil Thesis, Department of Engineering Science, Oxford University, 1989.

[38] O. Ore, *Graphs and Their Uses,* Mathematical Association of America, revised R.J. Wilson, USA, 1990.

[39] F.P. Preparata and M.I. Shamos, *Computational geometry.: an introduction,* Springer-Verlag, New York, 1985.

[40] R.C. Prim, "Shortest connection networks and some generalisations", *Bell System Technical Journal,* Vol. 36, Nov. 1957, pp. 1389–1401.

[41] R.F. Rashid, "Towards a system for the interpretation of moving light displays", *IEEE Trans. Computers,* Vol. PAMI-2, No. 6, Nov. 1980, pp. 574–581.

[42] J.O. Rawlings, *Applied Regression Analysis: A Research Tool,* Wadsworth and Brooks, USA, 1988.

[43] L.S. Shapiro, H. Wang and J.M. Brady, "A matching and tracking strategy for independently moving objects" in D. Hogg and R. Boyle (eds), *Proceedings BMVC'92,* Springer–Verlag, UK, 1992, pp. 139–148.

[44] L.S. Shapiro and J.M. Brady, "Rejecting outliers and estimating errors in an orthogonal regression framework", Tech. Report OUEL 1974/93, Dept. Engineering Science, University of Oxford, Feb. 1993. Submitted for publication.

[45] L.S. Shapiro, A. Zisserman and J.M. Brady, "What can one see with an affine camera?", Tech. Report 1993/93, Dept. Engineering Science, University of Oxford, June 1993.

[46] L.S. Shapiro, A. Zisserman and J.M. Brady, "Motion from point matches using affine epipolar geometry", Tech. Report 1994/93, Dept. Engineering Science, University of Oxford, June 1993. Submitted for publication.

[47] L.S. Shapiro, "Affine analysis of image sequences", PhD thesis, Oxford University, 1993.

[48] A. Shashua and S. Ullman, "Structural saliency: the detection of globally salient structures using a locally connected network", *Proceedings International Conference on Computer Vision (ICCV-2)*, Florida, 1988, pp. 321–327.

[49] S. Smith, "Feature based image sequence understanding", D. Phil thesis, Dept. Engineering Science, Oxford University, 1992.

[50] H. Spaïh, *Cluster Analysis Algorithms for Data Reduction and Classification of Objects*, Ellis Horwood Ltd., UK, 1980.

[51] G. Strang, *Linear Algebra and its Applications*, 3rd ed., Harcourt Brace Jovanovich Inc., USA, 1988.

[52] D.W. Thompson and J.L. Mundy, "Three dimensional model matching from an unconstrained viewpoint" in *IEEE Conference on Robotics and Automation*, Raleigh, NC, 1987, pp. 208–220.

[53] C. Tomasi and T. Kanade, "Shape and motion from image streams under orthography: a factorization method", *International Journal of Computer Vision*, Vol. 9, No. 2, Nov. 1992, pp. 137–154.

[54] S. Ullman, "Filling in the gaps: the shape of subjective contours and a model for their generation", *Biological Cybernetics*, Vol. 25, 1976, pp. 1–6.

[55] S. Ullman, *The Interpretation of Visual Motion*, MIT Press, USA, 1979.

[56] S. Ullman and R. Basri, "Recognition by linear combinations of model", *IEEE Trans. Pattern Anal. Machine Intell.*, Vol. 13, No. 10, Oct. 1991, pp. 992–1006.

[57] A. Verri and T. Poggio, "Against quantitative optic flow", *Proceedings International Conference on Computer Vision (ICCV-1)*, London, UK, May 1987, pp. 171–180.

[58] H. Wang, J.M. Brady and I. Page, "A fast algorithm for computing optic flow and its implementation on a transputer array", *Proceedings of the British Machine Vision Conference (BMVC90)*, Oxford, UK, Sept. 1990, pp. 175–180.

[59] H. Wang and J.M. Brady, "A structure–from–motion vision algorithm for robot guidance" in I. Masaki (ed.), *Proceedings IEEE Symposium on Intelligent Vehicles*, Detroit, June 1992.

[60] H. Wang and J.M. Brady, "Corner detection: some new results", *IEE Colloquium Digest of Systems Aspects of Machine Perception and Vision*, London, 1992, pp. 1.1–1.4.

[61] J. Walsh, "Videoconferencing comes of age", *Communications International*, Oct. 1991, pp. 157–159.

[62] J. Weng, T.S. Huang and N. Ahuja, "Motion and structure from two perspective views: algorithms, error analysis and error estimation", *IEEE Trans. Pattern Anal. Machine Intell.*, Vol. PAMI-11, No. 5, May 1989, pp. 451–476.

[63] R.J. Wilson and J.J. Watkins, *Graphs: An Introductory Approach*, John Wiley & Sons, USA, 1990.

[64] G. Xu, E. Nishimura and S. Tsuji, "Image correspondence and segmentation by epipolar lines: theory, algorithm and applications", Technical Report, Dept. Systems Engineering, Osaka University, July 1993.

[65] C.T. Zahn, "Graph–theoretical methods for detecting and describing Gestalt clusters", *IEEE Trans. Computers*, Vol. C–20, No. 1, Jan. 1971, pp. 68–86.

[66] Z. Zhang and O. Faugeras, *3D Dynamic Scene Analysis*, Springer–Verlag, 1992.

[67] A. Zisserman, *Notes on geometric invariance in vision: BMVC'92 tutorial*, Leeds, Sept. 1992.

3 Tracking and Measuring Drivers Eyes

David Tock and Ian Craw

3.1 Introduction

In this chapter we describe a computer vision system for tracking the eyes of a car driver in order to measure the corresponding blink rate. This measure is used as part of a larger system designed to detect when a car driver is becoming drowsy.

The requirements of such a system are very specific; it must not interfere with the driver's normal performance, and must require no co-operation from the driver.

There are already a number of systems specifically designed for tracking eye movements, but most are excluded by one or other of these requirements. For example a head mounted camera is viable for a combat pilot, who normally wears a helmet anyway; ophthalmologists and psychologists constrain the subject's head in some form of clamp while observations are made. Neither of these is acceptable in a vehicle, where either would restrict the movement of the driver and compromise safety.

A less restrictive technique involves directing laser light onto the eye, but again, this is ruled out for safety reasons, as is any technique that involves any lighting other than ambient. This also precludes the use of IR or UV lighting, as the potential effects may not be fully understood. A more intrusive approach is to use an electrooculogram; while this gives the driver the freedom of movement, it requires numerous electrodes to be attached to the face, and again is practicable only in test situations.

We are thus led to consider a simple vision system. The task is in principle feasible, since a dashboard mounted camera, pointing at the driver, provides an image from which a human observer can clearly identify blinks, and can estimate eyelid separation. Such a system is adaptable and autonomous; for the present we ignore the problems associated with working at night or in particularly poor light.

There are however additional constraints that mean we cannot use off-the shelf vision techniques. Although we wish to track features, many systems designed to do this, such as [7] and [11], do not perform well on people, and are even less effective on people in a car (see [10]). We have limited processing power available — taken to mean a Sun SparcStation 2 with associated framegrabber, but no other specialised processing hardware; we thus cannot use features that *can* be tracked on faces, such as [2] that use specialised hardware for the task. A further problem arises from the rapid lighting changes that seem to be characteristic of images from a moving car and which make anything but very robust tracking ineffective. A final difficulty comes from our need to detect events (blinks) that are completed within 0.1 of a second.

There are however particular constraints that can be incorporated to make the task easier. Although the system must adapt to different drivers in different driving positions, allowing for movements of the seat and steering wheel, once these have been fixed, they remain constant for long periods. A second simplification comes from noting that we are only interested in the long term change in the blink rate; the system does not need to identify 100% of blinks. Blink duration would also be of interest, but as the frame rate of conventional video is barely sufficient to catch blinks at all, it is beyond the capability of this system. Finally, as a simplification of the original problem, we assume that the system need not operate in the dark, that drivers will not we wearing heavily tinted glasses, but normal glasses may be worn.

The remainder of this chapter describes individually the various functional modules that make up the system. Their combined operation is then described, with a discussion of how performance can be evaluated in a system such as this. Results from various individual modules, and from the complete system are given. We then briefly describe the remainder of the driver monitoring system, and show some preliminary results. Finally, we propose a number of possible developments and other uses for similar systems.

3.2 Overview

Fig. 3.1 shows the overall structure of the current implementation, which consists of six independent modules. Communication between modules is via shared data, which in most cases consists of only a few bytes. A number of different techniques or implementations for each module can be incorporated into the program: the module to be used is selected at run time via a textual initialisation file, allowing rapid reconfiguration without recompiling.

Module 1 determines whether there is a driver in the vehicle, and by monitoring for a relatively long period of time (several hundred frames) identifies a region of interest within which the eyes can be expected to remain. The relatively long initialisation period allows the selected region to accommodate the small, frequent, movements made while driving, without being adversely affected by less frequent but larger excursions. Consequently, movements such as looking in all three mirrors or at the instrument cluster are acceptable, but looking out side windows or tuning the radio is not! If

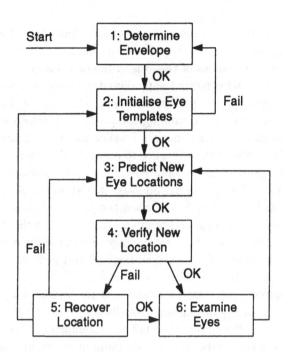

Figure 3.1
Block diagram showing structure of system.

the driver's eyes move outside the region of interest for more than a small number of frames, subsequent modules will fail, causing this module to re-evaluate the region of interest. The input required is a number of images, and the output is the coordinates of the selected region.

Module 2 makes the initial location of the eyes within the region of interest. This module could form part of the main loop, but for efficiency, the main loop makes use of temporal information and detailed information about the eyes that this module does not have available. At this stage the location of the eyes within the region of interest must be done *ab initio*. Whereas time is not a major consideration at this stage, the initial location must be determined rapidly enough that the main loop (modules 3-6) is accurately primed. The search for the initial location is restricted to the region of interest obtained from module 1, and the results are the coordinates of the two eyes and a small area of the image centered on those coordinates.

Module 3 makes use of the initialisation information, and subsequent verified locations to predict a new location. A number of techniques have been evaluated, ranging from the hypothesis that the eyes will not have moved, to Kalman filters. The 'no movement' hypothesis produces surprisingly good results under certain conditions, but the Kalman filter produces the most reliable results overall. The input consists of the initial location obtained from module 2 and subsequent locations from modules 4 to 6. The results are the predicted coordinates of the eyes in the next image.

Module 4 verifies and corrects the predicted position. A trade off is possible at this stage, between performance and tolerance. A large error is permissible if a large area surrounding the predicted location is examined, but doing so takes time. Examining a smaller surrounding area increases performance, but reduces the tolerance to errors in the prediction. As performance is the prime requirement, we choose a compromise that allows only a small error. The techniques adopted (based on template matching) are acceptable as they report *failure* when the predicted position is too inaccurate, rather than reporting *success* and the wrong result. The input is the predicted eye locations, the current image and the sub-images extracted by module 2. The output is either the corrected and verified eye locations, or an indication of failure.

Module 5 analyses the reason for failure of the verification stage. This may be due to a variety of reasons (described below) and the method of recovery depends on the cause of the failure. Examination of the image for characteristic properties often reveals the cause of the failure, and, for efficiency, this module can make use of additional intermediate results obtained from the processing done by module 4, rather than recomputing them itself. The input, therefore, is in principle limited to that of module 4, but may include other *ad hoc* parameters if available. Similarly, the output consists of a corrected and verified location, if possible, or an indication of failure. In this case, the failure is at one of two levels: one indicating a transient problem, and permitting the program to continue in the main tracking loop, the other indicating a more serious problem that requires the program to revert to module 2 for initialisation.

Module 6 examines the small area of image located, and positively identified as an eye, to determine whether it is open or closed. Additionally it measures the eyelid separation. As this is not alway possible for the current image, a short history of eye regions is maintained, so examination takes place one or more frames out of sync. The input is, once again, the current image, and the output from module 4 or 5.

3.3   Detailed description

3.3.1   Determine driver envelope

A study of recordings taken over long periods, with many drivers, operating in natural conditions, shows that each driver spends almost all of the time with the head in a relatively limited area of the field of view of the fixed camera. In order to reduce the processing times of subsequent modules, this *envelope* or *region of interest* is first determined. Of course, this region does not include every possible location of the driver's eyes; much head movement can occur from time to time, for example when at junctions, or parking. But it does define a region within which the eyes can be expected to remain most of the time, and which remains relatively constant for a given driver. We cannot however do this determination once and for all, since the envelope varies very considerably from driver to driver, and changes as a driver adjusts position.

The usefulness of the head envelope stems from its ability to predict initial search positions and limit the search area at future times, so it must reflect a time averaging process. Because of this, there is little to be gained by having individual accurate determinations of the head position such as are possible with standard feature location techniques [5] [12] [4]. We prefer rather to combine a large number of positions, each of which is obtained very quickly, and then determine the final location from an average.

A natural choice of method at this stage is frame differencing, defining the envelope in terms of those pixels at which movement have been observed. In practice two major difficulties limit the utility of this approach. The first is the problem of distinguishing driver movements from vehicle movements. Although the camera is rigidly mounted in the vehicle, some residual (random) relative motion of the vehicle remains. In addition, although the field of view of the camera is primarily within the vehicle the rest of the — apparantly moving — environment can be seen through the windows; where the drivers head occludes such a view, a simple motion detection becomes very unreliable, particularly when the driver himself remains static for several frames. A second problem, caused by the vehicle's motion, is that the prevailing lighting conditions can change rapidly, causing not only the overall illumination to change, but possibly changing shadows and reflections. Again this limits the usefulness of sequence analysis methods.

These difficulties are largely application specific, so our choice of method at this stage exploits another application specific feature of the problem. The interior of most vehicles, as seen by the dash mounted camera, is quite plain. The head lining, door pillars, seats, and occasionally the steering wheel are usually a mixture of black, once white or grey. Essentially there is little interior colour above the waistline of a car. Conversely, a driver has one of a range of well defined skin and hair colours. Although these change in appearance with illumination, their characteristic properties do not. Representing the image using the conventional RGB coding scheme reveals little about this range of colours, but when considered as an HSV image, the changing illumination is largely restricted to the V component. Representing hue as angle and saturation as radius, Fig. 3.2 shows how a range of skin tones form a cluster in HS space. Simple thresholding of the H and S components of the image allow us to identify potential skin regions within an image [1].

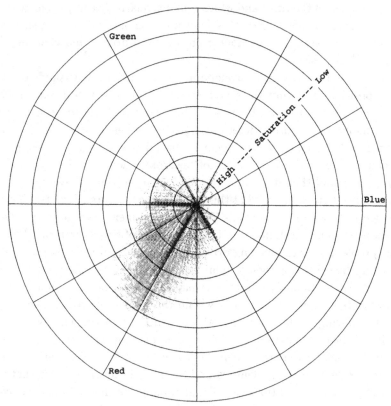

Figure 3.2
Distribution of skin coloured regions in HS space. (S=radius and H=angle.)

The thresholding is done at close to frame rates. We can thus easily average these over several hundred frames, and so eliminate any short duration movements, such as looking out side windows, or scratching or fidgeting. Fig. 3.3 show the result from one such average. Colour from the outside of the vehicle remains a problem, so the resulting image may contain more that one cluster of proposed skin regions. Nevertheless the face is expected to be the largest such feature, so the largest cluster is selected. Assuming this represents the locus of the whole face, we select a plausible region of interest for the eyes by rejecting pixels which occur at the boundaries of the region. Specifically we reject the bottom 50% of proposed pixels, and 5% from each of the top, left and right are rejected, and the remaining area is considered the region of interest. This can be seen on Fig. 3.4. If the area of the region of interest is too large, or if insufficient skin area is detected, the region is abandoned, and the process repeated.

Figure 3.3
Average face location displayed as frequency of occurence of skin coloured at given position in the image.

In an empty vehicle, this loop will continue indefinitely. When a driver enters the vehicle, the process does not stabilise for some time, as initially the driver's head movements are not just random perturbations from a fixed position. Thus frequent re-initialisation occurs. However, as the purpose of the system is to detect situations in which the driver *becomes* tired we do not regard such behaviour during the first few minutes as important. Once the driver has settled down, the system functions as designed, and spends most of its time in subsequent modules. Over a period of time the position of the driver can change slightly, causing the region of interest to become invalid. In such cases, subsequent modules fail, and the region is re-evaluated.

3.3.2   Initialise eye templates

Tests with existing eye detectors (e.g. [8],[6] or [3]) operating on images from the vehicle demonstrated shortcoming in each case: the most common was a trade off favouring accuracy over speed, which is inappropriate to our needs. We have adapted the most promising of the detectors tried to improve robustness, while retaining the rapid execution required to prime subsequent stages. The method adopted combines Robertson's eye proposer [9] with template matching for localisation. Although the results obtained are sometimes less accurate than those produced by other methods, they are sufficiently accurate for our needs, robust, and produced rapidly.

The eye proposer makes a single pass over the region of interest, considering it as an eight bit monochrome image. A pixel is selected if

- it is less than a fixed intensity threshold (75), and
- it is less than or equal in intensity to its eight connected neighbours, and
- a minimum gradient intensity (15) is detected within a fixed distance (four pixels) in at least four of the eight radials through the eight-connected neighbours.

Pixels that are selected by this process represent candidate eye regions, but do not necessarily correspond to the center of the eye. To reduce the number of selected pixels further, and to improve their location, a 9×9 region surrounding each pixel is examined using a 3×3 gaussian filter. The candidate pixel is allowed to move to the pixel with the minimum response. This localisation is repeated three times, allowing the candidate pixel to move up to twelve pixels. The end result is typically less than 20 pixels being flagged as candidate eye locations. Fig. 3.4 shows the proposed eye locations within the region of interest.

To reduce the number of candidates further, they are matched into pairs. A candidate may only form part of a pair if there is a corresponding candidate suitably far away and near enough in line. The actual distances obviously depend on image resolution, but for a 256×256 image would be a minimum horizontal spacing of 32 pixels, and a maximum vertical spacing of ten pixels. Apart from eliminating many candidates, this also identifies them as left or right candidates, further reducing subsequent processing.

To select between these candidates, a small surrounding area (31×15 pixels) is correlated against a set of stored eye templates. The correlation is performed for each position in a 5×5 neighbourhood centered on the candidate. Again, this allows the candidate pixel to move by a few pixels if necessary. The two candidates with the highest overall correlation are selected subject to that correlation being above a noise threshold.

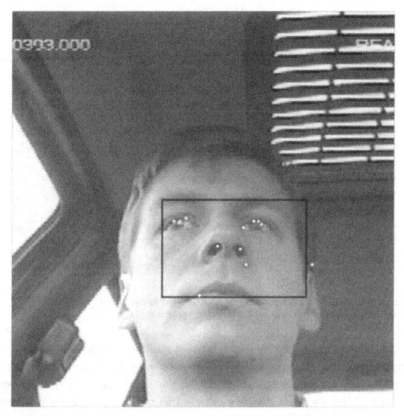

Figure 3.4
Typical image showing region of interest (black box) and twelve proposed eye
locations. The point on the right has migrated outside the region of interest while
localising.

The regions surrounding the selected eye locations are copied and used
for subsequent template matching operations. Fig. 3.5 shows the result of
this final stage by outlining the regions extracted for subsequent use. This
includes being used as one of the pairs for subsequent invocations of the eye
template initialiser.

3.3.3   Predict new eye location

In order to minimise the area to be examined during the next stage, we
attempt to predict where the eye will be in each successive image.

Two Kalman filters are used to predict new eye locations: a constant
velocity model is used for the position of the midpoint of the eyes, and a
constant distance model used for the horizontal and vertical separation. The
latter does not remain constant, as might be expected, and in fact varies considerably as the driver looks around or reacts to vehicle movement. Despite

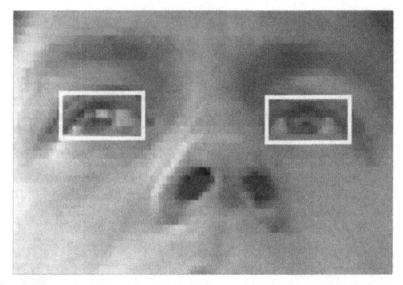

Figure 3.5
Enlarged portion of Fig. 3.4 showing regions selected as eye templates. The
enlarged region is *not* the region of interest in this example.

this, a driver's head may remain relatively still for considerable periods —
simply predicting the eyes will be where they were in the previous frame is
a surprisingly good approximation, so this was tried first. The effectiveness
diminished rapidly when the head started to move, as the movement was
obviously ignored. It also offered no simple way of imposing the constraints
required to ensure the predicted locations remain viable. This often resulted
in the predicted eyes locations converging to a single point, becoming ar-
ranged vertically, or exchanging places as a result of erroneous tracking.
Using the Kalman filters combats both of these problems.

For the purpose of the Kalman filter, the eyes are modelled as a single
mid-point, along with vertical and horizontal separation. By restricting
the horizontal and vertical distances, we can ensure the predicted locations
remain within viable limits. The limits are used more as a sanity check than
an active constraint, as they must be sufficiently generous to accommodate
drivers in a large range of positions. As the camera is very close to the
driver, this range of distances can vary by a factor of three. Consequently,
predictions that are infeasible for one driver may be quite feasible for another
and must be accepted.

Feedback is obtained from the verification and recovery stages described
below. The verification and prediction stages are allowed to track the eyes
outside the region of interest in the hope that the eyes move back into the
region. This is only allowed for a small number of frames before concluding

that the tracking has failed, or that the region of interest has changed. Either case calls for a reinitialisation.

Even when operating within the main tracking loop, feedback may not be possible on a regular basis because the verification and recovery stages do not take constant time to complete. By using frame numbers obtained from the frame grabber, the interval between processed images is determined, and the (sometimes irregular) time intervals obtained between consecutive successful locations are accommodated by the filter. The graph in Fig. 3.6 show the horizontal position of the center of the eyes over a period of time, along with the Kalman output. When compared to the zero-movement hypothesis, the Kalman prediction yields an acceptable result for significantly more of the time than the naive approach.

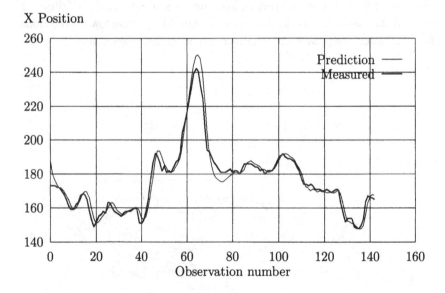

Figure 3.6
Predicted and measured osition of left eye over a ten second period. Despite the large movements, the prediction remains within ten pixels—the limit if verification is to succeed

3.3.4 Verification of prediction

The low frequency of sampling, combined with the speed of movement of the driver, often results in large movements between frames. At other times, the movements are so small that they can not be distinguished from movements attributable to image noise. In both cases, we expect the prediction to be inaccurate, so it must be verified, and corrected if necessary.

As we have already located the drivers eyes during earlier processing, and have recorded the eye regions of that earlier image, we are in an ideal position to apply template matching. The major difficulty normally associated with this approach is the lack of a good template, but we have access to an almost ideal template, specifically matched to the current driver.

Template matching can be performed over the entire region of interest, and doing so provides near maximal responses for the two eyes. This is illustrated in Fig. 3.7. As template matching is a computationally expensive operation however, we limit the area to a region surrounding the predicted location. Horizontal motion is more likely than vertical, so the search area is shaped accordingly. The left and right eyes are correlated individually, and the position in the search area with the maximum normalised correlation is chosen as the verified eye location. The correlation is normalised to lie between ±1.0, and a correlation of less than 0.8 is considered a failure. If either of the eyes lies outside the region of interest, or have low correlations, the verification stage fails and the recovery module is executed.

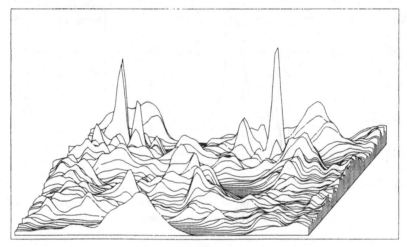

Figure 3.7
Result of correlating extracted eye templates over entire region of interest. The eyes correspond to the two largest peaks. For efficiency, only a small region surrounding the predicted location is correlated.

An alternate approach has been implemented, which improves execution speed at a slight expense of reliability. This takes the sum of absolute differences over the correlation area, rather than calculating a full normalised correlation. The execution of this algorithm is over twice as fast as full correlation, but it has a number of drawbacks. As it is less discriminating than the normalised correlation, it generates a number of near maximal responses which makes selecting the correct peak more error prone. This is especially the case when lighting levels have changed significantly since the initialisation. Also, once distracted from the correct location, it does not recover as well. The tradeoff is that with such a large improvement in speed, inter-frame movements are reduced significantly, so the prediction is likely to be more accurate, and hence the verification more likely to succeed. At present, the instability of this approach makes it less favourable than full correlation, but work continues with the idea.

3.3.5   Recovery from failed verification

When the verification stage does not yield a satisfactory location for the eyes, it can be for a variety of reasons. The recovery stage simply checks for specific symptoms characteristic of these modes of failure, and reacts accordingly. Possible causes, symptoms checked for and actions taken include the following.

Steering wheel blocking camera view due to cornering etc. This usually results in correlation scores very close to 0, which provides a good indication. Checking the range of gray levels over the bottom portion of the image is done for confirmation. As nothing can be done in this case, the missed image is counted as a missed frame, and execution continues with the next image. Should more than a predetermined number of consecutive images be missed (currently about 2 seconds worth), then it becomes impossible to predict the position of the eyes reliably. In such cases, the initial eye locator is used to reinitialise the tracking system.

Insufficient illumination. Usually caused by driving under a bridge or through a tunnel. Although the camera and the frame grabber can compensate automatically for a wide range of lighting levels, this range is far exceeded by the variations encountered during normal driving. Detection and response are essentially the same as the previous condition, but the entire image becomes very dark.

Driver moved out of region of interest. The excursion may be short or long lived. Short excursions are caused by looking anywhere other than straight forward, as happens at junctions. Longer excursions are caused by the driver adjusting the driving position, adjusting the steering wheel or seat, or by leaving the car completely. If the correlation is still high, then we note the excursion, but proceed to examine the eye region anyway, as the driver may return to the region of interest. A sufficient number of frames (longer this time, about 5 seconds worth) with verified locations outside the region of interest will cause the region to be re-evaluated. If a low correlation is obtained, no futher examination can take place. A sufficient number of frames with low correlation scores (again, about 2 seconds worth) will first cause the eye templates to be checked, and failing that, re-evaluation of the region of interest.

Eye partially or completely closed. The correlation of the eye template against a closed eye will be noticeably lower, but does not constitute a failure. In this case the the region is correlated against a number of closed eye templates. A significant correlation suggests the eyes were successfully located, so execution passes to the next stage.

As other causes for poor correlation scores are found, these can easily be added, while improvements to the verification stage result in the recovery stage being used correspondingly less.

3.3.6   Examine eyes

Two distinct outputs are produced: an indication of discrete blink events, and a continual estimate of eyelid separation, to allow the detection of a gradual closing of the eyes. The tracking system depends on matching a template of the drivers eye against the image, and as already noted this will produce a poor correlation if the eye is closed. This gives us a simple means of determining blink events. If the tracking system is working well, the predicted location will be accurate. If a good correlation is obtained for a series of images, then a poor correlation for one image, followed by a good correlation for subsequent images, this suggests that the tracking was working, but the template was simply a poor match, as is the case when the eye is closed. The correlation with closed eyes is performed in the recovery stage, so little more is involved at this stage.

Determining eyelid separation involves closer examination of the located region. Edge detection on the eyelids does not provide a reliable measure, but provisional results from examination of the boundary between iris and sclera appear more promising.

3.4   Operation and performance

The complete system is written in C++, and runs on a Sun SparcStation 2 with a Datacell S2200 24 bit frame grabber. The S2200 device driver has been modified to provide additional functionality to support some of the modules. Specifically, the device driver number frames allowing individual frames to be identified, and missing frames accounted for. It also handles the capture of multiple images in a slightly unusual manner, always keeping the current frame and the next completed frame available. This allows the program to start processing the next frame immediately after completing the current one, even if intervening frames have been lost.

The system will operate with images at any resolution provided by the hardware. There is little performance difference between them, other than initialisation, as the size of the templates are the same irrespective of image resolution. As the template size and the area used for correlation remains the same, working at a higher resolution does reduce the amount of movement that can be accommodated between frames.

Most work is conducted at a resolution of 256×256 pixels, as a compromise between clarity in the image, and reduced execution time. Where execution times are given, these will be for images of this size. Early results from examining the eyes suggests that a 256 pixel image is not enough to obtain all the information required about the eyes, but 512 pixel image is. The extra resolution is obtained for that module only by subsampling by a factor of 2, which involves virtually no overhead.

There are obvious difficulties testing a system like this live, so to facilitate testing, recordings are used. These consist of short drives (between 20 and 30 minutes) by different people, both male and female, and with and without glasses. Further sequences are obtained from time to time, under varying lighting and driving conditions. The only criteria are that there is sufficient light to operate the camera successfully, and that the sun does not shine or reflect onto the camera directly.

The first stage, determining the region of interest, is allowed to run for several hundred frames. As we are interested in the drivers position over a period of some minutes, the speed of this section is not critical. Each frame takes approximately 0.5 seconds to process, so a 500 frame average is compiled in under 5 minutes. The selection of the region of interest from the averaged image yields a satisfactory result in over 95% of cases, with most other cases yielding a region that is too generous.

Restricting the search to the area of interest, initial eye templates are located. This forms the first input to the tracking system, so a short execution time is necessary. Obtaining the correct location is critical to the remainder of the system, however, so a thorough, reliable system is required. The solution adopted executes in under 2 seconds. While this delay can permit considerable movement to take place, in practice this does not cause too much difficulty. If the tracking fails to lock on, the initialisation stage is repeated.

The performance of the prediction stage was given in the description earlier, in terms of success at directing the following stages of processing. Its success can be further quantified by measuring by how much the verification stage must adjust each *successful* prediction in order to correct it. An ideal predictor would yield a 100% prediction rate, with an average 0 pixel correction. The Kalman filter achieves almost a 100% prediction rate, and a small average correction requirement. This compares to the naive predictor, which scores between 80% and 90% prediction (very dependent on type of driver), and a larger pixel average correction. The prediction stage, including the feedback applied later in the cycle, takes approximately 2.5ms — this represents 15% of available processing time if all frames are to be analysed.

The remaining three stages, which combine with the prediction stage to form the main tracking/detection loop, are difficult to analyse separately. This is partly due to the speed at which they operate, and the significant change in behaviour of the system if run at a slower rate so that results can be analysed manually. A further difficulty is that maximum performance is achieved when all trace and debugging output is turned off, so the only result is the final output. A different approach to assessing the system is therefore adopted. As the operation is possibly less important than the final results, a measure of reliability of the final output is one measure of performance. This could be represented by the proportion of missed blinks, as these can easily be detected manually in real time and compared with the output from the system. Another way is to record how long the system can run within the main loop, without reverting to the eye initialiser, or the region of interest detector. This is the measure we prefer, as it allows for the system to *fail* at the prediction, verification or recovery stages, but recover automatically within a few images, and continue without significant loss. This is similar to the concept of MTBF often used to measure hardware reliability: a recoverable read error on a disk is not a failure.

The success of the main loop is largely determined by the initialisation stages. Only one good initialisation may be necessary, while a poor initialisation will rapidly lead to failure, and a re-initialisation. The main loop takes approximately 80ms per cycle, allowing about 12 images per second to be processed. This includes displaying intermediate results back on the frame grabber display. Of particular interest is the redisplay of the selected eye region in a fixed position on the display. The effect, when the tracking is performing correctly, is to display a pair of eyes on the screen that do not move, even though the driver may be. This at least allows a manual verification that the correct region is being tracked.

Several hundred frames are usually analysed, corresponding to a minute or more of driving, before the main loop is broken. The most common occurrence that makes re-initialisation necessary being the steering wheel obscuring the view of the driver. A threshold of 18 frames is set for non-recoverable failures from the verification module. This means less than

2 seconds of being obscured before re-initialisation takes place. This is easily achieved while driving in urban conditions, but becomes less of a problem on dual carriageways and motorways. The second most common occurrence is the driver looking out of a side window. Although this too is more common in urban conditions, it happens for different reasons on open roads, where a driver may look around out of boredom. Evidence suggests this happens less as the driver becomes tired, making it less of a problem as the output from the monitoring system becomes more important.

3.5 Description of monitoring system

The blink detection and eye monitoring system described above forms one of a number of inputs into the driver monitoring system. The goal is to be able to detect changes in driver status by monitoring existing vehicle sensors, or simple additional sensors. These include the brakes, throttle, steering, engine speed and load, inside and outside temperature and humidity, ambient light and time of day, all of which are already instrumented on many modern cars. Additional sensors include strain gauges in the drivers seat, and other engine parameters. For the initial study, the test vehicle has been equipped with a number of additional sensors which would currently be impractical in a production vehicle. These include lane-tracking, electroencephalogram (EEG) and electrocardiogram (ECG).

Tests have been carried out, in a simulator, on private roads, and on public roads. In the simulator and on the private roads, drivers were deprived of sleep before being ask to drive for several hours. The data obtained is compared with data obtained from a similar drive carried out without sleep deprivation. For obvious safety reasons, this kind of comparative test could not be performed on public roads, but there are significant differences between behaviours in the three different environments.

The system described in this chapter is intended to supplement or ideally replace the EEG and ECG equipment, which is impractical for long term testing. If a sufficiently reliable system can be developed, the prospect of building it into production vehicles opens up a number of security and convenience possibilities.

3.6 Further developments

A number of suggestions have been made for other potential uses, all based round the same theme. The intention is only to provide the necessary correlation during the development of the driver monitoring system—a final production version would use other vehicle sensors, as already described.

This is partly due to anticipated reluctance by drivers to have a camera watching them, and partly for economic reasons. In other *driving* environments, there would be more potential for including the camera. These include trains, aircraft, HGVs etc. Here the professionals tend to welcome the prospect of a system that could warn them of impending fatigue. It has been suggested that a similar system operating on a wider field of vision could find widespread use in lecture theatres.

Interest has also been shown by a driving simulator manufacturer. Here the problem is how to provide realistic rearward vision through the door and interior mirrors. The driver is free to move with in the vehicle, and often does so to temporarily adjust his view in the mirror. To accommodate this movement, there must be a large display to the rear, only a small portion of which is ever required. By being able to track the position of the drivers eyes within the vehicle, it would be possible to determine what would be seen in the mirror, and rather than use a mirror, a small display could be provided that always showed the correct *reflection*. As the driver moved, so would the apparent image in the display. It would probably be necessary to use two cameras to cover the wider range of acceptable movements, and to obtain a 3D position which would almost certainly be required.

In the more immediate future, improving the performance of the existing system, with the hope of attaining frame rate operation, is one of the aims. As a relatively large proportion of accidents take place at night, finding a way of operating in extremely low lighting would be a great gain. Passive IR is one possibility, but so far our experience of IR images has suggested a high sensitivity camera may be a better solution.

References

[1] S. Akamatsu, T. Sasaki, H. Fukamachi, N. Masui, and Y. Suenaga. An accurate and robust face identification scheme. In *ICPR 92*, 1992.

[2] A. Azarbayejani, T. Starner, B. Horowitz, and A. Pentland. Visually controlled graphics. *IEEE: Transactions on Pattern Analysis and Machine Intelligence*, 15(6):602–605, June 1993.

[3] A. Bennett and I. Craw. Finding image features using deformable templates and detailed prior statistical knowledge. In Peter Mowforth, editor, *British Machine Vision Conference 1991*, pages 233–239, 1991.

[4] R. Brunelli and T. Poggio. Face recognition through geometrical features. In *Proceedings of the Second Eurpoean Conference on Computer Vision*, 1992.

[5] I. Craw, D. Tock, and A. Bennett. Finding face features. In Giulio Sandini, editor, *Proceedings of ECCV-92*, number 588 in Lecture Notes on Computing Science, pages 92–96. Springer-Verlag, 1992.

[6] P. W. Hallinan. Recognizing human eyes. *SPIE - Geometric Methods in Computer Vision*, 1991.

[7] C. Harris and C. Stennett. RAPID - a video rate object tracker. In *Proceedings of the British Machine Vision Conference*, pages 73–77, 1990.

[8] M. Nixon. Eye spacing measurement for facial recognition. *Proceedings of SPIE*, August 1985.

[9] G. Robertson and K.C. Sharman. Object location using proportions of the directions of intensity gradient - PRODIGY. In Canadian Image Processing and Pattern Recognition Society, editors, *Proceedings Vision Interface 92, Vancouver Canada*, pages 189–195, 1992.

[10] D. Tock and I. Craw. Blink rate monitoring for a driver awareness system. In *Proceedings of the British Machine Vision Conference*, 1992.

[11] S. Vinther and R. Cipolla. Towards 3D object model acquisition and recognition using 3D affine invariants. In *Proceedings of the British Machine Vision Conference*, 1993.

[12] A. Yuille, D. Cohen, and P. Hallinan. Feature extraction from faces using deformable templates. In *Proceedings of the IEEE Conference on Computer Vision and Pattern Recognition*, 1989.

II Model-Based Vision and Exploration

17 Model-Based Vision and Exploration.

4 Model-Based Vision for Traffic Scenes Using the Ground-Plane Constraint

Geoff Sullivan

4.1 Introduction

This chapter presents an overview of a model-based vision system able to locate, recognise and track multiple vehicles in complex traffic scenes, from monocular cameras[1]. Individual technical developments have been reported extensively in conference and research papers. The aim of this chapter is to summarise the various techniques, and draw them together into a description of the overall approach. It also discusses the main processing bottlenecks, and reports ongoing work that we believe will soon allow the system to run comfortably in real-time.

The current system already operates in near real-time with quite modest computing requirements. There are four main stages of processing:

1. Detection of image movement to obtain initial foci of attention (FOA) and to reduce the number of possible object classes

2. Analysis of extended edge features in the vicinity of an FOA to generate initial hypotheses of specific vehicles and their approximate poses

3. Hypothesis-based pose refinement to obtain the optimal fit between a hypothesised vehicle and the image local to the initial pose

4. Hypothesis-based tracking of vehicle position and orientation through extended image sequences.

Each of these processing stages depends crucially on the use of the ground-plane constraint (GPC), which stipulates that vehicles stand on a known planar surface - the road. The GPC makes computationally feasible the use of high- level reasoning about 3D vehicles, moving in a 3D scene, which greatly helps to solve many challenging tasks for the visual analysis of traffic.

4.2 Visual analysis of traffic

An important application area for machine vision is the detection and identification of road traffic vehicles, and the monitoring of their positions and interactions over time. Existing systems have largely concentrated on the measurement of traffic density in simple traffic scenes. They have sought to characterize information in images that can be used directly to infer the

[1] The system has been developed under UK and European Union funding, successively from SERC (Alvey MMI-007), Esprit (P2152 VIEWS) and SERC-DTI LINK (TIO-68).

presence of individual vehicles (e.g. [1][7][10]). This approach is computationally simple, but is essentially limited in its performance.

Typical methods seek out regions of change in the image by use of temporal differentiation, either from frame to frame, or with respect to a slowly adapting reference image. Regions in the image are tracked over time, most simply by using a greatest-overlap criterion to establish inter-frame correspondences between regions. Such methods work well in situations where vehicles are well separated in the image, but may fail in the presence of irrelevant moving objects, occlusion between different vehicles, variations in lighting conditions, and instability of the camera. More importantly, image-based methods are unable to recover the object class or the pose of objects accurately. Such detail is crucial for high-level interpretations of interactions between vehicles, and the behaviour that they execute [5][8].

The system described here takes a radically different approach. Instead of finding and tracking 2D image features, it uses 3D computer models to locate vehicles in the image, and to reason about their positions with respect to a known 3D world [2][12]. Model-based vision makes extensive use of a priori knowledge, encoded implicitly in CAD-like geometrical models, about the objects to be recognised and the scene in which they appear. The exercise becomes one of fitting *a priori* models to low-level image data, rather than inferring objects from complexes of image features. Since the models are 3D, it is straightforward to take 3D effects into account, and thus to overcome many of the classic problems in object recognition. In particular, 3D algorithms are far more robust to variations in illumination and colour, and to the size and shape of the image of an object in different poses; they deal properly with occlusion between objects, and make it possible to incorporate object-centred dynamic constraints; they may also easily be adapted to deal with camera movement, and to fuse data from multiple cameras [17].

The benefits of model-based vision are well known, but there is a significant computational cost. Unconstrained search for a rigid object in an image involves six degrees of freedom (most easily described as translations and rotations with respect to a fixed world coordinate frame). However road vehicles are normally constrained to move with their wheels in contact with a 2D surface - the road. Vehicles therefore possess only three local degrees of freedom - the position on the 2D surface (x, y) and the angle of rotation about the vertical θ. This "ground-plane constraint" (GPC) can be exploited to greatly simplify many visual problems in traffic analysis. In particular, if the position of the camera is known with respect to the ground plane, the GPC makes it computationally feasible to use iterative "hypothesis and test" methods, under the control of the evolving scene interpretation. We can then make highly specific predictions about the likely appearance of the image, based on detailed 3D models of vehicles moving in the scene subject to the GPC.

4.3   Camera calibration

The use of the GPC requires the position and orientation of the camera to be known with respect to a world reference frame. Conventionally, camera calibration is done by fitting a known 3D model of the scene to the image, and solving the resultant set of equations to recover the projection transformation of the imager [16]. In our work we have sometimes been able to model the road markings and visible landmarks on building for this purpose [14]. However, traffic scenes are difficult to model without recourse to a detailed survey, which is both expensive and likely to disrupt the traffic flow. We have therefore also developed a more qualitative approach to camera calibration, using interactive software tools. This approach is less accurate than can be achieved from a well- surveyed scene, but since it relies only on two measurements on the roadway, it is far more applicable in practice.

The problem is to recover ten camera parameters - the six extrinsic parameters (the 3D positions and orientations of the camera, with respect to the scene coordinate frame) and the four intrinsic parameters (the piercing point — the 2D point in the image where the ray from the focus is perpendicular to the image plane, and the two scale factors for the image coordinates[2]. In practice, the piercing point is rarely far from the centre of the image, and any error has only second order effects on our processing. The ratio of the image scale factors can easily be estimated, simply by viewing a square target on axis and parallel to the image plane - once again, any errors have only second order effects. Of the intrinsic parameters, only the focal length then remains to be determined.

To recover the extrinsic parameters, we start by identifying two parallel stretches of road markings, from which we can define the vanishing point in the image for all lines parallel to the road, see Fig. 4.1. We then set both the focal length and the nominal height of the camera to some approximate values, and place on an image of the scene a simulated reference model, comprised of a rectangular grid with attached normals, whose projection in the image is always constrained to lie between the parallel lines. The operator then uses a slider bar to roll the model about an axis through the vanishing point, until the model appears to be square with respect to the

---

[2] Using video cameras, there is often a marked difference between the horizontal and vertical scaling factors, corresponding to a non-unity aspect ratio of the pixels, commonly introduced by poor control of the horizontal scanning electronics.

Figure 4.1
Typical traffic scene, with parallel road markings identified.

road. To a very good approximation, the visual effect of this rotation is independent of the assumed focal length and height of the camera. The operator's visual task turns out to be surprisingly simple. His perception is dominated by the frame of reference he instinctively recovers from the image of the roadway, and it is fairly easy to identify when the calibration model looks square. Fig. 4.2 gives an impression of the perceptual task — at this stage the vertical lines should be ignored, since they are affected by the assumed focal length and height.

This procedure completely locates the ground-plane, given the initial assumptions. These parameters can now be estimated from knowledge of two distances on the ground-plane, which are most conveniently aligned with the calibration model. We use a longitudinal distance given by white line markings, and a lateral distance, given by the lane width; at least in principle, these distances conform to highway standards and known in advance. We first apply a uniform scale and compute the height of the camera above the road plane needed to make the lateral distance correct. We can now compute the apparent length of the longitudinal distance. A second slider bar now allows us to vary the assumed focal length, each time recomputing the corresponding tilt of the ground-plane towards the vanishing point and

Figure 4.2
Calibration model rolling −5 degrees (top) through the perceived veridical (centre)
to +5 degrees (bottom) about a line through the vanishing point of the road.

Figure 4.3
Calibration model after estimating the scale and focal length.

the camera height (always maintaining the other ground-plane settings and the lateral distance), until the longitudinal distance also becomes correct. The result is shown in Fig. 4.3, where (by way of confirmation) the verticals of the calibration model now seem well-aligned with the lampposts.

Geometrically, the final stage can be thought of as swinging the camera in the plane of the ray to the vanishing point perpendicular to the ground (as set by eye), subject to the constraint that the depth to the lateral measurement remaining fixed in focal units, until the foreshortening of the longitudinal measurement due to the focal length and camera height has the desired effect.

The whole process takes a few minutes, and gives a standard of calibration that has proved quite sufficient for our purposes. This interactive approach to camera calibration requires minimal work at the traffic site, and decouples the camera parameters in a way that is very easy to appreciate. It has removed a major operational difficulty that stands in the way of practical applications of vision systems for traffic analysis.

4.4   Movement cues for vehicles

The first visual task for the traffic understanding system is to identify areas
of the image where vehicles might be. The primary cue we use is that of
detecting coherent movement in the image having approximately the right
properties. We use two main methods for detecting and tracking movement
in image sequences, which were developed by collaborators in the Esprit
VIEWS project.

4.4.1   Blob-tracking.

The first approach was developed by the IITB of the Fraunhofer Institute,
Karlsruhe, Germany. Blobs (smoothed Laplacian extrema) are first detected
in single images at frame rates by means of a special-purpose pipelined
processor. Using nearest-neighbour correspondence, the track of each ex-
tremum over five successive frames is analysed, and only those showing
consistent movement over this time period are considered further. Nearby
blobs, all having similar image displacement vectors, are then grouped into
local clusters, to form extended spatio-temporal movement cues. A number
of tuning parameters controlling the initial blob-size and displacement and
the variance of the clustering process allow the system to be configured to
suit the local traffic conditions.

The movement sub-system runs in real-time, using 512×512 pixel video
image sequences taken at 25Hz. Its main benefits are that it recovers coherent regions of image movement in a way that is relatively insensitive to
lighting changes. Its main disadvantage is the need for a dedicated pipelined
processor to achieve real-time operation.

The method has also been extended: (i) to use multi-scale Laplacian
filtering, so that strong foreshortening in images can be taken into account,
and (ii) to compensate for camera movement (of known angular velocity)
in the initial blob tracking phase.

4.4.2   Region tracking

The second approach to movement detection was developed by Marconi
Radar and Control Systems, Frimley, UK. A slowly adapting approximation of the temporal median image is maintained, using an iterative updating
method with a typical time constant of 20 sec. The median image is subtracted from each incoming image, and the result is thresholded and then
cleaned up, using morphological operators to reject details below a certain
size. Significant regions of change in the resulting image are then identified
by connected component analysis, and are tracked between frames using an
iterative algorithm that provides some immunity to region fragmentation

and fusion. A major advantage of this approach is that the binary regions can be used as masks to obtain the original image detail relating to the moving object. A major defect is its excessive sensitivity to camera motion and lighting changes that have time- constants of less than 10 sec (e.g. passing clouds, or changes of camera iris).

The region tracker currently works in a little under real time on a SUN 10/30 computer, using 256×256 video images (undersampled vertically and horizontally by a factor of two), taken at 5Hz. An alternative implementation based on a network of transputers is capable of carrying out the region-finding processes comfortably at (5Hz) real-time. Shape, size and velocity characteristics of the tracked regions are also measured to provide initial indications of the class and pose of isolated vehicles (see next section).

Both of these movement detection algorithms provide powerful means to establish isolated foci of attention (FOAs) in the image for subsequent, more computationally expensive, processing. However, the FOAs obtained are unstable, and fail to isolate individual vehicles if the image movement is due to multiple over-lapping objects; this is a very common problem in traffic applications. Furthermore, simple movement detection loses vehicles that slow to a stop. But the main deficiency of all methods based purely on image movement is that they have very limited ability to classify vehicles. Without knowledge of the 3D structure of vehicles, they are unable to compensate for the changing shape of the image as a vehicle moves and rotates in the scene.

On the other hand, reasoning about the 3D shape of vehicles is far more computationally expensive, and can only be applied if a strong sense of visual context is available that allows processing to concentrate on highly specific interpretations. The role of 2D movement detection in the system is to perform the essential first step of pre-attentive analysis, which, together with the GPC, makes it possible for 3D visual algorithms to attend only to the most plausible "initial hypotheses".

4.5   Initial object hypothesis generation

It is straightforward to project either type of movement cue from the image plane to the ground-plane. We may hope that these fairly accurately reflect the silhouettes of vehicles, as seen from the camera. In typical wide-area traffic scenes, silhouettes for a single object class vary considerably in shape and size, and cannot easily be used to instantiate object hypotheses (e.g. [7]). However, under the GPC, it is simple to pre-compute expected attributes of the silhouettes that can be stored in discrete tables. This stage is carried out off-line, once the camera calibration is known.

The image is first tessellated into small regions, whose centres correspond to a set of discrete points on the ground-plane (x_i, y_j). A model of each major expected vehicle type is instantiated at each point at a discrete set of orientations θ_k, and a set of shape attributes is obtained from its silhouette. At present the shape measurements consist of the overall area, the aspect ratio, and the dominant orientation, so that in effect each silhouette is approximated by an oriented ellipse. The tables are then inverted, so that the image location and shape attributes may be used to index all compatible object classes and orientations.

This technique is far from reliable. It is easily upset by lighting changes (causing changes in shadows) or wet conditions (causing specular reflections off the roadway) both of which distort the regions obtained from the image-movement phase. Moreover, it cannot deal with occlusion between vehicles. However, once the tables are compiled, it is very cheap to apply. It efficiently reduces the number of initial hypotheses of class identity and gives a very approximate estimate of the pose of a vehicle within the FOA.

4.6 Pose recovery

An initial hypothesis makes a 3D model-based approach to pose recovery computationally feasible, carried out in two separate algorithms. The first uses a form of parameter voting (much like the Hough transform) to find vehicle types and poses that are most compatible with extended edge features in the vicinity of the FOA. The second then evaluates the hypothesis - i.e. associates it with a goodness-of-fit score, which measures the degree to which edge features predicted by the hypothesis are found in the image. The initial hypothesis is then refined, by searching in the (x, y, θ) pose space for a local peak in the evaluation score.

The voting algorithm occurs in two phases, illustrated in Fig. 4.4. These successively identify the most likely orientation of the vehicle (θ), and its location on the ground (x, y). Firstly, the image around the FOA (Fig. 4.4(a)) is subjected to a conventional line description algorithm, based on the Canny edge- detector [4] (b) followed by a reduction to a set of straight lines (c). Strong lines of significant length in (c) are then compared against each of the hypothesised vehicle models to find sets of lines that are all consistent with one view of a model (cf. the View Consistency Constraint [9]).

Each line of the line description is paired in sequence with each line of a hypothesised object model. In general, the end-points of image lines recovered in this way are very unstable, because (i) thresholds used in edge-detection frequently cause drop-out near the smooth corners of the vehicle,

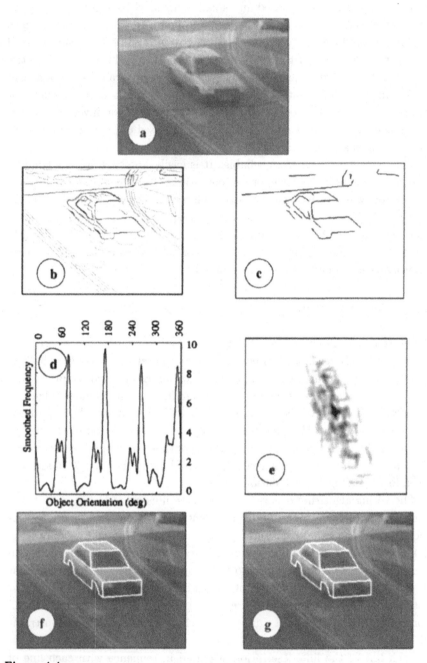

Figure 4.4
(a) Image; (b) Canny edges; (c) Line description; (d) Orientation histogram; (e)
(x, y) accumulator at 174 degrees; (f) Recovered pose; (g) Pose after iconic
refinement.

and (ii) the line-description process is itself very inaccurate. Only the orientation and the lateral location of the recovered lines are at all reliable.

Under the GPC, the image line orientation is normally sufficient to determine the orientation of the vehicle θ up to a two-fold ambiguity (for details of the geometry, see [13][15]). It may be that the model line is invisible at such an orientation, because of self-occlusion, in which case it is discarded. We consider in succession all possible image-line to model-line matches, and accumulate all possible vehicle orientations into a histogram (Fig. 4.4(d)), with each "vote" distributed among the θ bins according to an analytic error function computed from the length of the image line, the angle of the model line, and the camera parameters (see [13] — note in particular that a model line perpendicular to the ground-plane provides no constraint on object orientation). Typical results show several distinct peaks, often orthogonal to each other, reflecting the strong rectilinear symmetries of vehicles.

Each peak is then investigated in turn. Some may be discarded because they are incompatible with the estimate of orientation given by the movement cueing system, or because of a priori knowledge of the road scene (e.g. a motorway with strongly pre-determined vehicle orientations). Any surviving peak determines the subset of image-to-model line-matches which contributed to it, and which therefore are all mutually compatible with that orientation.

In a separate voting procedure we then seek the most compatible position of the vehicle, by considering how each line-match in the subset constrains the origin of the vehicle coordinate frame on the ground plane (x, y), taking into consideration the uncertainty about the line ends. A line-match is considered valid if the mid-point of the image line falls somewhere on the projected model line. A given line-match therefore allows the instantiated model to slide along the image line. The origin of the vehicle coordinate system thus traces a segment of straight line in the (x, y) plane parallel to the instantiated model line, which is easily calculated. Taking each line-match in turn, we assemble an accumulator array in (x, y) that is then slightly blurred to account for lateral uncertainty in the image line (see Fig. 4.4(e)). Peaks of the accumulator array show where multiple image-to-model line-matches for this orientation are also mutually compatible in translation. The pose corresponding to the dominant peak in Fig. 4.4(e) is shown in Fig. 4.4(f).

Fig. 4.5 shows typical examples obtained in a cluttered traffic scene. The parameter-space approach, coupled with the GPC, makes it possible quickly and reliably to identify mutually compatible labeled groups of line features, and to enforce the Viewpoint Consistency Constraint ([9]) efficiently and effectively.

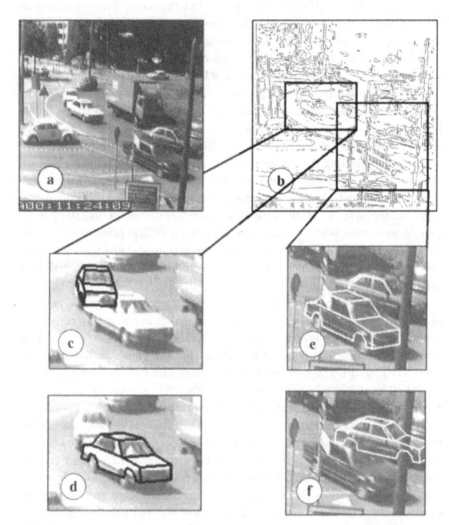

Figure 4.5
(a) Image (512 × 512); (b) Line description with FOA (here identified by hand);
(c-f) final vehicle poses recovered.

The performance of the pose-recovery algorithm has proved extremely good. It is also fast, since all processing is done only on small regions of interest (ROI) of the image. In our current serial implementation on a SUN workstation, by far the slowest component of the algorithm is the edge-detection and line description stage. Work is now in hand to adapt the algorithms for use with special-purpose image pre-processing boards (see Section 4.11).

4.7 Pose refinement

The final step in the vehicle location process is to evaluate the pose hypothesis and refine it to seek the best local fit between the vehicle and the image. This phase allows the object model as a whole to be compared with the original image, independently of any edge-detection thresholds or line description processes. It relies entirely on top-down methods and involves no context-free image processing. It uses the prevailing object and pose hypothesis to compute a scalar "objective function", which measures the quality of the match with the grey-level image — a process we have called "iconic evaluation" ([3]). For the first time in the system, it also allows occlusion by fixed objects in the scene, or by other already processed vehicles, to be taken into account.

For any given pose of a known vehicle (an "instance"), the model can be transformed before the camera and projected into the image in the form of a wire-frame similar to the overlays shown in Fig. 4.4 and Fig. 4.5. Each visible line on the model is evaluated in the image by measures based on the average strength of image derivatives orthogonal to the line (see [2][12] for details). The model specifies the type of line expected (e.g. bars or edges) and the circumstances in which it becomes visible (e.g. whenever it is not occluded, or only as an occluding boundary). The raw measures of aggregated edge strength are converted to probabilities, by means of look-up tables derived empirically. These are assembled off-line using Monte Carlo methods to determine probability distributions for scores obtained by randomly placed lines of given length and type.

A typical object instantiation contains 10-40 lines to evaluate. The individual probability scores are assumed to be independent, and pooled by standard methods to give an aggregate score having a χ^2 distribution[3] [3]. Each pose is thereby associated with a measure of its fit in the image. Given

---

[3] The independence assumption is clearly false, since the presence of one good feature is obviously correlated with the presence of others. We therefore obtain wildly significant χ^2 scores, but we have found the technique to be very effective as a qualitative measure in practice.

an initial pose estimate, based on features obtained by context-free image analysis (e.g. Fig. 4.4(f)), a search can then be carried out in pose space (x, y, θ) for the local peak (Fig. 4.4(g)). The final scores obtained for multiple initial object and pose hypotheses may then be used to discriminate between alternative object classes.

A number of different search methods have been investigated. The most robust uses the current pose estimate to define a local object coordinate frame, and searches in discrete steps separately along the forward-back, lateral, and rotational variables in object space. The best pose found becomes the seed for the next iteration, and so on, until a local peak is found. A somewhat cheaper, but usually effective, search routine is based on the simplex algorithm [11].

Pose refinement is computationally expensive, since each evaluation requires the model to be instantiated with hidden lines removed. However a very large saving can be made by assuming that the topology of the wireframe model will not change much within the space to be searched. At the start of the process, we compute a "2.5D" model containing only those features visible at the seed pose, and this is transformed (linearly) in all subsequent evaluations in this search. Depending on the model's complexity, speed improvements of up to 10 have been obtained.

4.8   Active vs. passive models

More recently, we have explored an alternative technique for pose refinement in which the model is "active" and interacts dynamically with the image. Given a starting pose, the image is searched to find strong edge-points near each line of the wireframe model as before, but now the edge-points contribute elemental forces acting on the model line in 3D. A strong edge-point in an image gives no indication either of the depth of a (3D) edge along the ray or where it might act along the (3D) model line. We therefore consider the force to act along the mutual perpendicular between the ray and the model line - hence what we have called the spring and smooth rods analogy [18].

The elemental forces derived from the 2D image act in 3D on a 3D model, so they can easily be combined using simple mechanics. Under the GPC, these forces can only rotate the model about θ, and translate it in (x, y). The aggregate torque and lateral forces are allowed to act for a nominal time step to pull the model into a better fit with the image. The whole process then iterates. The new technique is somewhat similar to the previous method, but now the model fitting becomes an active process in which the model is pulled by the image, as distinct from the search for a local maximum, using

Figure 4.6
Fragment of image, with scene model and "true" vehicle hypothesis superimposed.

a passive model to evaluate each pose.

A major problem in designing complex vision systems is finding reliable ways to compare alternative algorithms [6]. The performance of different pose refinement algorithms can only be studied in the context of a complete system. One technique is to consider how the algorithms behave when the initial "seed" pose is subjected to small perturbations (see also [2]). Ideally, the final pose will return quickly and accurately to the "true" pose, for a wide range of seed poses. The performance of the active and passive algorithms when applied to Fig. 4.6 have been compared in this way with the results illustrated in Fig. 4.7.

The image in Fig. 4.6 shows a car partially hidden by street furniture, with the scene model and the "true" pose of the vehicle shown superimposed. The occlusions and the road markings make this image particularly prone to misinterpretation. Seed poses close to the true pose were selected exhaustively from 11 samples each within ± 0.5 metre bounds in x and y, and ± 12.5 degree bounds in θ, making 1331 trials for each algorithm. The poses recovered are shown in Fig. 4.7, for the passive (left) and active (right) techniques. The top diagrams show the recovered poses as short vectors, indicating the position and orientation of the pose. The bottom replots the same data as histograms of (x, y) position, and with the orientation collapsed. (Both representations are shown in a $\pm - 1$ metre square.)

It can be seen that the active algorithm shows significantly better convergence than the passive technique; the recovered poses are far less scattered. The active algorithm is also potentially faster, since the number of iterations required is smaller: in this example the number of iterations of the passive

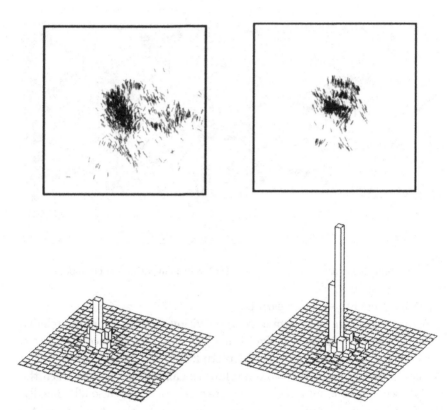

Figure 4.7
Comparison between "passive" (left) and "active" (right) pose refinement
algorithms. Top: Scatter plot showing recovered poses, after deliberate
perturbation of the seed pose (see text) Bottom: (x,y) histograms of the same data.

algorithm was fixed at 30 (though nearly as good performance is obtained
with only 10), whereas the simplex search used in the passive case typically
used 50-100 pose evaluations. Since the complexity of the two algorithms
is about the same, we can expect to obtain significant speed improvements
for the process. However, the code used in the active algorithm has not
been properly optimised, and we cannot yet make a direct comparison of
processing time.

4.9   Vehicle tracking

At this stage of the vision system we have one or more vehicle-and-pose
hypotheses, together with their "iconic scores". Any score that exceeds a
fairly low threshold is allowed to survive, to become what we might call a
percept. Unfortunately, even despite the complexity of the preceding algo-

rithms, we may still have multiple percepts, each corresponding to an initial hypothesis generated by the movement cueing process, which continues to survive on the basis of its fit to a single image. The final stage of the system therefore seeks to resolve the conflict by analysis of the temporal behaviour of the competing percepts. Fortunately it is far easier to maintain a percept than to initiate one: we simply use the pose from the first image to be the seed pose for the next image, re-apply the pose refinement algorithm, and continue.

The final discrimination between competing percepts can then be based on the consistency obtained in both the iconic scores and the apparent dynamics of the vehicle. For example, a percept that makes "impossible" movements from frame to frame (e.g. jumps sideways, or accelerates violently) ought to be questioned in favour of one with more plausible behaviour. These ideas are somewhat speculative and have not been properly tested, mainly because adequate test data has only recently become available.

Once "boot-strapped" over several images in this way, the tracking process can switch in a 3D dynamic model embedded in a Kalman filter to predict the seed pose for the next search. In this phase of operation the 3D tracker runs entirely "top-down" under the control of current model hypotheses; the only image-processing is the context-specific iconic evaluation.

4.10   Performance

The model-based traffic understanding system has been demonstrated on a wide range of sequences of traffic taken in natural scenes, under different weather and lighting conditions. A major application area for the Esprit VIEWS project concerned ground traffic at airports, whose behaviour was to be compared against known servicing schedules. We have successfully detected, identified, located, tracked and analysed the behaviour of all vehicles in a typical airport scene, involving aircraft, articulated fuel-tankers, baggage handlers, tractors, moving staircases and service vans, over a sequence of images lasting for 30 minutes. By way of illustration, a still from the system's output is given in Fig. 4.8, which shows an instantiated interpretation, together with the view of the interpreted scene from above. The single camera is about 200 metres from the aircraft, and the accuracy of recovery of the aircraft is about to within ±1 metre. The smaller vehicles (here clustered under the belly of the aircraft) subtend as little as 20-25 pixels in the image, but are still recovered with reasonable accuracy.

Traffic understanding requires analysis of the spatio-temporal behaviour of multiple interacting vehicles [8]. A major advantage of the model-based

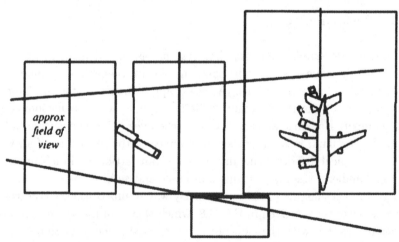

Figure 4.8
(a) Section of image, showing instantiated models; (b) view of 3D scene from above

methods described here is that we are able to recover a full 3D understanding of the scene. It is therefore a simple matter to answer 3D questions, which are not explicit in the image itself: Where are the vehicles in the scene? How near each other are two vehicles? What is their relative orientation? It is also possible to assess the dynamics of vehicles (in physical, not image-based, terms), which provides essential information with which to identify the unfolding behaviour of vehicles.

The model-based vision system we have developed for traffic understanding demonstrates the huge benefit of using high-level knowledge to assist in the solution of vision tasks. The use of the GPC enormously simplifies the pose recovery problem, and makes possible fast, efficient interpretation of complex traffic scenes. The prototype implemented at the end of the Esprit VIEWS project comprised three SUN 10 workstations, one each to carry out the image movement and model-based processing, and the third to arbitrate between the two knowledge sources, and to reason about high-level behaviours (these algorithms have not been discussed here; the work within VIEWS on high-level reasoning is reported in [5]). This version is now capable of running in real- time for simple traffic scenes contining a single vehicle; the current update time per object is about 200 ms, and tracking is usually successful with images sampled at 5Hz [17].

4.11   Current work

Predictably, the model-based algorithms currently represent the main processing bottleneck in the system, and we are currently working on a number of improvements. The key to processing efficiency lies in the effective interaction between the context-dependent (top-down) vision algorithms and the context-free (bottom-up) image processing. The latter are essentially simple and can usually easily be parallelised and delegated to dedicated co-processors. There are two main ways to improve the efficiency of the existing system.

Firstly, the pose-refinement methods we have developed (both the active and the passive methods) achieve much of their speed by avoiding unnecessary image pre-processing — image derivatives are only computed if they are needed to evaluate a specific hypothesis. This strategy has proved dramatically successful for conventional serial processors, where the cost of globally-applied, pre-attentive image processing tends to dominate over the attentive vision algorithms. However, searching also brings its own inefficiencies: during pose refinement, we consider many instances of the model that are close in pose space. We often therefore need to repeat the same (or very nearly the same) measurement. For example, the front bumper of a car may project to (effectively) the same image line from many different nearby poses.

Some form of memory to keep track of the work already done, together with an explicit discretisation of the image-processing operations, is needed to avoid this unnecessary repetition. One way with which we have had some success operates at the line evaluation level. To evaluate a model (passive), or to compute the forces on a model (active), we first consider each projected feature of the model in isolation. A feature is defined by a line segment in the image, and has four degrees of freedom - most conveniently expressed as the location of its centre, its length and its orientation in the image. We can quantize this space into discrete features, so that when a particular test is invoked we actually use the nearest allowed feature. The result can then be stored so that any subsequent re-use of the same feature can simply look up the value. This scheme is simple to implement using a hashing mechanism. We have found that more than 50% of the feature tests can thereby be avoided, though the saving greatly depends on the resolution used to sample the feature space: coarser sampling leads to more saving, but performance degrades because of the sampling errors introduced.

An alternative approach is to try to increase the amount of work carried out by ancillary processors. It is totally unrealistic to hope to achieve this by pre-computing the line features: each feature test requires the aggregation of highly specific directional derivatives in the image. It would be infeasible, even within a very limited ROI, to compute all such derivatives, let alone aggregate them along lines of arbitrary length and position. However, a very useful saving can be made by using a fixed, small number of directional derivatives. Other directions can then be interpolated (effectively making the assumption that the image is smooth), or even more simply, they can simply be approximated by the nearest pre-computed value.

We can also effect a major saving on the inner loops of the evaluation process by searching for derivative maxima along the vertical and horizontal raster lines, instead of along the true normals to a feature; we thus avoid having to compute sub-pixel positions and interpolate grey-levels values. This simplification has the further major advantage that it allows more of the image processing to be carried out by context-free pre-processing. We first pre-compute approximations to the vertical and horizontal derivatives in the image, using Sobel operators. A morphological dilation is then applied to replace each pixel in the vertical derivatives with the maximum value found nearby in the same raster column (and similarly for the horizontal derivatives).

During pose evaluation, we then classify a linear feature either as H or V, according to whether it is nearer the horizontal or the vertical in the image.

An H feature obtains its image derivatives from the vertically differentiated image (and similarly, a V feature uses the horizontally differentiated one). But now there is no need to search along the normals for local maxima, since this is already recorded in the dilated images. This technique greatly simplifies the computation at the heart of the feature evaluation algorithm, and therefore gives huge speed improvements in exchange for relatively simple pre-processing hardware. However, in our simulations of the new approach we have noted some additional instability in the pose refinement algorithm. Careful analysis will be required to determine if this is a price worth paying.

4.12   Conclusions

The model-based traffic understanding system described here integrates many different machine vision algorithms. The main drive has been to exploit high- level knowledge about traffic scenes, including the structure and dynamics of vehicles, and the geometry of the cameras being used. Such knowledge defines the semantics of the visual task, and is a pre-requisite for visual interpretation. However, high-level knowledge also constrains the visual problem, and thereby makes it computationally tractable.

Traffic analysis has been a very rewarding domain in which to explore model-based algorithms, since although the objects encountered are very limited, it nevertheless presents a rich set of visual problems with demanding requirements for real-time computer vision.

Acknowledgements

The work reported here has been carried out over many years in a succession of SERC and Esprit projects, jointly supervised by Prof. K D Baker and the author. It is a pleasure to record my deep gratitude to the long list of past associates and research students who have contributed to the work.

Special thanks are due to Dr. A D Worrall, without whose software wizardry the system would be little more than a fragmented patchwork of nice ideas.

References

[1] A. T. Ali and E. L. Dagless. Alternative practical methods for moving object detection, 4th International Conf on Image Processing and its Applications, IEE 354, April 1992, 77-80.

[2] K. D. Baker and G. D. Sullivan. Performance assessment of model-based tracking. Proc of IEEE Workshop on Applications of Computer Vision, Palm Springs, California, 1992, 28-35.

[3] K. S. Brisdon. Hypothesis Verification Using Iconic Matching, PhD Thesis, University of Reading, November 1990.

[4] J. F. Canny. A computational approach to edge detection. IEEE T-PAMI 8(6) pp679- 698, 1986.

[5] D. R. Corrall, A. N. Clark and A. G. Hill. Airside ground movements surveillance. NATA-AGARD Symposium on Machine Intelligence in Air Traffic Management. (Berlin, May 1993).

[6] R. M. Haralick. Performance characterisation in computer vision. Proc. Brit. Machine Vision Conf 1992, pp 1-8. Springer-Verlag.

[7] M. Kilger. Video-based Traffic Monitoring, 4th International Conference on Image Processing and its Applications, IEE 354, April 1992, 89-92.

[8] D. Koller, K. Daniilidis and H-H. Nagel. Model-based object tracking in Monocular image sequences of road traffic scenes. Int Journ of Computer Vision 10:3, 357- 281 (1993).

[9] D. Lowe. The viewpoint consistency constraint. Int J. Computer Vision, Vol 1, 1987, 57-72.

[10] S. W. Lu. A multiple target tracking system. Proc of the SPIE 1388, 1991, 299-305.

[11] W. H. Press et al. Numerical Recipes; Cambridge University Press, Cambridge, 1986.

[12] G. D. Sullivan, Visual interpretation of known objects in constrained scenes, Phil. Trans. Royal Soc. London, Series B: Biol. Sci., vol.337, 1992, pp.361-370.

[13] T. N. Tan, G. D. Sullivan and K. D. Baker. Recognising objects on the ground plane. Image and Vision Computing, 12:3 pp 164-172 (1994).

[14] T. N. Tan, G. D. Sullivan and K. D. Baker. On Computing the perspective transformation matrix and camera parameters. British Machine Vision Conference 1993 pp 125-134.

[15] T. N. Tan, G. D. Sullivan and K. D. Baker, Line-Based Object Scale and Pose Recovery, Proc. of Asian Conf. on Computer Vision, Osaka, Japan, 1993.

[16] R. Y. Tsai Synopsis of recent progress on camera calibration for 3D machine vision in The Robotics Review. O Khatib, et al. (Eds) MIT Press, 1989.

[17] A. D. Worrall, G. D. Sullivan and K. D. Baker. Advances in Model based Traffic Vision. British Machine Vision Conference 1993 pp 559-568.

[18] A. D. Worrall, G. D. Sullivan and K. D. Baker. Pose refinement of active models using forces in 3D. Procedings of the Third European Conference on Computer Vision, ECCV94 (in press).

5 Active Exploration of Dynamic and Static Scenes

David W. Murray, Ian D. Reid, Kevin J. Bradshaw, Philip F. McLauchlan, Paul M Sharkey, and Stuart M. Fairley

5.1 Introduction

In recent work we have described the construction of an agile camera platform, a high-bandwidth parallel vision system, and several real-time motion and vergence processes that enable an active camera to perform motion saccades to "capture" moving targets, and thereafter to track them [17, 9, 11, 13, 3, 1]. These capabilities have been developed within the context of active surveillance, where the system must react and attend quickly to the unexpected as well as expected motion of people and vehicles in a scene.

In this chapter, we review some of that work, and then describe a technique devised by Reid *et al* [14] that recovers in real time the trajectories of moving objects tracked on a plane in the scene. The trajectories are described using 2D Cartesian coordinates defined in the plane itself. The transformation from joint angles in the camera platform to these coordinates is derived by self-calibration by active observation of static scene geometry, geometry which has been stored earlier as a model.

As well as demonstrating an immediate application to surveillance, we indicate the potential of using of a steerable camera as a pointing device in projective coordinates, with the camera platform's rotation centre providing the centre of projection.

5.2 The visuo-control loop and head mechanism

At the lowest level, the purpose of gaze movements is first to establish and then to maintain the projection of a certain part of the scene onto a certain part of the image. In our work that special part is a small central foveal subimage, occupying laterally some 6° of the camera's 50° field of view. Processing for the small redirections of gaze involved in tracking or pursuit is carried out only within this fovea, whereas processing to initiate saccades is carried out on the entire but subsampled image, dubbed the periphery.

The parallel architecture we have developed, sketched in Fig. 5.1, supports multiple concurrent vision processes in both fovea and periphery. We regard each vision process as independently supplying the gaze controller with visual knowledge that it can either utilize or ignore. In this way, control in our system is split between two sites. The gaze controller is concerned with selecting an appropriate response (saccade, tracking, etc), with choos-

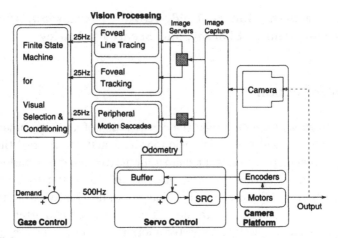

Figure 5.1
An overview of the architecture of the visuo-control loop.

ing a visual input to drive it, and with transforming the visual signal into an appropriate error signal for the servo-controller. The various responses are coded as states in a finite state machine. The input side of the gaze controller operates asynchronously at a rate determined by the availability of vision results, whereas the output stage runs prediction and interpolation processes, so that a predicted visual signal is available synchronously at 500Hz. In general, both 2D position and velocity visual signals $(\mathbf{r}, \dot{\mathbf{r}})$ are generated, each relative to the camera's optical axis. As the external demand is always a zero vector (ie the demand is to place something in the centre of the image, $\mathbf{r} = \mathbf{0}$, and track it so that its relative velocity is nulled, $\dot{\mathbf{r}} = \mathbf{0}$), the error signal into the servo-controller is obtained simply by inverting the sign of the visual signal.

The servo-controller in its turn converts the error signals into errors in joint angles and velocities $(\boldsymbol{\theta}, \dot{\boldsymbol{\theta}})$ via the camera platform's inverse kinematics, and generates outputs to drive the motors. The servo itself receives 500Hz position and velocity feedback from encoders on the motor shafts. This inner feedback loop allows the head to move as a pointing device without visual feedback, at much higher gains and speeds. The servo-controller also acts as system clock. The need to combine prompt head data with delayed vision results for prediction makes timing an important issue, the more so as different visual sensors may have different rates and will almost certainly have different latencies. As part of its 500Hz control loop therefore, the servo maintains a ring buffer of mount status data such as position and velocity and response mode at the time of image capture — data that can be interrogated by the vision processes and the prediction stage of the gaze controller.

Our system is presently implemented using Inmos T805 Transputers for vision and control processing (some twenty cpu's are used in this work), Datacube MaxVideo boards for image capture and smoothing, and a Sparc 2 as host, running an X-windows interface for overall control and monitoring. A portable system is currently being constructed that utilizes C40 processors hosted by a i486 PC.

Our camera platform, "Yorick", has five powered axes, each with the same modular design, configured as a common elevation platform in which the two elevation axes are mechanically linked [17]. In this chapter all the processing uses a single camera, and uses just two axes which we will refer to as elevation (up-down) and vergence (left-right). Our work on making saccadic reactions to motion has made clear to us the need for mounts capable not only of high speed, but also of high acceleration, in addition to the usual desiderata of mechanical stiffness, precision and simplicity. In Fig. 5.2 we show the camera platform and its axis performances obtained in dynamic tests carried out on the unloaded mount. The high acceleration figures achieved using geared DC motors are exploited routinely during saccades — indeed high acceleration/velocity ratios are characteristic of such camera movements. Further members of a small Yorick family have been built in the laboratory using the same technology. The smallest has a mass of less than 2kg and can be carried by a robot arm.

5.2.1   Visual feedback signals

Suppose that the camera's optic axis lies along $\hat{o}(t)$ and the visual target lies along a unit direction $\hat{g}(t)$, both referred to a fixed world coordinate frame whose origin lies at the centre of projection. Our camera platform's mechanism provides no cyclotorsional degree of freedom about the optic axis, and so the movement required to transform $\hat{o}$ to $\hat{g}$ can be determined from the 2D image position $\mathbf{r}$, the intersection of $\hat{g}$ with the image plane. (The intersection of $\hat{o}$ with the image defines $\mathbf{r} = \mathbf{0}$.) Thus, all that is necessary to redirect the camera is image position $\mathbf{r}$, the camera's focal length f, and $\hat{o}$, from which the servo-controller can implicitly find $\hat{g}$ and via the device's inverse kinematics find the set of joint angles required to align $\hat{o}$ with $\hat{g}$. (The camera's focal length is obtained by an online calibration process described in [8]. A point to note is that although a feedback system provides some immunity from mis-calibration, changing the assumed focal length the camera effectively changes the *gain* of the system leading to over- or under-damped response during saccade.)

Whilst such control using position alone is satisfactory in many situations, it has limitations in gaze control because of latency: limitations that become severe for control of saccades and tracking at high velocities, as the

Description	Vergence	Elevation	Pan
Axis Range	360°	360°	360°
90° Slew Time	0.28 s	0.29 s	0.76 s
360° Slew Time	0.95 s	0.97 s	1.69 s
Max Slew Rate	400°/s	400°/s	300°/s
Max Acceleration	6000°/s²	5000°/s²	500°/s²
Max Deceleration	10000°/s²	9000°/s²	800°/s²
Backlash	0.0075°	0.0075°	0.0025°
Angle Resolution	0.00036°	0.00036°	0.00018°
Repeatability	0.0075°	0.0075°	0.0025°
Min Velocity	0.027°/s	0.027°/s	0.014°/s

Figure 5.2
The Yorick camera platform and the measured performance of its axes: vergence
($\times 2$), elevation and pan (or neck). The work discussed in this chapter is driven
monocularly, and uses only the elevation axis and left camera's vergence axis.

resulting error is proportional to the product of velocity and latency. The latency of visual processing $\Delta t_{\text{process}}$ is large compared with the intrinsic time constants of the controlled plant (ie the camera platform) and the scene. Typically in our work the latency between a scene event and a visual result being available to the gaze controller is $\Delta t_{\text{process}} \sim 100\text{--}150\text{ms}$. One way of maintaining stability in the face of such delayed feedback is to reduce the gain, effectively lengthening the time constants associated with the camera platform. The more satisfactory solution which we adopt here is to employ prediction to compensate for the delay. To effect this, an estimate of $d\hat{\mathbf{g}}/dt$ is required. (Higher temporal derivatives are also relevant of course, but their computation from the visual data and use in control in the short time between detection of motion and firing a saccade are impracticable given a 25Hz image sampling rate.) Thus our aim is to estimate the prompt desired gaze direction from measurements made time $\Delta t_{\text{process}}$ earlier as

$$\hat{\mathbf{g}}(t) = \hat{\mathbf{g}}(t^-) + \left[\frac{d\hat{\mathbf{g}}}{dt}\right]_{t^-} \Delta t_{\text{process}} , \qquad (5.1)$$

where $t^- = t - \Delta t_{\text{process}}$ and where the gaze velocity is assumed constant.

During saccades the problem of delay is more severe. Because visual feedback is useless during saccade, further visual results may not be available for 100–400ms. Again, our solution is to use prediction, firing a capture saccade ballistically using precomputed position and velocity.

While velocity is useful in making predictions, it is also useful in the control process itself. The servo-controller generates a motor torque τ using both position *and* velocity errors,

$$\tau = K_p[\theta_{err}]^{\frac{1}{2}} + K_v[\dot{\theta}_{err}]^{\frac{1}{2}} + \tau_{int} \qquad (5.2)$$

where θ_{err} is the difference between the demand and current joint angle, and similarly for the velocity, where K_p and K_v are the associated gains, and where τ_{int} is an integral torque. Further discussion of the controller can be found in [17] and [18].

5.3   Capture saccades

Motion that is unexpected is in general not being tracked by the camera, and so is likely to be large. Our starting point for firing a capture saccade in response to motion in the scene is therefore the video-rate computation of optical flow $\dot{\mathbf{r}}$ at coarse scale across the periphery. Components of the optical flow field $\dot{\mathbf{r}}$ are derived from the spatio-temporal gradients of the smoothed and subsampled image irradiance $E(\mathbf{r}, t)$ using the motion constraint equation [5, 6] $E_t + \dot{\mathbf{r}} \cdot \nabla E = 0$, from which components $\mathbf{v} = -E_t \nabla E / |\nabla E|^2$ of $\dot{\mathbf{r}}$ along the gradient direction can be found.

To segment out objects moving independently of the background we subtract components of the image motion $\dot{\mathbf{r}}_h$ induced by known motion of the camera on the head platform. If the rectilinear and angular velocities of the camera with respect to the static background are $\mathbf{V}$ and $\mathbf{\Omega}$, then the image motion due to head motion is

$$\frac{\dot{\mathbf{r}}_h}{f} = \frac{1}{Z}(\mathbf{V} + \frac{\mathbf{r}}{f}(\mathbf{V} \cdot \hat{\mathbf{z}})) - \mathbf{\Omega} \wedge \frac{\mathbf{r}}{f} - \frac{\mathbf{r}}{f}(\mathbf{\Omega} \wedge \frac{\mathbf{r}}{f} \cdot \hat{\mathbf{z}}) \qquad (5.3)$$

where f is the camera's focal length. If the body carrying the head has motion $(\mathbf{V}_{body}, \mathbf{\Omega}_{body})$ then $(\mathbf{V}, \mathbf{\Omega})$ are found from the forward kinematics as nonlinear functions of body motion, joint angles $\boldsymbol{\theta}$ and joint velocities $\dot{\boldsymbol{\theta}}$ as

$$\mathbf{V} = \mathbf{f}(\boldsymbol{\theta}, \dot{\boldsymbol{\theta}}, \mathbf{\Omega}_{body}) + \mathbf{V}_{body} \qquad \mathbf{\Omega} = \mathbf{g}(\boldsymbol{\theta}, \dot{\boldsymbol{\theta}}) + \mathbf{\Omega}_{body} \ . \qquad (5.4)$$

In our work there is no gross body translation, and the only translation is that induced from rotation by the small offset δ of the rotation axis from the optic centre. The corresponding translational image motion terms are scaled by δ/Z_{ave} compared to the rotational terms, where Z_{ave} is a typical depth. This factor is $\approx 10^{-2}$ for our geometry, and we can safely neglect translation.

The motion and its components arising from the scene alone are then

$$\dot{\mathbf{r}}_s = \dot{\mathbf{r}} - \dot{\mathbf{r}}_h \qquad\qquad \mathbf{v}_s = \mathbf{v} - (\dot{\mathbf{r}}_h \cdot \hat{\mathbf{v}})\hat{\mathbf{v}} \ , \qquad (5.5)$$

where $\hat{\mathbf{v}}$ is a unit vector in the direction of $\mathbf{v}$.

The next step is to decide, using the scene normal flow $\mathbf{v}_s$, which image regions are background and which are independent moving objects. Aside from gross error, the background has $\mathbf{v}_s \sim \mathbf{0}$, and so we aggregate areas of the image that exhibit coherent motion of substantial size, and declare them as foreground objects.

Given such an object, an attempt is made using least squares to fit a constant velocity field $\langle \dot{\mathbf{r}}_s \rangle$ to all the flow components belonging to that object. The position of the moving object $\mathbf{r}_s$ is found as the weighted centroid of the motion vector positions contributing to the object.

The detection and segmentation algorithms run at the video rate of 25Hz using five Inmos T805 Transputers [9]. Because the motion may be large, we use non-interlaced image fields which, to fit the available bandwidth, are subsampled down to 64×32 pixels, commensurate with the scale of objects and size of motion we wish to detect. Although computation of the spatio-temporal gradients is performed in fixed time, the time required for the segmentation and fitting stage depends on the data volume, but the timing data stored by the servo-controller enables the exact latency for every frame of data to be derived. Typically, the peripheral latency Δt_p from image capture, through detection and segmentation to the fitted motion field is $\Delta t_p \sim 110$ms.

To illustrate the detection and segmentation process, Fig. 5.3 shows 5 frames with 80ms separation of two people walking past each other on the street. The outline of each detected moving region is shown along with the velocity vector and the error ellipse, both magnified six times for clarity. At the start of the displayed sequence the people are just passing each other and are detected as one moving region (frames 5,7). Note that the estimated error is large as here the constant velocity assumption is violated. When the regions split at frame 9 the constant velocity fit improves considerably. The error ellipse is obtained directly from the residual of the least squares fit and its eccentricity, obtained from the covariance matrix, indicates the degree to which the aperture problem has been overcome, a large eccentricity indicating little constraint in the direction of the major axis. The final frame of Fig. 5.3 shows motion detection and segmentation from a car on the road.

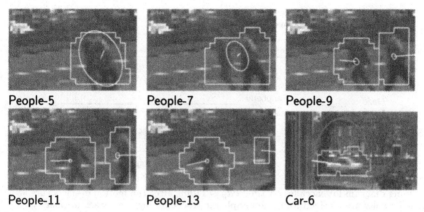

People-5   People-7   People-9

People-11   People-13   Car-6

Figure 5.3
Real-time motion detection and segmentation results for a sequence of two people
passing on a pavement next to the road outside our laboratory. The last frame
shows motion segmentation for a car moving right to left on the road.

We have performed several tens of experiments, each involving several
hundred motion measurements, to assess the performance of the motion
computation as the image subsampling, and size, speed, rigidity and texture
of the target object are changed. The important outcome of these is that the
measurements are repeatable with characterizable distributions, enabling
processing to be tuned if the class of visual targets is known a priori.

5.4   Firing saccades

The sequence of events followed when the gaze controller fires a capture
saccade is shown in Fig. 5.4. When the coarse motion sensor detects a
new region moving independently of the background, the high-level gaze
controller initiates a constant velocity filter, which takes both the position
and velocity of that region as input. Because of the visual latency, the
filter output at time t actually refers to scene and image activity at $t^- =
t - \Delta t_{process}$, but after a number of frames of integration (typically three)
we use the filter output to predict the current image position and velocity
of the target, and these are sent as a demand to the servo-controller to start
the head saccading.

During periods of high camera velocity results from the vision system
are ignored by the gaze controller. The gaze controller continues however
to generate a new *prediction* of current position and velocity every 2ms
to satisfy the 500Hz synchronous servo-controller. To test saccades only,
without pursuit, this prediction is carried on until well after the saccade
is ended, and so the rapid redirection when the errors between actual and

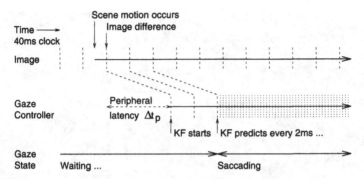

Figure 5.4
Timing diagram for saccades. A time $\Delta t_p \sim 110$ms after the motion event occurs visual results are received from the peripheral processing by the gaze controller which then starts up a constant velocity Kalman Filter, and after n, usually 3, frames, begins to predict at 500Hz the target's *current* position and velocity, and sends these as feedback to the servo controller.

demanded position and velocity are high is followed by a period of constant velocity coasting as the errors approach zero.

Fig. 5.5 charts the progress of a saccade by logging one second's worth of 500Hz data from the servo-controller. From the graphs of angular position and velocity for the vergence axis it can be seen that the camera platform is stationary for the first 600ms of the sequence, then receives a saccade initiation with demands of some $-15°$ in position, and $12°\text{s}^{-1}$ in velocity. The saccade is completed after 80ms. A peak velocity of $240°\text{s}^{-1}$ and an acceleration as large as $7000°\text{s}^{-2}$ are attained by the axis. As noted earlier, saccades routinely exploit the high acceleration achievable by the platform, but because of their short duration tend not to approach the axis velocity limit. Fig. 5.5 also shows four foveal images captured every 40ms from the start of the saccade. The camera is initially stationary, waiting for a result from the periphery to indicate that a target has appeared. Some two frames (80ms) after the saccade has been initiated, the target enters the foveal region. During the coasting period after saccade the target remained in the fovea for over 15 frames (not shown) even though no tracking occurred. The result shows first that for a constant velocity target the estimates from the peripheral motion processes and prediction from the Kalman filter are indeed of sufficient accuracy to allow target capture in the small fovea (here subtending a solid angle of only 1.5% of that of the whole image) and, secondly, that the extrapolation of the demand at the end of the saccade makes timing of the start of the pursuit process non-critical.

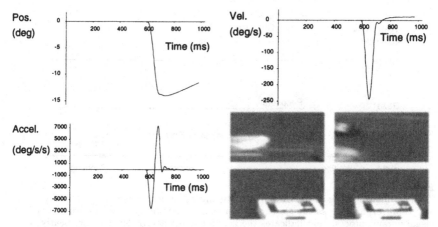

Figure 5.5
Servo-controller data for the vergence (left-right) axis logged at 500 Hz during a saccade. The images are taken through the fovea at 0,40,80 and 120 ms after the saccade is fired, showing the moving target entering the fovea.

5.5   Saccade to pursuit

As explained above, the prediction mechanism causes the camera to coast at the end of a saccade, as its position and velocity approach that of a target with an assumed constant velocity. To trigger the transition from the saccade state to the pursuit state, the gaze controller monitors the odometry from the camera platform fed back with the foveal vision results to determine a point at which the demands are satisfied, after which the gaze controller starts using the foveal motion and position as error signals to the servo-controller. The timing involved is shown in Fig. 5.6.

It is intuitive that the use of velocity information becomes the more important when the saccade is to be followed by tracking using only the small fovea. Matching the position and velocity of the camera to that of the target by the end of the saccade means that in the latency interval between the end of the saccade and the availability of the first *foveal* vision results the camera will keep up with a constant velocity target even though no visual feedback is available.

To test this experimentally we measured the variation of success fraction of saccade to pursuit transitions as the target velocity is increased, with and without the use of velocity information, and with and without velocity filtering. To remove velocity feedback within the same controller we simply used $\dot{r} = 0$ in the visual signal, which immediately satisfies the external demand. The target was a model train running around an oval track, but only one portion of straight track was visible to ensure that the constant velocity model was realistic as far as possible. Separate runs were performed

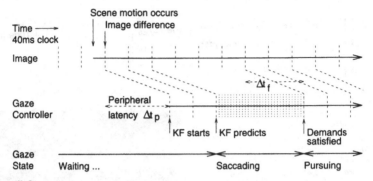

Figure 5.6
Timing diagram for saccade to pursuit. The initiation of the saccade is as in Fig.
5.4. However, as soon as the gaze controller receives odometry data from the foveal
visual pursuit process that indicates the position and velocity demands are nearly
satisfied, it enters pursuit mode, and uses the foveal data to control the head
thereafter. Δt_f is the foveal processing latency.

at each speed setting with the camera stationary to determine the angular
speed of the target prior to saccade.

Fig. 5.7 shows the results. Each datum represents the outcome of 500
trials. For all three cases the success rate approaches 100% at low target
velocities. As the target velocity increases the success rate for positional
feedback alone falls gracelessly to zero (curve (a)). Now, positional feedback alone should work for saccade to pursuit provided the target is in the
fovea at the end of saccade. If this is the case, our results should be easily interpreted using simple kinematics. Let us assume that the target has
zero acceleration and represent the lack of velocity feedback as a velocity
"error", $\delta\dot{\theta}$. The maximum target velocity is then related to the size of the
fovea by $\frac{1}{2}\alpha = \delta\dot{\theta}_{max}\Delta t$ where $\alpha = 6°$ is the fovea's width and $\Delta t \sim 300\text{ms}$,
the total delay. This predicts that positional feedback alone will fail for tar-
get velocities above $10°\text{s}^{-1}$ or, equivalently, as the fovea has a width of 70
pixel, $\sim 117\text{pixel.s}^{-1}$. This estimate agrees very well with experiment. The
success rate using both velocity and position feedback continues at a high
value, with the results from the filtered data still above 70% at 250pixel.s^{-1}.
The gradual fall off at higher velocities is a result of the increasing uncertainty in the velocity measurements made in the periphery, which could in
principle be compensated for by increasing the size of the fovea.

5.6   Pursuit using affine transfer

Using our head platform we have explored two different methods of tracking
objects in the fovea. One uses a fine scale copy of the peripheral optical flow
process to recover an average velocity and position [1]. The second, which

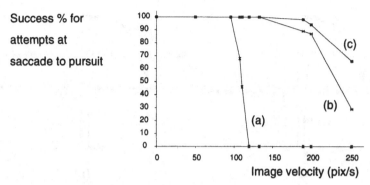

Figure 5.7
 The percentage success rate of transitions from saccade to pursuit as a function of image velocity: (a) without velocity feedback, (b) with velocity feedback but without filtering before saccade, and (c) with velocity feedback and with filtering before saccade.

we outline here, uses motion and position obtained from discrete corner features [13].

We shall not discuss the detection and tracking of corner features, but review how to obtain a stable fixation point from tracked corners. On first consideration, an image corner seems an ideal feature for providing the single position $r(t)$ to fixate on over time. However a number of problems frustrate their naïve use. The first is segmentation: which corners belong to the target, which to the background? We currently use a segmentation based on velocity that assumes that there is only one moving object in the fovea.

The second and considerably more important problem is that while a corner may provide a stable track for a few frames, either noise or occlusion will inevitably cause it to disappear. Thus positional control alone using a single corner feature is not feasible, as shown in Fig. 5.8(a). Our first attempts at overcoming this problem used the heuristics quite often seen in motion segmentation algorithms of using either the centroid of the points or the centroid of points on the convex hull. While these panacea might give an acceptable appearance to a motion segmentation, they fail hopelessly to give an acceptable foveal fixation position, as shown in Fig. 5.8(b). Another palliative tried was to use velocity control so that when one corner disappeared, the fixation point did not immediately switch to the nearest available corner but did so gradually. While this produced an acceptable smooth response, the response became sluggish.

Despite individual corners or simplistic measures on corners such as the centre-of-mass providing poor positional data, a cluster of corners arising from a moving object exhibits surprising temporal coherence in position and

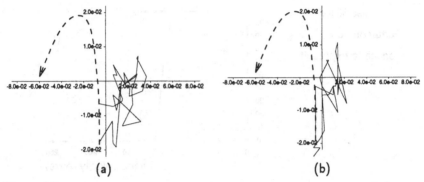

Figure 5.8
Gaze demands for two different methods of computing a desired fixation point. The
x and y axes represent azimuth and elevation demands, respectively. The dotted
line shows the actual target motion, while the solid lines represent the demands
generated by the single corner method (a) and the centroid of moving corners (b).

motion, even though the sets of corners in view at any two different times
may be substantially different. This temporal coherence can be exploited
within a structure from motion framework to supply a stable gaze direction related to a physical position on the target that need not correspond
to a detectable feature such as a corner or edge. Our algorithm derives
from recent work ([7, 12, 4, 2]) that explores the possibility of recovering
structure alone, rather than structure and motion simultaneously, from a
sequence of images. These papers show that structure can be recovered up
to a 3D global linear transformation (affine or projective). Such recovered
structure is sufficient to compute images from arbitrary novel viewpoints, a
process known as *transfer* [10], which forms the basis for our gaze direction
algorithm.

In what follows we assume an affine or weak perspective camera projection. This is a valid assumption for our work where object relief will always
be small in comparison to depth. Algebraically, an affine projection can be
represented by the equation [10]:

$$\mathbf{x} = [\mathbf{M}]\mathbf{X} + \mathbf{t} \tag{5.6}$$

where $\mathbf{x}$ is a 2×1 image position vector, $[\mathbf{M}]$ is a 2×3 matrix, $\mathbf{X}$ is a 3×1
world position vector, and $\mathbf{t}$ is a 2×1 translation vector.

5.6.1   Affine transfer

Consider a set of four points, $\mathbf{O}, \mathbf{A}, \mathbf{B}$ and $\mathbf{C}$, in general position (ie non-
coplanar and no three of which are collinear) on an object under surveillance
(see Fig. 5.9). The four points define a basis set, say $\{\mathbf{A} - \mathbf{O}, \mathbf{B} - \mathbf{O}, \mathbf{C} - \mathbf{O}\}$,
into which coordinates for any point on the object (or for that matter any

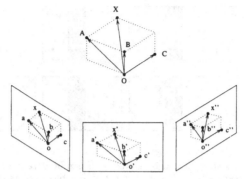

Figure 5.9
The world positions and affine projections of five points (four basis points and one other) in three views.

point in the world), $\mathbf{X}$, may be uniquely defined by three *affine coordinates*, α, β, γ:

$$\mathbf{X} = \alpha(\mathbf{A} - \mathbf{O}) + \beta(\mathbf{B} - \mathbf{O}) + \gamma(\mathbf{C} - \mathbf{O}) + \mathbf{O} \ . \tag{5.7}$$

These coordinates are invariant to the affine projection in the sense that the projected coordinates of the point $\mathbf{X}$ are the same linear combination of the projected basis vectors:

$$
\begin{aligned}
\mathbf{x} &= [\mathbf{M}]\mathbf{X} + \mathbf{t} \\
&= \alpha([\mathbf{M}]\mathbf{A} + \mathbf{t} - [\mathbf{M}]\mathbf{O} - \mathbf{t}) + \beta([\mathbf{M}]\mathbf{B} + \mathbf{t} - [\mathbf{M}]\mathbf{O} - \mathbf{t}) + \quad (5.8) \\
&\quad \gamma([\mathbf{M}]\mathbf{C} + \mathbf{t} - [\mathbf{M}]\mathbf{O} - \mathbf{t}) + [\mathbf{M}]\mathbf{O} + \mathbf{t} \\
&= \alpha(\mathbf{a} - \mathbf{o}) + \beta(\mathbf{b} - \mathbf{o}) + \gamma(\mathbf{c} - \mathbf{o}) + \mathbf{o} \ . \quad (5.9)
\end{aligned}
$$

Moreover, given two views of the four "basis" points ($\mathbf{a}, \mathbf{b}, \mathbf{c}, \mathbf{o}$ and $\mathbf{a}', \mathbf{b}', \mathbf{c}', \mathbf{o}'$), we can compute the affine coordinates of the fifth point, $\mathbf{X}$ in the two views by solving the overconstrained system of linear equations

$$
\begin{bmatrix} \mathbf{x} - \mathbf{o} \\ \mathbf{x}' - \mathbf{o}' \end{bmatrix} = \begin{bmatrix} \mathbf{a} - \mathbf{o} & \mathbf{b} - \mathbf{o} & \mathbf{c} - \mathbf{o} \\ \mathbf{a}' - \mathbf{o}' & \mathbf{b}' - \mathbf{o}' & \mathbf{c}' - \mathbf{o}' \end{bmatrix} \begin{bmatrix} \alpha \\ \beta \\ \gamma \end{bmatrix} \tag{5.10}
$$

for α, β and γ.

Having computed the affine coordinates of the point $\mathbf{X}$, it is then a straightforward matter, using the process known as *transfer* [10], to determine its projection in a novel view, given the projected positions of the reference (basis) points in the novel view, as

$$\mathbf{x}'' = \alpha(\mathbf{a}'' - \mathbf{o}'') + \beta(\mathbf{b}'' - \mathbf{o}'') + \gamma(\mathbf{c}'' - \mathbf{o}'') + \mathbf{o}'' \ . \tag{5.11}$$

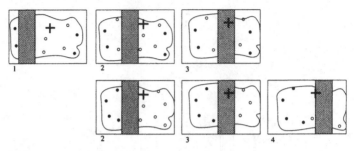

Figure 5.10
The desired fixation point, indicated by a cross-hair can be determined in frame 3
from its position in frames 1 and 2 using the set of four basis points marked in
black. In order to determine its position in frame 4, a different set of four points
present in frames 2, 3 and 4 is used. Note that the fixation point on the object need
not be visible; it is recovered in frame 3 even though the object point is occluded.

5.6.2   Transfer of gaze direction

As noted earlier, gaze holding can be achieved by the continuous generation
of a demand based on the relative position of the target to the current
gaze direction. In the image, this demand will correspond to the difference
between the desired fixation point, and the centre of the image (the current
fixation point). Clearly a prerequisite for smooth tracking is that the same
point on the target should be identified from frame to frame and used to
generate the demand. Under the affine structure from motion paradigm it
turns out to be relatively straightforward even if the actual desired fixation
point on the target is invisible.

Suppose that while tracking an object undergoing a linear transformation
(more general than a rigid one), the desired fixation point was $\mathbf{g}$ in frame t
and $\mathbf{g}'$ in frame t'. We can compute its affine coordinates $[\alpha_g, \beta_g, \gamma_g]^\top$ using
Equation 5.10 above. Then in frame t'', a short time later, the positions
of the four basis points project to new positions, $\mathbf{a}'', \mathbf{b}'', \mathbf{c}''$ and $\mathbf{o}''$, and
Equation 5.11 gives a position for the desired fixation point $\mathbf{g}''$ in the new
frame. Note that neither $\mathbf{G}$, the gaze point in the scene, nor its projections
$\mathbf{g}, \mathbf{g}', \mathbf{g}''$ need correspond to a physical feature: the desired fixation point
can be virtual.

Therefore, with *any* four corner correspondences (provided that the scene
points are in general position) in three frames we can reconstruct the position of the desired fixation point given its image coordinates in the first
two frames. The four corners used need not be the same over time, there
must merely be *one* set of four corner correspondences between each set
of three consecutive frames. As the set used varies, we are effectively performing a change of basis relative to which world and image coordinates
are computed. Unlike other tracking/fixation methods such as correlation

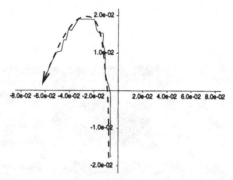

Figure 5.11
Gaze demands for the affine transfer method of computing a desired fixation point.
The x and y axes represent azimuth and elevation demands, respectively. The
dotted line shows the actual target motion, while the solid line represents the
demands generated by the algorithm (cf Fig. 5.8).

matching, the method is viewpoint invariant, and will work even if the fixation point in space is occluded (see Fig. 5.10).

The superiority of this method is clear when we compare it to single corner
and centroid methods illustrated in Figure 5.8 using the same visual simulus.
Unlike these other methods the affine transfer method is undistracted and
matches the true trajectory extremely well, as seen in Fig. 5.11.

Fig. 5.12 shows a sequence as a poster was moved in front of the camera.
The three basis points, shown in white, are seen to jump around, but the
recovered gaze position using transfer, marked with a cross hair, is stable.
Fig. 5.13 shows tracks of a moving train overlaid on an image taking from
the resting direction.

5.7   Recovering planar trajectories

The problem we address now is how to recover Cartesian trajectories of
tracked objects as they move on a plane in the scene. The camera and
scene geometry under consideration is sketched in Fig. 5.14. The elevation
and vergence joint angles (θ_e, θ_v) together define a gazing direction that
intersects the "frontal plane" at point x. The frontal plane is perpendicular
to the resting gaze direction $(\theta_e = \theta_v = 0)$, and lies an arbitrary distance in
front of the rotation centre of the camera. The gazing direction goes on to
strike a planar surface in the scene at point **X**.

Any pair of corresponding points on the two planes is related by an homography

$$\mathbf{X} = [\mathbf{P}]\mathbf{x} , \qquad (5.12)$$

where the vectors are expressed in homogeneous coordinates $\mathbf{x} = (x, y, 1)^{\top}$

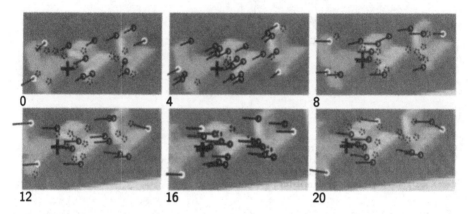

Figure 5.12
Defining a gaze direction using affine structure: Dotted circles show the positions of unmatched corners, solid circles show the positions of matched corners, each with a velocity vector, white solid circles indicate the current basis set and a crosshair indicates the desired fixation point. (Every fourth frame is shown from a 1120ms sequence.)

Figure 5.13
A test scene of a toy train travelling around a track (highlighted in the picture) with the gaze angles of the system superimposed on a resting reference frame.

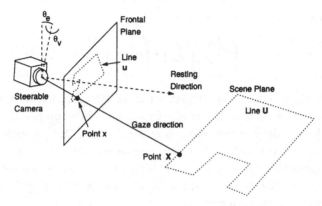

Figure 5.14
The geometrical relationship between steerable camera, the frontal plane and the scene plane.

and $\mathbf{X} = (X, Y, 1)^\top$, and $[\mathbf{P}]$ is 3×3 matrix which, because the scale is arbitrary, has only eight degrees of freedom. The homography $[\mathbf{P}]$ can be recovered by establishing the correspondence between (at least) four known points, or four known lines, in each of the two planes (eg [10]). Here we will use lines, as they conveniently incorporate multiple point measurements in the scene without having to establish multiple point correspondences.

The equivalent homography between lines is readily obtained from the dual relationships between lines and points in both planes, $\mathbf{u}^\top \mathbf{x} = 0$ and $\mathbf{U}^\top \mathbf{X} = 0$, as

$$\mathbf{U} = [\mathbf{P}^\top]^{-1}\mathbf{u} , \tag{5.13}$$

or reversing the direction of transformation, as is most natural for the calibration phase,

$$\mathbf{u} = [\mathbf{P}^\top]\mathbf{U} = [\mathbf{L}]\mathbf{U} . \tag{5.14}$$

The homogeneous representation of a line in the ground plane is given in terms of the normal to the line $\hat{\mathbf{N}} = (\cos\Phi, \sin\Phi)^\top$ and the distance D (which may be negative) along the normal from Cartesian origin to the line as

$$\mathbf{U} = (U, V, W)^\top = (\cos\Phi, \sin\Phi, -D)^\top . \tag{5.15}$$

Similarly for lines in the frontal plane,

$$\mathbf{u} = (u, v, w)^\top = (\cos\phi, \sin\phi, -d)^\top . \tag{5.16}$$

However, the equivalence implicit in the homogeneous representation $(u, v, w)^\top \equiv (\lambda u, \lambda v, \lambda w)^\top$, where λ is some arbitrary scalar, requires that we solve not $\mathbf{u} = [\mathbf{L}]\mathbf{U}$, but rather

$$\begin{pmatrix} \lambda u \\ \lambda v \\ \lambda w \end{pmatrix} = [\mathbf{L}] \begin{pmatrix} U \\ V \\ W \end{pmatrix} . \tag{5.17}$$

In addition, the scale uncertainty means that only 8 of the 9 matrix elements are recoverable. Several methods of solution have been proposed. All first eliminate λ, and the simplest goes on to set $L_{33} = 1$ [16]. A more sophisticated method retains all matrix elements as variables, but uses singular value decomposition to discover the null space, so avoiding problems that occur if $L_{33} = 0$. Here we use the former method, as the $L_{33} = 0$ condition rarely [1] occurs on physical grounds.

A little working shows that each line i for which correspondence $\mathbf{u}_i \leftrightarrow \mathbf{U}_i$ is established contributes two equations to the system

$$[\mathbf{A}]\mathbf{l} = \mathbf{b} \tag{5.18}$$

where

$$[\mathbf{A}] = \begin{bmatrix} \vdots & \vdots & \vdots & \vdots & \vdots & \vdots & \vdots & \vdots \\ U_i w_i & V_i w_i & W_i w_i & 0 & 0 & 0 & -U_i u_i & -V_i u_i \\ 0 & 0 & 0 & U_i w_i & V_i w_i & W_i w_i & -U_i v_i & -V_i v_i \\ \vdots & \vdots & \vdots & \vdots & \vdots & \vdots & \vdots & \vdots \end{bmatrix} \tag{5.19}$$

$$\mathbf{l} = (L_{11}, L_{12}, L_{13}, L_{21}, L_{22}, L_{23}, L_{31}, L_{32})^{\top} \tag{5.20}$$

and

$$\mathbf{b} = \begin{pmatrix} \vdots \\ W_i u_i \\ W_i v_i \\ \vdots \end{pmatrix} . \tag{5.21}$$

The unknown matrix elements in vector $\mathbf{l}$ can be recovered exactly using four lines, or by least squares using the pseudo-inverse method, $\mathbf{l} = [\mathbf{A}^{\top}\mathbf{A}]^{-1}[\mathbf{A}]\mathbf{b}$, for more than four lines.

Once $[\mathbf{L}]$ is acquired, the gaze direction $\mathbf{x}(t)$ at any time t can be transformed to homogeneous coordinates in the ground plane using

$$\mathbf{X}(t) = [\mathbf{P}]\mathbf{x}(t) = [\mathbf{L}^{\top}]\mathbf{x}(t) . \tag{5.22}$$

Again because of the equivalence of any homogeneous coordinate under multiplication by a scalar, Cartesian coordinates in the plane (X_C, Y_C) are recovered by renormalizing the recovered third component of $\mathbf{X} = (X, Y, Z)^{\top}$ to unity:

$$X_C = X/Z \qquad Y_C = Y/Z . \tag{5.23}$$

---

[1] It occurs if an observed line at the horizon of the ground plane is mapped to the line through the origin of the frontal plane.

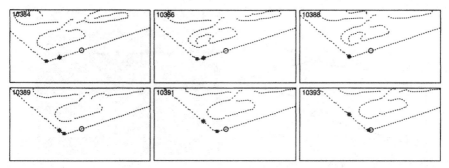

Figure 5.15
A sequence of video-rate (25Hz) foveal edgemaps obtained as the camera traces
around around a string. The near-centre string is marked with a circle, the
nth-neighbour edgel that is creating the positional demand to drive the camera
motion is marked with a star. A point of high curvature on the traced string is
marked with a square.

5.7.1   Active tracing of static lines

Underlying the line tracing process used in the calibration phase is 25Hz
implementation in the fovea of the Canny edge detection and hysteresis
linking algorithms. An initial state in the finite state machine makes the
camera perform a search pattern until it finds a long straight edge in the
fovea, and it then directs the camera onto that line. The finite state machine
then enters the tracing state. At each frame, after computing edgels and
linking them together into strings, the edgel nearest the centre of the fovea is
located and its parent string identified. The gaze controller then traverses
the string to find the nth-neighbour of the central edgel, and sends its
position as a demand to the servo-controller, and so on as the next image is
received. The effect of this is to cause the camera to trace smoothly along
an extended edge, even though no correspondence is sought from frame to
frame.

(At present if the nth-neighbour does not exist, *i.e.* is off the end of the
string, the $(n-1)$th or lower is substituted. This causes the camera simply
to stop at the end of an edge. Of course, a panoply of techniques might be
devised to allow intelligent search to continue.)

Fig. 5.15 shows the line tracing process, and it is apparent that the
edgel linking process allows continuation of a single strong edge around
corners. In order to fit to straight lines, we need to determine these points
of high curvature. This could be done within the frontal plane by looking
for high curvature points in **x** contours, but data are already available for
this purpose in the linked strings. In each frame, we determine points of
high curvature along the central string by looking for significant changes in
the local edgel orientation using a 5×1 gradient mask. Fig. 5.15 shows

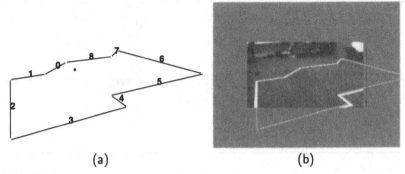

(a)   (b)

Figure 5.16
(a) The straight lines $\mathbf{u}_i, i = 0, \ldots, 8$ fitted to gaze directions $\mathbf{x}$ obtained by active line tracing during the calibration stage. (b) The same lines overlaid on a image taken by the camera viewing (nominally) along the resting direction. Notice that the active head accesses a wider field of view than the 50° of the camera. (The grey surround is merely to provide contrast.)

one such point marked by a square. When the camera is pointing close to a high curvature point a flag is set indicating a non-straight portion and this flag is passed by the vision process along with the joint angles (θ_e, θ_v) from the odometry packet to the process that builds a calibration map in the frontal plane. The joint angles are converted into the position $\mathbf{x}$ and if a continuous succession of $\mathbf{x}$ values are deemed by the vision process to be from a straight edge, a straight edge is fitted recursively in the frontal plane. As soon as an $\mathbf{x}$ value is received tagged by a non-straight flag, indicating the end of a straight section, the most recently fitted straight line is stored as a line $\mathbf{u}$ to be used for calibration.

Fig. 5.16(a) shows eight straight edges $\mathbf{u}_i$ fitted to the contours $\mathbf{x}$ in the frontal plane recovered by tracing the set of scene calibration lines. For convenience in the laboratory these were created by laying white tape onto the floor tiles. In Fig. 5.16(b) these have been overlaid on an image taken by the camera viewing nominally along the resting direction. We stress that this image has taken no part in the analysis. Its 50° field of view is much less than the near 180° field of view accessible to the active camera. The wider the field of view, the more accurate the calibration.

The lines $\mathbf{u}_i$ measured in the frontal plane are matched to the model lines $\mathbf{U}_i$. This is presently done by hand, but work in model recognition using projective invariants [15] shows there are ways to automate this process.

The set of matched lines and the resulting projective matrix are given in Fig 5.17, as is the Cartesian reconstruction of the calibration lines. They are obtained by transforming the endpoints of the straight lines measured in the frontal plane using $[\mathbf{L}^\top]$. The small circle is the origin of ground plane coordinates (this need not, and here does not, coincide with the inter-

#	u	v	w	U	V	W
0	4.854e-1	8.743e-1	3.555e+1	-1.	1.	-2.
1	1.442e-1	9.895e-1	-1.426e-1	0.	1.	0.
2	1.000e+0	-1.800e-5	2.199e+2	-1.	0.	-3.
3	2.612e-1	9.653e-1	-1.642e+2	0.	-1.	-2.5
4	5.794e-1	-8.151e-1	-2.854e+0	-1.	0.	-1.
5	2.163e-1	9.763e-1	-1.094e+2	0.	-1.	-2.
6	2.540e-1	-9.672e-1	-9.728e+1	1.	0.	-2.
7	7.142e-1	7.000e-1	-5.984e+1	-1.	1.	0.
8	1.145e-1	9.934e-1	2.758e+1	0.	1.	-1.

$$[\mathbf{L}^T] = \begin{bmatrix} 8.33e-03 & -1.81e-02 & -1.04e+00 \\ -4.38e-03 & -2.99e-02 & 7.70e-05 \\ 1.90e-04 & 6.04e-03 & 1.00e+00 \end{bmatrix}$$

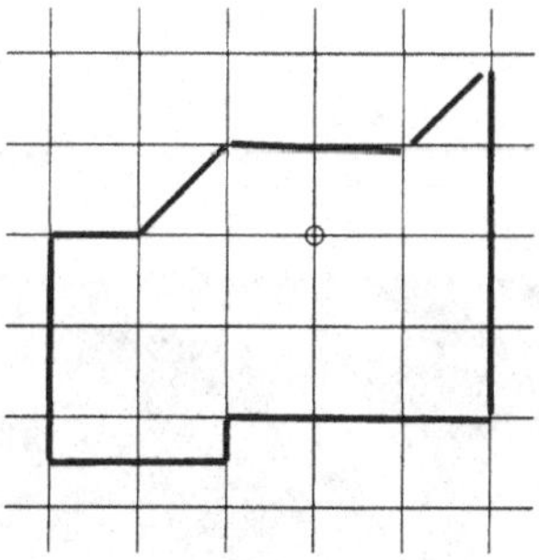

Figure 5.17
The measured equations of the matched lines in the frontal and scene planes, the computed homography $[\mathbf{L}^T]$, and the resulting Cartesian reconstruction of the calibration pattern.

section of the resting direction with the ground plane). The grid indicates the underlying Cartesian grid used to generate the model line descriptions (U, V, W). It follows the mesh of floor tiles on the lab floor. The recovered lines are so close to the model that we do not show the model lines explicitly.

5.8   Putting it together

As noted in Section 5.2, the high level gaze controller is implemented as a finite state machine. On startup the gaze controller enters a state where it tracks straight lines and creates the calibration matrix. It continues in this mapping state until distracted by a movement in the scene. The controller then fires a saccade, and then initiates tracking.

As tracking of a target proceeds, the time varying joint angles $(\theta_e(t), \theta_v(t))$ of the camera platform are mapped into $\mathbf{x}(t)$ in the frontal plane, and then by applying $[\mathbf{L}^T]$ and normalizing, mapped into the Cartesian coordinate system as a trajectory $\mathbf{X}(t)$.

Fig. 5.18(a) shows the track $\mathbf{x}(t)$ obtained while the camera tracks a small radio-controlled buggy being driven around the laboratory floor. It is overlaid on an image taken from the resting direction. Fig. 5.18(b) shows the Cartesian view of the recovered trajectories.

5.9   Conclusion

In this chapter we have described a combination of real-time processes that allows the detection of an object moving in the scene and the rapid redirection of a foveal region of attention onto that target. The motion saccade is followed by tracking, where we have given a brief outline of an algorithm

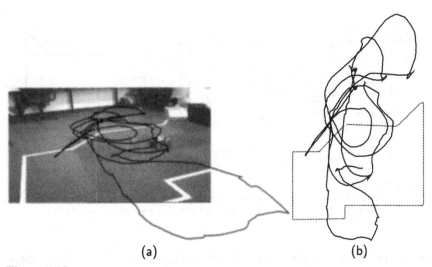

(a)   (b)

Figure 5.18
(a) A scene of a buggy with the gaze angles of the system superimposed on a resting
reference frame and (b) the rectified trajectory of the buggy and the floor markings.

that allows a stable gaze direction to be established from a set of corner
features that may disappear and reappear over time.

We then described a method of calibrating the transformation from head
platform joint angles into 2D Cartesian coordinates based in a plane in
the 3D scene. The calibration was obtained by following lines in the scene
whose coordinates had been stored as a model. The processing involved the
real-time detection of Canny edges in the foveal region.

The recovery of Cartesian coordinates of tracked objects has obvious applications in traffic surveillance, and part of our current work aims to describe those trajectories, feeding back learned motion trajectories to the
tracking stage.

Another interesting aspect of the calibration work is that the active camera is being used a pointing stick in a projective frame where the centre of
rotation, rather than the optic centre, is the centre of projection. By building geometry in the plane normal to the resting direction we effectively
construct a projective camera with an unlimited angle of view.

Acknowledgements

This work has been funded by Grants GR/G30003 and GR/J65372 from
the UK Science and Engineering Research Council and by the EC's Esprit
Project 5390. KJB and SMF gratefully acknowledge the receipt of SERC
research studentships.

References

[1] K. J. Bradshaw, P. F. McLauchlan, I. D. Reid, and D. W. Murray. Saccade and pursuit on an active head/eye platform. *Image and Vision Computing (In Press)*, 12(3), 1994.

[2] S. Demey, A. Zisserman, and P. Beardsley. Affine and projective structure from motion. In D. Hogg and R. Boyle, editors, *Proceedings of the 3rd British Machine Vision Conference, Leeds*, pages 49–58. Springer-Verlag, September 1992.

[3] S. M. Fairley. Obtaining initial disparity estimates for coarse vergence control of a real-time stereo head/eye platform. First Year Report, Department of Engineering Science, University of Oxford, July 1993.

[4] O. D. Faugeras. What can be seen in three dimensions with an uncalibrated stereo rig? In G. Sandini, editor, *Proceedings of the 2nd European Conference on Computer Vision, Santa Margharita Ligure, Italy*, pages 563–578. Springer-Verlag, 1992.

[5] C. L. Fennema and W. L. Thompson. Velocity determination in scenes containing several moving objects. *Computer Graphics and Image Processing*, 9:301–315, 1979.

[6] B. K. P. Horn and B. G. Schunck. Determining optical flow. *AI Journal*, 17:185–203, 1981.

[7] J. J. Koenderink and A. J. van Doorn. Affine structure from motion. *J. Opt. Soc. Am. A*, 8(2):377–385, 1991.

[8] P. F. McLauchlan and D. W. Murray. Variable state dimension filter applied to active camera calibration. In *Proc SPIE Sensor Fusion VI, Boston MA*, pages 14–25, September 1993.

[9] P. F. McLauchlan, I. D. Reid, and D. W. Murray. Coarse motion for saccade control. In D. Hogg and R. Boyle, editors, *Proceedings of the 3rd British Machine Vision Conference, Leeds*, pages 357–366. Springer-Verlag, September 1992.

[10] J.L. Mundy and A. Zisserman. Projective geometry for machine vision. In J. L. Mundy and A. Zisserman, editors, *Geometric Invariance in Computer Vision*, pages 463–519. MIT Press, Cambridge MA, 1992.

[11] D. W. Murray, P. F. McLauchlan, I. D. Reid, and P. M. Sharkey. Reactions to peripheral image motion using a head/eye platform. In *Proceedings of the 4th International Conference on Computer Vision, Berlin*, pages 403–411, Los Alamitos, CA, 1993. IEEE Computer Society Press.

[12] L. Quan and R. Mohr. Towards structure from motion for linear features through reference points. In *Proceedings of the IEEE Workshop on Visual Motion*, 1991.

[13] I. D. Reid and D. W. Murray. Tracking foveated corner clusters using affine structure. In *Proceedings of the 4th International Conference on Computer Vision, Berlin*, pages 76–83, Los Alamitos, CA, 1993. IEEE Computer Society Press.

[14] I. D. Reid, D. W. Murray, and K. J. Bradshaw. Towards active exploration of static and dynamic scene geometry. Submitted to IEEE International Conference on Robotics and Automation, San Diego CA, 1994.

[15] C. A. Rothwell, A. Zisserman, D. A. Forsyth, and J. L. Mundy. Projective geometry for machine vision. In J. L. Mundy and A. Zisserman, editors, *Geometric Invariance in Computer Vision*, pages 463–519. MIT Press, Cambridge MA, 1992.

[16] C.A. Rothwell, A. Zisserman, C.I. Marinos, D.A. Forsyth, and J.L. Mundy. Relative motion and pose from arbitrary plane curves. *Image and Vision Computing*, 10(4):250–262, 1992.

[17] P. M. Sharkey, D. W. Murray, S. Vandevelde, I. D. Reid, and P. F. McLauchlan. A modular head/eye platform for real-time reactive vision. *Mechatronics*, 3(4):517–535, 1993.

[18] P.M. Sharkey and D.W. Murray. Coping with delays for real-time gaze control. In *Proc SPIE Sensor Fusion VI, Boston MA*, September 1993.

6 Robust Shape Recovery from Occluding Contours Using a Linear Smoother

Richard Szeliski and Richard Weiss

6.1 Introduction

Most visually-guided systems require representations of surfaces in the environment in order to integrate sensing, planning, and action. The task considered in this chapter is the recovery of the 3D structure (shape) of objects with piecewise-smooth surfaces from a sequence of profiles taken with known camera motion. The *profile* (also known as the *extremal boundary* or *occluding contour*) is defined as the image of the *critical set* of the projection map from the surface to the image plane. Since profiles are general curves in the plane without distinguished points, there is no *a priori* pointwise correspondence between these curves in different views. However, given the camera motion, there is a correspondence based on the *epipolar constraint*. For two images, i.e., classical *binocular stereo*, this epipolar constraint is a set of straight lines that are the intersection of the *epipolar planes* with the image plane. The epipolar plane through a point is determined by the view direction at that point and the instantaneous camera translation direction.

In the case of contours that are not view dependent, e.g., creases (tangent discontinuities) and surface markings, many techniques have been developed for recovering the 3D contour locations from two or more images under known camera motion [28, 26, 3, 6, 5, 29]. Techniques have also been developed for simultaneously estimating contour locations and camera positions [37, 17, 22]. However, for smooth curved surfaces, the critical set that generates the profile is different for each view. Thus, the triangulation applied in two-frame stereo will not be correct along the occluding contour for smooth surfaces. For the same reason, it is often not possible to determine the camera motion from the images unless some assumptions are made either about the surface or the motion [2, 19]. On the other hand, the fact that the critical sets sweep out an area means that the connectivity of the surface points can be determined, i.e., one obtains a surface patch rather than a set of points.

The problem of reconstructing a smooth surface from its profiles has been explored for known planar motion by Giblin and Weiss [20] and subsequently for more general known motion by Vaillant and Faugeras [39, 40] and Cipolla and Blake [7, 12, 2]. These approaches are either based on a differential formulation and analysis, or they use curve fitting but still only use three frames. First order temporal derivatives are usually computed as differences from pairs of frames, and second order derivatives from triples. Unfortunately, determining differential quantities reliably from real images in this way is difficult. Even fitting curves to data from three images can be unsatisfactory. This has led Cipolla and Blake to use relative measurements in order to cancel some of the error due to inadvertent camera rotation. Their approach approximated image contours with B-snakes which require initialization for each contour that is tracked. In addition, B-snakes implicitly smooth the contours in the image. Since the recovery of 3D points is a linear problem (as we will show in this chapter), the smoothing can be done in 3D on the surface, where more context can be used in the detection of discontinuities so that detailed structure can be preserved.

It is natural to consider surface reconstruction as an optimal estimation problem. To overcome the limitations of previous algorithms, the approach we develop in this chapter applies standard techniques from estimation theory (Kalman filtering and smoothing) to make optimal use of each measurement without computing differential quantities. First, we derive a *linear* set of equations between the unknown shape (surface point positions and radii of curvature) and the measurements. We then develop a robust linear smoother ([18, 9]) to compute statistically optimal current and past estimates from the set of contours. Smoothing allows us to combine measurements on both sides of each surface point.

Our technique produces a complete surface description, i.e., a network of linked 3D surface points, which provides us with a much richer description than just a set of 3D curves. Some parts of the surface may never appear on the profile. In some cases this is due to occlusion either by the same surface or another one. In other cases, it is due to limitations of the camera trajectory [21]. Since the method presented here also works for arbitrary surface markings and creases, a larger part of the surface can be reconstructed than from occluding contours of the smooth pieces alone. Our approach also addresses the difficult problem of contours that merge and split in the image, which must be resolved if an accurate and complete 3D surface model is to be constructed.

The method we develop has applications in many areas of computer vision, computer aided design, and visual communications. The most traditional application of visually based shape recovery is in the reconstruction of a mobile robot's environment, which allows it to perform obstacle avoidance and planning tasks [5]. Visually based shape recovery can also be used to develop strategies for robotics grasping and manipulation tasks, or as an off-line technique to "learn" object descriptions for object automatically or pose recognition tasks. In less traditional applications, our system could be used to perform *reverse engineering*, i.e., to automatically acquire 3D computer aided design (CAD) description of real-world objects or prototypes, or even to construct a "3D fax" for transmitting 3D object descriptions and images between desktops.

This chapter is structured as follows. We begin in Section 6.2 with a description of our edge detection, contour linking, and edge tracking algorithms. In Section 6.3, we discuss the estimation of the epipolar plane for a sequence of three or more views. Section 6.4 presents the linear measurement equations that relate the edge positions in each image to the parameters of the circular arc being fitted at each surface point. Section 6.5 then reviews robust least squares techniques for recovering the shape parameters and discusses their statistical interpretation. Section 6.6 shows how to extend least squares to a time-evolving system using the Kalman filter, and develops the requisite forward mapping (surface point evolution) equations. Section 6.7 extends the Kalman filter to the linear smoother, which optimally refines and updates previous surface point estimates from new measurements. Section 6.9 presents a series of experiments performed both on noisy synthetic contour sequences and on real video images. We close with a discussion of the performance of our new technique and a discussion of future work.

6.2   Contour detection and tracking

The problem of edge detection has been extensively studied in computer vision [27, 11]. The choice of edge detector is not crucial in our application, since we are interested mostly in detecting strong edges such as occluding contours and visible surface markings.[1] For our system, we have chosen the *steerable filters* developed by Freeman and Adelson [16], since they provide good angular resolution at moderate computation cost, and since they can find both step and peak edges. We have used both the G_1 and (G_2, H_2) sets of filters, with the default parameters suggested by Freeman and Adelson. An example of our edge detector operating on the input image in Fig. 6.1a is shown in Fig. 6.1b.

Once discrete edgels have been detected, we use local search to link the edgels into contours. We find the two neighbors of each edgel based on proximity and continuity of orientation. Note that in contrast to some of the previous work in reconstruction from occluding contours [12, 2, 8], we do not fit a smooth parametric curve to the contour since we wish to use all of the edgels in the shape reconstruction directly, without losing detail.[2] The curve fitting problem is essentially one of detecting outliers. Since the 3D

---

[1] Unlike many edge detection applications, however, our system provides us with a quantitative way to measure the performance of an edge detector, since we can in many cases measure the accuracy of our final 3D reconstruction.

[2] However, we do perform a small amount of curvature-dependent smoothing along the curves to reduce noise. This can be viewed as part of the edge extraction stage.

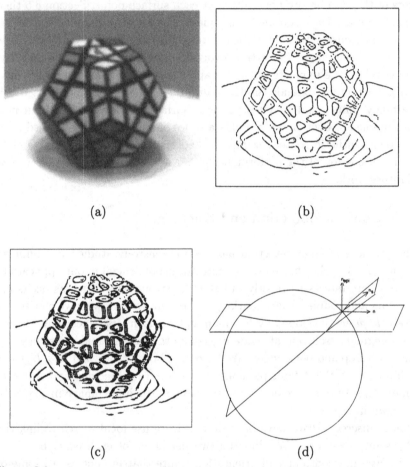

(a)   (b)

(c)   (d)

Figure 6.1
Input processing: (a) sample input image (dodecahedral puzzle), (b) estimated
edgels and orientations (maxima in $|G_1|^2$), (c) tracked edgels, (d) correspondence of
points on the occluding contours using the epipolar constraint.

reconstruction provides more context, smoothing in 3D should be preferred.

We then use the known epipolar line constraints (Section 6.3) to find the best matching edgel in the next frame. Our technique compares all candidate edgels within the epipolar line search range (defined by the expected minimum and maximum depths), and selects the one that matches most closely in orientation, contrast, and intensity (see Fig. 6.1c). Once an initial estimate for the 3D location of an edgel has been computed, the search range can be dramatically reduced (see Section 6.5.3).

Since contours are maintained as a list of discrete points, it is necessary to resample the edge points in order to enforce the epipolar constraint on each track. We occasionally start new tracks if there is a sufficiently large (2 pixel wide) gap between successive samples on the contour. While we do not operate directly on the spatiotemporal volume, our tracking and contour linking processes form a virtual surface similar to the *weaving wall* technique of Harlyn Baker [4]. Unlike Baker's technique, however, we do not assume a regular and dense sampling in time.

6.3   Reconstructing surface patches

The surface being reconstructed from a moving camera can be parametrized in a natural way by two families of curves [20, 12]: one family consists of the critical sets on the surface; the other is tangent to the family of rays from the camera focal points. The latter curves are called *epipolar curves* and together with the critical sets form the *epipolar parametrization*. This parametrization can always be used except when the profile is singular or when the normal to the surface is perpendicular to the direction of camera translation [21]. For a pair of stereo images, each viewing direction together with the translation vector from one camera center to the other determines a plane called an *epipolar plane*. The same construction holds in the case of motion: in the limit, as the time between samples goes to zero, the plane determined by a view direction and the camera translation velocity will also be called an epipolar plane. For a more detailed discussion of epipolar curves see [21].

The problem is that any smooth surface reconstruction algorithm that is more than a first order approximation requires at least three images and, that in general, the three corresponding tangent rays will not be coplanar. However, there are many cases when this will be a good approximation. One such case is when the camera trajectory is almost linear. If the camera trajectory is linear, then the epipolar planes form a pencil of planes containing that line. Under orthographic projection, if the camera motion is planar, then all of the epipolar curves will be planar as well.

Cipolla and Blake [12, 2] and Vaillant and Faugeras [39, 40] noticed that to compute the curvature of a planar curve from three tangent rays, one can determine a circle that is tangent to these rays. See Fig. 6.2. The necessary assumption is that the surface remains on the same side of the tangent rays. This is true for intervals of the curve that do not have a singularity or zero curvature.

Given three or more edgels tracked with our technique, we would like to compute the location of the surface and its curvature by fitting a circular arc to the lines defined by the view directions at those edgels. In general, a non-singular space curve has a unique circle that is closest to the curve at any given point. This is called the *osculating circle*, and the plane of this circle is called the *osculating plane*. It is easy to see that if the epipolar curve is non-singular, then the epipolar plane is an estimate of its osculating plane [2], and the lines defined by the view directions are close to this plane and can be projected onto it. The accuracy of the computation of the radius of curvature depends on the conditioning of this projection. Since in the limit, the epipolar plane is the osculating plane for the epipolar curve, the epipolar curves should be the most robust to reconstruct by projecting onto this plane.

The relationship between the curvature of a curve such as the epipolar curve and the curvature of the surface is determined by the angle between the normal to the curve and the normal to the surface. The curvature of the curve scaled by the cosine of this angle is the *normal curvature*. The curvature of a surface can be thought of as a function that assigns to every tangent direction v a value which is the curvature k_v of the normal slice in that direction. If v is the tangent to the epipolar curve, k_{epi} is the curvature of the epipolar curve, and ϕ is the angle between the epipolar plane and the plane containing v and the surface normal, then the relationship among them is given by the equation

$$k_v = k_{epi} \cos \phi \qquad (6.1)$$

This gives Meusnier's Theorem which says that the normal curvature is the same for all curves on the surface with a given tangent direction. Since the normal to the surface can be determined from the image, the normal curvature can be obtained from the epipolar curve.

6.4   Measurement equations

Once we have selected the epipolar plane as the reconstruction plane for fitting the circular arc, we must compute the set of lines in this plane which should be tangent to the circle. This can be done either by projecting the

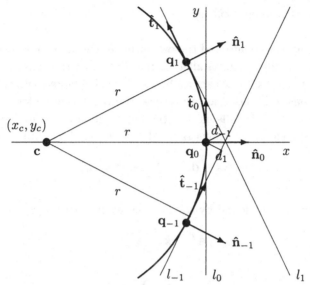

Figure 6.2
Local coordinate axes and circle center point calculation In this figure, the points
p_i and q_i are coincident. In general, the q_i will lie somewhere along the tangent
rays, and the p_i will be the points of tangency to the osculating circle.

3D lines corresponding to the linked edgels directly onto the plane, or by
intersecting the tangent planes (defined by the edgels and their orientations)
with the reconstruction plane.

We represent the 3D line corresponding to an edgel in frame i by a 3D
point q_i and a direction $\hat{t}_i$. The point q_i is chosen to be the intersection
of the viewing ray with a reference plane $z = z_0$. The direction is given by
$\hat{t}_i = \mathcal{N}(q_i - c_i)$, where c_i is the camera center and $\mathcal{N}()$ normalizes a vector.
We choose one of these lines as the *reference frame* $(\hat{n}_0, \hat{t}_0)$ centered at q_0
(where $\hat{n}_0 = \hat{t}_0 \times \hat{n}_{epi}$), e.g., by selecting the middle of n frames for a batch
fit, or the last frame for a Kalman filter. This line lies in the reconstruction
plane defined by $\hat{n}_{epi}$.

If we parameterize the osculating circle by its center $c = (x_c, y_c)$ and
radius r (Fig. 6.2), we find that the tangency condition between line i and
the circle can be written as

$$c_i x_c + s_i y_c + r = d_i \qquad (6.2)$$

where $c_i = \hat{t}_i \cdot \hat{t}_0$, $s_i = -\hat{t}_i \cdot \hat{n}_0$, and $d_i = (q_i - q_0) \cdot \hat{n}_i$. *Thus, we have a
linear estimation problem in the quantities* (x_c, y_c, r) *given the known mea-
surements* (c_i, s_i, d_i). This linearity is central to the further developments
in the chapter, including the least squares fitting, Kalman filter, and linear
smoother, which we develop in the next three sections.

6.5   Least squares fitting

While in theory the equation of the osculating circle can be recovered given
the projection of three non-parallel tangent lines onto the epipolar plane, a
much more reliable estimate can be obtained by using more views. Given the
set of equations (6.2), how can we recover the best estimate for (x_c, y_c, r)?
Regression theory [1, 9] tells us that the minimum least squared error estimate of the system of equations $\mathbf{Ax} = \mathbf{d}$ can be found by minimizing

$$e = |\mathbf{Ax} - \mathbf{d}|^2 = \sum_i (\mathbf{a}_i \cdot \mathbf{x} - d_i)^2. \tag{6.3}$$

This minimum can be found by solving the set of *normal equations*[3]

$$(\mathbf{A}^T\mathbf{A})\hat{\mathbf{x}} = \mathbf{A}^T\mathbf{d} \tag{6.4}$$

or

$$(\sum_i \mathbf{a}_i\mathbf{a}_i^T)\hat{\mathbf{x}} = \sum_i \mathbf{a}_i d_i.$$

A statistical justification for using least squares will be presented shortly
(Section 6.5.1).

In our circle fitting case, $\mathbf{a}_i = (c_i, s_i, 1)$, $\mathbf{x} = (x_c, y_c, r)$, and the normal
equations are

$$\begin{bmatrix} \sum_i c_i^2 & \sum_i c_i s_i & \sum_i c_i \\ \sum_i s_i c_i & \sum_i s_i^2 & \sum_i s_i \\ \sum_i c_i & \sum_i s_i & \sum_i 1 \end{bmatrix} \begin{bmatrix} x_c \\ y_c \\ r \end{bmatrix} = \begin{bmatrix} \sum_i c_i d_i \\ \sum_i s_i d_i \\ \sum_i d_i \end{bmatrix}. \tag{6.5}$$

If we solve the above set of equations directly, the estimates for x_c and r will
be very highly correlated and both will be highly unreliable (assuming the
range of viewpoints is not very large). This can be seen both by examining
Fig. 6.2, where we see that the location of $\mathbf{c}$ is highly sensitive to the exact
values of the d_i, or by computing the covariance matrix $\mathbf{P} = (\mathbf{A}^T\mathbf{A})^{-1}$
(Section 6.5.1).

We cannot do much to improve the estimate of r short of using more
frames or a larger camera displacement, but we can greatly increase the
reliability of our shape estimate by directly solving for the *surface point*
(x_s, y_s), where $x_s = x_c + r$ and $y_s = y_c$.[4] The new set of equations is thus

$$c_i x_s + s_i y_s + (1 - c_i)r = d_i. \tag{6.6}$$

---

[3] Alternative techniques for solving the least squares problem include *singular value
decomposition* [30] and Householder transforms [9].
[4] While the point (x_s, y_s) will not in general lie on the line $(\mathbf{q}_0, \hat{\mathbf{t}}_0)$, the tangent to the
circle at (x_s, y_s) will be parallel to $\hat{\mathbf{t}}_0$.

While there is still some correlation between x_s and r, the estimate for x_s is much more reliable (Section 6.5.1). Once we have estimated (x_s, y_s, r), we can convert this estimate back to a 3D surface point,

$$\mathbf{p}_0 = \mathbf{q}_0 + x_s \hat{\mathbf{n}}_0 + y_s \hat{\mathbf{t}}_0, \tag{6.7}$$

a 3D center point

$$\mathbf{c} = \mathbf{q}_0 + (x_s - r)\hat{\mathbf{n}}_0 + y_s \hat{\mathbf{t}}_0 = \mathbf{p}_0 - r\hat{\mathbf{n}}_0, \tag{6.8}$$

or a surface point in the ith frame

$$\mathbf{p}_i = \mathbf{c} + r\hat{\mathbf{n}}_i = \mathbf{p}_0 + r(\hat{\mathbf{n}}_i - \hat{\mathbf{n}}_0), \tag{6.9}$$

where

$$\hat{\mathbf{n}}_i = \hat{\mathbf{t}}_i \times \hat{\mathbf{n}}_{\text{epi}}$$

is the osculating circle normal direction perpendicular to line l_i (Fig. 6.2).

6.5.1 Statistical interpretation

The least squares estimate is also the *minimum variance* and *maximum likelihood* estimate (optimal statistical estimate) under the assumption that each measurement is contaminated with additive Gaussian noise [9]. If each measurement has a different variance σ_i^2, we must weight each term in the squared error measure (6.3) by $w_i = \sigma_i^{-2}$, or, equivalently, multiply each equation $\mathbf{a}_i \cdot \mathbf{x} = d_i$ by σ_i^{-1}.

In our application, the variance of d_i, σ_i^2, can be determined by analyzing the edge detector output and computing the angle between the edge orientation and the epipolar line

$$\sigma_i^2 = \sigma_e^2 / (\hat{\mathbf{l}}_i \cdot \hat{\mathbf{n}}_{\text{epi}})^2 = \sigma_e^2 / (1 - (\hat{\mathbf{m}}_i \cdot \hat{\mathbf{n}}_{\text{epi}})^2),$$

where σ_e is the variance of $\mathbf{q}_i$ along the surface normal $\hat{\mathbf{m}}_i$. This statistical model makes sense if the measurements d_i are noisy and the other parameters (c_i, s_i) are noise-free. This is a reasonable assumption in our case, since the camera positions are known but the edgel locations are noisy. The generalization to uncertain camera locations is left to future work.

When using least squares, the covariance matrix of the estimate can be computed from $\mathbf{P} = (\mathbf{A}^T \mathbf{A})^{-1}$. We can perform a simple analysis of the expected covariances for n measurements spaced θ apart. Using Taylor series expansions for $c_i = \cos i\theta$ and $s_i = \sin i\theta$, and assuming that $i \in [-m \ldots m]$, $n = 2m + 1$, we obtain the covariance matrices

$$P_3^c \approx \begin{bmatrix} 6\theta^{-4} & 0 & -6\theta^{-4} \\ 0 & \frac{1}{2}\theta^{-2} & 0 \\ -6\theta^{-4} & 0 & 6\theta^{-4} \end{bmatrix} \quad \text{and} \quad P_3^s \approx \begin{bmatrix} 1 & 0 & -2\theta^{-2} \\ 0 & \frac{1}{2}\theta^{-2} & 0 \\ -2\theta^{-2} & 0 & 6\theta^{-4} \end{bmatrix}$$

where P_3^c is the 3 point covariance for the center-point formulation, and P_3^s is the 3 point covariance for the surface-point formulation. As we can see, variance of the surface point local x estimate is four orders of magnitude smaller than that of the center point. Similar results hold for the overdetermined case ($n > 3$). Extending the analysis to the asymmetrical case, $i \in [0 \ldots 2m]$, we observe that the variance of the x_s and y_s estimates increases.

6.5.2   Robustifying the estimate

To improve the quality and reliability of our estimates further, we can apply *robust statistics* to reduce the effects of *outliers*, which are due to grossly erroneous measurements as well as large changes in the surface curvature [23]. Many robust techniques are based on first computing *residuals*, $r_i = d_i - \mathbf{a}_i \cdot \mathbf{x}$, and then re-weighting the data by a monotonic function

$$(\sigma_i')^{-2} = \sigma_i^{-2} g(|r_i|)$$

or throwing out measurements whose $|r_i| \gg \sigma_i$. Alternatively, least median squares can also be used to compute a robust estimate, but at an increased complexity.

In our application, outliers occur mainly from gross errors in edge detection (e.g., when adjacent edges interfere) and from errors in tracking. Currently, we compute residuals after each batch fit, and keep only those measurements whose residuals fall below a fixed threshold.

6.5.3   Predicting 2D locations for tracking

Once a 3-D estimate for an edgel location has been computed, it can be used to predict where the edgel would appear in the next frame, and hence to improve the correspondence produced by the tracking stage. When no 3-D information is available, we project the viewing ray passing through a 2-D edgel into the next frame to give us the epipolar search line. We use the intersection of the viewing ray with a minimum and maximum depth plane to determine the endpoints that limit the search range.

When a 3-D position estimate is available, we project the 3-D position and covariance estimate into the new reconstruction plane. The position on the screen of the edgel then gives us the middle of the search range, while a multiple of the standard deviation in the local x direction (which is parallel to the image plane and in the reconstruction plane and hence along the epipolar line) times the epipolar line determines the limits of the search range. More formally, the endpoints of the search line are

$$\mathcal{P}_i(\mathbf{p}_i \pm \alpha \sigma_x \hat{\mathbf{n}}_0)$$

where $\mathcal{P}_i$ projects points in 3-D onto the ith frame, and σ_x^2 is the variance in the local x direction.

Our approach is similar in spirit to the *validation gate* approach used by Blake *et al.* for their Kalman-filter snake tracking [8]. Even more sophisticated data association techniques could be used to disambiguate multiple intersecting tracks [10].

6.6   Kalman filter

The Kalman filter is a powerful technique for efficiently computing statistically optimal estimates of time-varying processes from series of noisy measurements [18, 9, 25]. In computer vision, the Kalman filter has been applied to diverse problems such as motion recovery [32], multiframe stereo [29], and pose recovery [24]. In this section, we develop a Kalman filter for contour-based shape recovery in two parts: first, we show how to perform the batch fitting of the previous section incrementally; second, we show how surface point estimates can be predicted from one frame (and reconstruction plane) to another.

The *update* or *data processing* part of a Kalman filter takes a current estimate $\tilde{\mathbf{x}}_i$ with its associated covariance $\tilde{\mathbf{P}}_i$ and produces an updated estimate $\hat{\mathbf{x}}_i$ and covariance $\hat{\mathbf{P}}_i$ by processing a single measurement

$$d_i = \mathbf{a}_i \cdot \mathbf{x}_i. \qquad (6.10)$$

The traditional Kalman filter formulation [18] first computes a Kalman gain matrix

$$\mathbf{K}_i = \tilde{\mathbf{P}}_i \mathbf{a}_i (\mathbf{a}_i^T \tilde{\mathbf{P}}_i \mathbf{a}_i + \sigma_i^2)^{-1}, \qquad (6.11)$$

where σ_i^2 is the variance associated with measurement i. It then increments the state estimate by adding a weighted residual

$$\hat{\mathbf{x}}_i = \tilde{\mathbf{x}}_i + \mathbf{K}_i (d_i - \mathbf{a}_i \cdot \tilde{\mathbf{x}}_i). \qquad (6.12)$$

and decrements the covariance matrix

$$\hat{\mathbf{P}}_i = \tilde{\mathbf{P}}_i - \mathbf{K}_i \mathbf{a}_i^T \tilde{\mathbf{P}}_i. \qquad (6.13)$$

Applying this Kalman filter to our circular arc fitting task is straightforward, since each of our tangent lines is of the required form (6.10), $d_i = \mathbf{a}_i \cdot \mathbf{x}_i$. More numerically stable or computationally efficient forms of the Kalman filter have also been developed [9], but we have not yet implemented them to see if they improve our performance.

The update part of the Kalman filter is derived directly from the measurement equation (6.2) [18]. It provides an incremental technique for estimating quantities in a *static* system, e.g., for refining a set of (x_s, y_s, r) estimates as more edgels are observed. For our application, however, we need to produce a series of surface points that can be linked together into a complete surface description. If we were using batch fitting, we would perform a new batch fit centered around each new 2D edgel. Instead, we use the complete Kalman filter, since it has a much lower computational complexity. The Kalman filter provides a way to deal with *dynamic* systems where the state $\mathbf{x}_i$ is evolving over time. We identify each measurement $\mathbf{x}_i$ with the surface point (x_s, y_s, r) whose local coordinate frame is given by $(\hat{\mathbf{n}}_i, \hat{\mathbf{t}}_i, \hat{\mathbf{n}}_{\mathrm{epi}})$ centered at $\mathbf{q}_i$ in frame i.

The second half of the Kalman filter requires a *system model* or *process model* that predicts the evolution of state variables over time [18]. For our smooth surface model, we assume that r (the third component of $\mathbf{x}$) can vary slowly over time, but that the other two components have no associated process noise, i.e., $\mathbf{s} = (0, 0, s_r)$.

The overall sequence of processing steps is therefore the following. Initially, we perform a batch fit to $n \geq 3$ frames, using the last frame as the reference frame. Next, we convert the local estimate into a global 3D position (6.7) and save it as part of our final surface model. We use this 3D estimate to construct a reduced search range for edgels during the tracking phase. Then, we project the 3D surface point and its radius onto the next frame, i.e., into the frame defined by the next 2D edgel found by the tracker.[5] Then, we update the state estimate using the local line equation and the Kalman filter updating equations. We repeat the above process (except for the batch fit) so long as a reliable track is maintained (i.e., the residuals are within an acceptable range). If the track disappears or a robust fit is not possible, we terminate the recursive processing and wait until enough new measurements are available to start a new batch fit.

6.7   Linear smoothing

The Kalman filter is most commonly used in control systems applications, where the current estimate is used to determine an optimal control strategy to achieve a desired system behavior [18]. In certain applications, however, we may wish to refine old estimates as new information arrives, or, equivalently, to use "future" measurements to compute the best current estimate. Our shape recovery application falls into this latter category, since the accuracy of the estimate depends on the range of viewing angles for the measurements, and this can be increased by taking measurements from both

---

[5] For even higher accuracy, we could use the 2D projection of our 3D surface point as the input to our tracker.

sides of the 3D curve corresponding to a given visible occluding contour. In addition, it should be noted that if the curvature of the epipolar curve is not constant, then for each interval over which it is monotonic, filtering rather than smoothing will introduce a bias.

The generalization of the Kalman filter to update previous estimates is called the *linear smoother* [18]. The smoothed estimate of x_i based on all the measurements between 0 and N is denoted by $\hat{x}_{i|N}$. Three kinds of smoothing are possible [18]. In *fixed-interval smoothing*, the initial and final times 0 and N are fixed, and the estimate $\hat{x}_{i|N}$ is sought, where i varies from 0 to N. In this case, each point in the model is estimated from all of the data in a track. In *fixed-point smoothing*, i is fixed and $\hat{x}_{i|N}$ is sought as N increases. Each point is updated as new data is obtained, i.e. there is a separate smoother for each point. In *fixed-lag smoothing*, $\hat{x}_{N-L|N}$ is sought as N increases and L is held fixed. This has the advantage that each point is estimated within a fixed amount of time from when it appears on the profile, and it is only estimated once. Since the lag time is non-zero, information on both sides of the critical set are used.

For surface shape recovery, both fixed-interval and fixed-lag smoothing are of interest. Fixed-interval smoothing is appropriate when shape recovery is performed off-line from a set of predetermined measurements. The results obtained with fixed-interval smoothing should be identical to those obtained with a series of batch fits, but at a much lower computational cost. The fixed-interval smoother requires a small amount of overhead beyond the regular Kalman filter in order to determine the optimal combination between the outputs of a forward and backward Kalman filter [18, 9].

For our contour-based shape recovery algorithm, we have developed a new fixed-lag smoother, which, while sub-optimal, allows us to predict the position of the contour in successive images and simplifies the tracking problem. Our fixed-lag smoother begins by computing a *centered* batch fit to $n(\geq 3)$ frames. The surface point is then predicted from frame $i-1$ to frame i as with the Kalman filter, and a new measurement from frame $i+L$, $L = \lfloor n/2 \rfloor$ is added to the predicted estimate. The addition of measurements ahead of the current estimate is straightforward using the projection equations for the least-squared (batch) fitting algorithm.

Our modified fixed-lag smoother and the optimal fixed-lag smoother incorporate the same information into the current estimate, but use slightly different relative weightings of the data. Intuitively, the optimal smoother weights the data most heavily towards the middle (inversely proportional to the distance from the current estimate), while our modified smoother weights the data most heavily towards the front (most recent measurement). For systems where the process noise σ_s^2 is much smaller than the

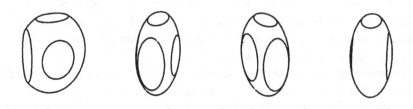

Figure 6.3
Four images from synthetic truncated ellipsoid sequence. The top and left hand
side are truncated (cut off), while the front and back sides are inscribed with an
ellipse (surface marking).

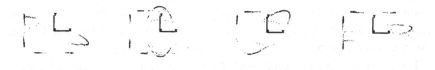

Figure 6.4
Top view of reconstructed 3D curves. The surface markings and ridges are
stationary, while the occluding contours (ellipse) sweeps around the object.

measurement noise σ_i^2, the results should be similar. We examine the relative performance of the batch estimator, Kalman filter, and sub-optimal
linear smoother in Section 6.9.

6.8 Building a complete surface description

The batch fitting, Kalman filter, and linear smoothers all produce a series
of surface point estimates, one for each input image. Because our reconstruction takes place in object space, features such as surface marking and
sharp ridges are stationary in 3D (and have $r = 0$). For these features, we
would prefer to produce a single time-invariant estimate. While the detection of stationary features could be incorporated into the Kalman filter or
smoother itself, we currently defer this decision to a post-processing stage,
since we expect the estimates of position and radius of curvature to be more
reliable after the whole sequence has been processed. The post-processing
stage collapses successive estimates that are near enough in 3D (say, less
than the spacing between neighboring sample points on the 3D contour).

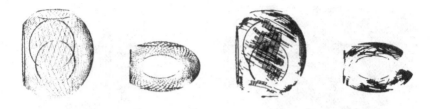

Figure 6.5
Oblique and top view of reconstructed 3D surface (all 3D curves are superimposed).
The left pair shows only the reconstructed profile curves, while the right pair shows
the profiles linked by the epipolar curves (only a portion of the complete meshed
surface is shown for clarity). A total of 72 images spaced 5° apart were used.

algorithm	n	σ_i	$n_f \geq 3$	$n_f \geq 7$	$n_f \geq 7 \wedge \sigma_x^2 < 0.5$
smoother	7	0.0	.0074 (77%)	.0046 (45%)	.0044 (38%)
smoother	7	0.1	.0114 (74%)	.0054 (41%)	.0051 (36%)
batch	7	0.0	.0042 (79%)	.0036 (56%)	.0035 (43%)
batch	7	0.1	.0074 (77%)	.0054 (53%)	.0051 (42%)
batch	3	0.0	.0008 (77%)		
batch	3	0.1	.0159 (75%)		

Table 6.1
Root median square error and percentage of edges reconstructed for different
algorithms, window sizes (n), input image noise σ_i, and criteria for valid estimates
(n_f: minimum number of frames in fit, σ_x^2: covariance in local x estimate). These
errors are for an ellipse whose major axes are $(0.67, 0.4, 0.8)$ and for a 128×120
image.

It adjusts the neighbor (contour) and temporal (previous/next) pointers to
maintain a consistent description of the surface.

To fit a complete surface to the data while interpolating across small
gaps, a variety of techniques could be used. Traditionally, physically-based
deformable models [38, 31] have been used to fit such sparse and incom-
plete 3-D data. An alternative, which does not suffer from the restrictions
on topology imposed by previous techniques, is to use a self-triangulating
system of particles to model and interpolate the surface [33]. We plan to
investigate the intergration of this system with our multiframe stereo algorithm in future work.

(a)   (b)

(c)   (d)

Figure 6.6
Sample real image sequences used for experiments: (a) dodecahedron (b) soda can
(c) coffee (d) tea.

6.9   Experimental results

To determine the performance of our shape reconstruction algorithm, we
generated a synthetic motion sequence of a truncated ellipsoid rotating
about its z axis (Fig. 6.3). The camera is oblique (rather than perpendicular) to the rotation axis, so that the epipolar curves are not planar, and
the reconstruction plane is continuously varying over time. We chose to use
a truncated ellipsoid since it is easy to compute its projections analytically
(they are ellipses, even under perspective), and since its radius of curvature
is continuously varying (unlike a cylinder).

When we run the edge images through our least-squares fitter or Kalman
filter/smoother, we obtain a series of 3D curves. The curves corresponding

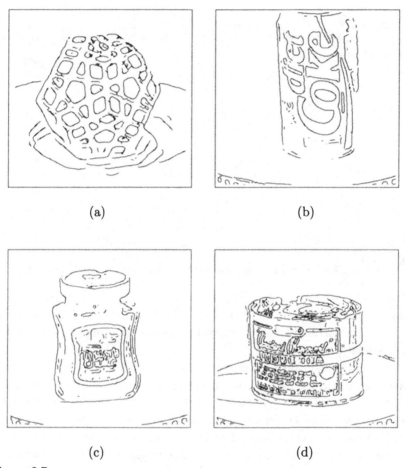

(a)   (b)

(c)   (d)

Figure 6.7
Extracted edges: (a) dodecahedron (b) soda can (c) coffee (d) tea.

to the surface markings and ridges (where the ellipsoid is truncated) should be stationary and have zero radius, while the curves corresponding to the occluding contour should continuously sweep over the surface.

We can observe this behavior using a three-dimensional graphics program we have developed for displaying the reconstructed geometry. This program allows us to view a series of reconstructed curves either sequentially (as an animation) or concurrently (overlaid in different colors), and to vary the 3D viewing parameters either interactively or as a function of the original camera position for each frame. Fig. 6.5 shows all of the 3D curves overlaid in a single image. As we can see, the 3D surface is reconstructed quite well. The left hand pair of images shows an oblique and top view of a noise-free

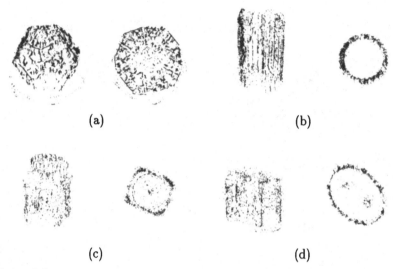

(a)   (b)

(c)   (d)

Figure 6.8
3D reconstructed points from (a) dodecahedron, (b) soda can, (c) coffee, and (d) tea.

data set, using the linear smoother with $n = 7$ window size. The right-hand pair shows a portion of the reconstructed surface, showing both the profile and epipolar curves.

To obtain a quantitative measure of the reconstruction algorithm performance, we can compute the root median square error between the reconstructed 3D coordinates and the true 3D coordinates (which are known to the synthetic sequence generating program). Table 6.1 shows the reconstruction error and percentage of surface points reconstructed as a function of algorithm choice and various parameter settings. The table compares the performance of a regular 3-point fit with a 7-point moving window (batch) fit, and a linear fixed-lag smoother with $n = 7$. Results are given for the noise-free and $\sigma_i = 0.1$ pixels case. The different columns show how by being more selective about which 3D estimates are considered valid (either by requiring more frames to have been successfully fit, or lowering the threshold on maximum covariance), a more reliable estimate can be obtained at the expense of fewer recovered points. For noise free data, the 3 point algorithm is better because it is less sensitive to curvature variation. However, for noisy data, the 7 point algorithms are better, with batch fitting performing slightly better than linear smoothing.

We have also applied our algorithm to the four real image sequences shown in Fig. 6.6. These sequences were obtained by placing an object on a rotating mechanized turntable whose edge has a Gray code strip used for reading back the rotation angle [35, 36]. The camera motion parameters

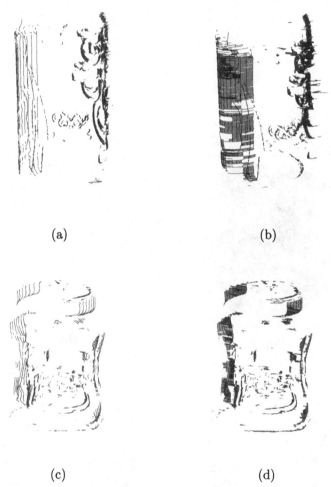

(a)   (b)

(c)   (d)

Figure 6.9
Profile and epipolar curves for: (a–b) soda can (c–d) coffee.

for these sequences were obtained by first calibrating the camera intrinsic
parameters and extrinsic parameters to the turntable top center, and then
using the computed turntable rotation. Fig. 6.7 shows the edges extracted
from each of these images.

Fig. 6.8 shows two views of each set of reconstructed 3D curves. We can
see that the overall shape of the objects has been reconstructed quite well.
We show only the profile curves, since the epipolar curves would make the
line drawing too dense for viewing at this resolution. Fig. 6.9 shows both
the profile curves and the epipolar curves for selected portions of the soda
can and coffee objects.

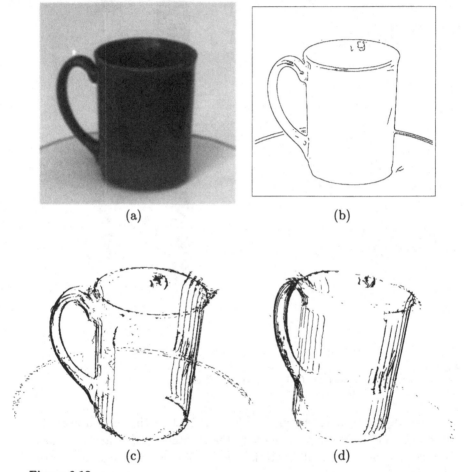

(a)   (b)

(c)   (d)

Figure 6.10
Another example: coffee cup. Note that objects with interior holes (non-trivial topology) can be easily handled by this method.

As a final example, Fig. 6.10 shows some partial results (10 reconstructed profile curves) from an image sequence of a coffee mug. This example demonstrates that our method can handle objects with interior holes, since we are not limited to only following the external silhouettes of the objects. In future work, we plan to study the events that occur when multiple silhouette curves obscure each other in the image sequence (which corresponds to points of bitangency in 3D).

6.10   Discussion and Conclusion

This chapter extends previous work on both the reconstruction of smooth surfaces from profiles (edge-based multiframe stereo) and on the epipolar analysis on spatiotemporal surfaces. The ultimate goal of our work is the construction a complete detailed geometric and topological model of a surface from a sequence of views together with an estimate of uncertainty. Towards this end, our observations are connected by tracking edges over time as well as linking neighboring edges into contours. The information represented at each point includes the position, surface normal, and curvatures (currently only in the viewing direction). In addition, error estimates are also computed for these quantities. Since the sensed data does not provide a complete picture of the surface, e.g., there can be self-occlusion or parts may be missed due to coarse sampling or limitations on the camera trajectory, it is necessary to build partial models. In the context of active sensing and real-time reactive systems, the reconstruction needs to be incremental as well.

Because our equations for the reconstruction algorithm are linear with respect to the measurements, it is possible to apply statistical linear smoothing techniques, as we have demonstrated. This satisfies the requirement for incremental modeling, and provides the error estimates that are needed for integration with other sensory data, both visual and tactile. The application of statistical methods has the advantage of providing a sound theoretical basis for sensor integration and for the reconstruction process in general [34, 15].

In future work, we intend to develop a more complete and detailed surface model by combining our technique with regularization-based curve and surface models. We also plan to investigate the integration of our edge-based multiframe reconstruction technique with other visual and tactile techniques for shape recovery.

References

[1] A. Albert. *Regression and the Moore-Penrose Pseudoinverse*. Academic Press, New York, 1972.

[2] E. Arborgast and R. Mohr. An egomotion algorithm based on the tracking of arbitrary curves. In *Second European Conference on Computer Vision (ECCV'92)*, pages 467–475, Santa Margherita Liguere, Italy, May 1992. Springer-Verlag.

[3] R. D. Arnold. Automated stereo perception. Technical Report AIM-351, Artificial Intelligence Laboratory, Stanford University, March 1983.

[4] H. H. Baker. Building surfaces of evolution: The weaving wall. *International Journal of Computer Vision*, 3(1):50–71, 1989.

[5] H. H. Baker and R. C. Bolles. Generalizing epipolar-plane image analysis on the spatiotemporal surface. *International Journal of Computer Vision*, 3(1):33–49, 1989.

[6] R. C. Bolles, H. H. Baker, and D. H. Marimont. Epipolar-plane image analysis: An approach to determining structure from motion. *International Journal of Computer Vision*, 1:7–55, 1987.

[7] A. Blake and R. Cipolla. Robust estimation of surface curvature from deformation of apparent contours. In *First European Conference on Computer Vision (ECCV'90)*, pages 465–474, Antibes, France, April 23–27 1990. Springer-Verlag.

[8] A. Blake, R. Curwen, and A. Zisserman. A framework for spatiotemporal control in the tracking of visual contour. *International Journal of Computer Vision*, 11(2):127–145, October 1993.

[9] G. J. Bierman. *Factorization Methods for Discrete Sequential Estimation*. Academic Press, New York, New York, 1977.

[10] Y. Bar-Shalom and T. E. Fortmann. *Tracking and data association*. Academic Press, Boston, 1988.

[11] J. Canny. A computational approach to edge detection. *IEEE Transactions on Pattern Analysis and Machine Intelligence*, PAMI-8(6):679–698, November 1986.

[12] R. Cipolla and A. Blake. The dynamic analysis of apparent contours. In *Third International Conference on Computer Vision (ICCV'90)*, pages 616–623, Osaka, Japan, December 1990. IEEE Computer Society Press.

[13] R. Cipolla and A. Blake. Surface shape from the deformation of apparent contours. *International Journal of Computer Vision*, 9(2):83–112, November 1992.

[14] R. Curwen, A. Blake, and A. Zisserman. Real-time visual tracking for surveillance and path planning. In *Second European Conference on Computer Vision (ECCV'92)*, pages 879–883, Santa Margherita Liguere, Italy, May 1992. Springer-Verlag.

[15] J. J. Clark and A. L. Yuille. *Data Fusion for Sensory Information Processing Systems*. Kluwer Academic Publishers, Boston, Massachusetts, 1990.

[16] W. T. Freeman and E. H. Adelson. The design and use of steerable filters. *IEEE Transactions on Pattern Analysis and Machine Intelligence*, 13(9):891–906, September 1991.

[17] O. D. Faugeras, F. Lustman, and G. Toscani. Motion and structure from motion from point and line matches. In *First International Conference on Computer Vision (ICCV'87)*, pages 25–34, London, England, June 1987. IEEE Computer Society Press.

[18] A. Gelb, editor. *Applied Optimal Estimation*. MIT Press, Cambridge, Massachusetts, 1974.

[19] P. J. Giblin, J. E. Rycroft, and F. E. Pollick. Moving surfaces. In *Mathematics of Surfaces V, Inst of Math and its Applications Conference*. Cambridge University Press, Sept 1992.

[20] P. Giblin and R. Weiss. Reconstruction of surfaces from profiles. In *First International Conference on Computer Vision (ICCV'87)*, pages 136–144, London, England, June 1987. IEEE Computer Society Press.

[21] P. J. Giblin and R. S. Weiss. Epipolar fields on surfaces. In *Third European Conference on Computer Vision (ECCV'94)*, Stockholm, Sweden, (to appear) 1994. Springer-Verlag.

[22] B. K. P. Horn. Relative orientation. *International Journal of Computer Vision*, 4(1):59–78, January 1990.

[23] P. J. Huber. *Robust Statistics*. John Wiley & Sons, New York, New York, 1981.

[24] D. G. Lowe. Fitting parameterized three-dimensional models to images. *IEEE Transactions on Pattern Analysis and Machine Intelligence*, 13(5):441–450, May 1991.

[25] P. S. Maybeck. *Stochastic Models, Estimation, and Control*, volume 1. Academic Press, New York, New York, 1979.

[26] J. E. W. Mayhew and J. P. Frisby. The computation of binocular edges. *Perception*, 9:69–87, 1980.

[27] D. Marr and E. Hildreth. Theory of edge detection. *Proceedings of the Royal Society of London*, B 207:187–217, 1980.

[28] D. C. Marr and T. Poggio. A computational theory of human stereo vision. *Proceedings of the Royal Society of London*, B 204:301–328, 1979.

[29] L. H. Matthies, R. Szeliski, and T. Kanade. Kalman filter-based algorithms for estimating depth from image sequences. *International Journal of Computer Vision*, 3:209–236, 1989.

[30] W. H. Press, B. P. Flannery, S. A. Teukolsky, and W. T. Vetterling. *Numerical Recipes: The Art of Scientific Computing*. Cambridge University Press, Cambridge, England, 1986.

[31] A. Pentland and S. Sclaroff. Closed-form solutions for physically-based shape modeling and recognition. *IEEE Transactions on Pattern Analysis and Machine Intelligence*, 13(7):715–729, July 1991.

[32] P. Rives, E. Breuil, and B. Espiau. Recursive estimation of 3D features using optical flow and camera motion. In *Conference on Intelligent Autonomous Systems*, pages 522–532. Elsevier Science Publishers, December 1986. Also appeared in 1987 IEEE International Conference on Robotics and Automation.

[33] R. Szeliski, D. Tonnesen, and D. Terzopoulos. Modeling surfaces of arbitrary topology with dynamic particles. In *IEEE Computer Society Conference on Computer Vision and Pattern Recognition (CVPR'93)*, pages 82–87, New York, New York, June 1993.

[34] R. Szeliski. *Bayesian Modeling of Uncertainty in Low-Level Vision*. Kluwer Academic Publishers, Boston, Massachusetts, 1989.

[35] R. Szeliski. Shape from rotation. In *IEEE Computer Society Conference on Computer Vision and Pattern Recognition (CVPR'91)*, pages 625–630, Maui, Hawaii, June 1991. IEEE Computer Society Press.

[36] R. Szeliski. Rapid octree construction from image sequences. *CVGIP: Image Understanding*, 58(1):23–32, July 1993.

[37] R. Y. Tsai and T. S. Huang. Uniqueness and estimation of three-dimensional motion parameters of rigid objects with curved surfaces. *IEEE Transactions on Pattern Analysis and Machine Intelligence*, PAMI-6(1):13–27, January 1984.

[38] D. Terzopoulos and D. Metaxas. Dynamic 3D models with local and global deformations: Deformable superquadrics. *IEEE Transactions on Pattern Analysis and Machine Intelligence*, 13(7):703–714, July 1991.

[39] R. Vaillant. Using occluding contours for 3D object modeling. In *First European Conference on Computer Vision (ECCV'90)*, pages 454–464, Antibes, France, April 23–27 1990. Springer-Verlag.

[40] R. Vaillant and O. D. Faugeras. Using extremal boundaries for 3-D object modeling. *IEEE Transactions on Pattern Analysis and Machine Intelligence*, 14(2):157–173, February 1992.

III Visual Control

7 Visual Robot Guidance from Uncalibrated Stereo

Roberto Cipolla and Nicholas J. Hollinghurst

7.1 Introduction

When humans grasp and manipulate objects, they almost invariably do so with the aid of vision. Visual information is used to locate and identify things, and to decide how (and if) they should be grasped. Visual feedback helps us guide our hands around obstacles and align them accurately with their goal. *Hand–Eye Coordination* gives us a flexibility and dexterity of movement that no machine can match.

Most vision systems for robotics usually need to be *calibrated*. Camera geometry — the focal length, principal point and aspect ratio of each camera [17], the relative position and orientation of the cameras (epipolar geometry) [15] and their relation to the robot coordinate system [16] — must be measured to a high degree of accuracy. A well-calibrated stereo rig can accurately determine the position and shape of things to be grasped in all three dimensions [14]. However, if calibration is erroneous or the cameras are disturbed, the system will usually fail gracelessly.

For hand–eye applications where a manipulator moves to a visually-specified target, an alternative approach is to use visual feedback to match manipulator and target positions *in the image*. Exact spatial coordinates are not required, and a well-chosen feedback architecture can correct for quite serious inaccuracies in camera calibration (as well as inaccurate kinematic modelling) [19]. Visual feedback alone without exploiting or learning the relationship between the robot kinematics and the stereo cameras, however, can lead to inefficient motions [10].

In this chapter we describe a system that combines stereo vision with a robotic manipulator to enable it efficiently to locate and reach simple unmodelled objects in an unstructured environment. The system is initially uncalibrated; it "calibrates" itself automatically by tracking the gripper during four deliberate exploratory movements in its workspace and is able to operate successfully in the presence of errors in the modeled kinematics of the robot manipulator and unknown changes in the position, orientation and intrinsic parameters of the stereo cameras during operation.

The system exploits an *affine stereo* algorithm – a simple but robust approximation to the geometry of stereo vision – (described in Section 2) which, though of modest accuracy, requires minimal calibration and can tolerate small camera movements. We show that, in some circumstances, this simplified camera model is less sensitive to image measurement error since it avoids computing parameters required in the full perspective stereo that are inherently ill-conditioned [4]. Closed-loop control is achieved by tracking the gripper's movements across the two images to estimate its position and orientation relative to the target object. This is done with a form of *active contour model* resembling a B-spline snake [3] but constrained to deform only affinely (described in Section 3) to produce a more reliable tracker that is less easily confused by background contours or partial occlusion. Inevitable errors in aligning the gripper and target object position and orientation are corrected by an image-based feedback mechanism (Section 4). Preliminary results of a realtime implementation are presented (Section 5) and show the system to be remarkably immune to unexpected movements of the cameras and focal lengths even after the initial self-calibration.

7.2 Affine stereo

7.2.1 Perspective and projective camera models

The full perspective transformation between world and image coordinates is conventionally analysed using the *pinhole camera* model, in which image-plane coordinates (u, v) are ratios of world coordinates (x_c, y_c, z_c) in a camera-centred frame, thus: $u = f x_c / z_c$, $v = f y_c / z_c$. The relation between the camera-centred and some other world coordinate frame consists of *rotation* ($\mathbf{R}$) and *translation* ($\mathbf{t}$) components representing the camera's orientation and position. Using homogeneous coordinates (with scale factor s for convenience),

$$\begin{bmatrix} su \\ sv \\ sf \end{bmatrix} = \begin{bmatrix} r_{11} & r_{12} & r_{13} & t_1 \\ r_{21} & r_{22} & r_{23} & t_2 \\ r_{31} & r_{32} & r_{33} & t_3 \end{bmatrix} \begin{bmatrix} x_w \\ y_w \\ z_w \\ 1 \end{bmatrix}. \qquad (7.1)$$

The relation between image plane coordinates (u, v) and pixel addresses (X, Y) can be modelled by an affine transformation (to represent offsets, scaling and shearing). Combining this with (7.1) yields a general 3D to 2D projection, with 11 degrees of freedom:

$$\begin{bmatrix} \sigma X \\ \sigma Y \\ \sigma \end{bmatrix} = \begin{bmatrix} m_{11} & m_{12} & m_{13} & m_{14} \\ m_{21} & m_{22} & m_{23} & m_{24} \\ m_{31} & m_{32} & m_{33} & m_{34} \end{bmatrix} \begin{bmatrix} x_w \\ y_w \\ z_w \\ 1 \end{bmatrix}. \qquad (7.2)$$

This is the usual camera model for many stereo vision systems. Although it neglects effects such as lens distortion that are significant in some high-accuracy applications [15], it correctly predicts image distortion due to perspective effects (*e.g.*, parallel 3D lines projecting to intersect a vanishing point) and it preserves the invariance of the cross ratio (not ratio) of lengths.

7.2.2 Weak perspective and affine camera models

Consider a camera viewing a compact scene of interest from distance h. For convenience, we can translate the world coordinate system so that the scene lies close to the world origin. The component of t along the optical axis, t_3, will then equal h. As distance increases relative to the extent of the scene, sf/h will tend to unity for all points, and equation (7.1) becomes:

$$\begin{bmatrix} u \\ v \end{bmatrix} = \frac{f}{h} \begin{bmatrix} r_{11} & r_{12} & r_{13} & t_1 \\ r_{21} & r_{22} & r_{23} & t_2 \end{bmatrix} \begin{bmatrix} x_w \\ y_w \\ z_w \\ 1 \end{bmatrix}. \tag{7.3}$$

This formulation assumes that images are not distorted by variations in depth, and is known as *weak perspective* [13]. It is equivalent to orthographic projection scaled by a factor inversely proportional to the average depth, h. It can be shown that this assumption results in an error that is, at worst, $\Delta h/h$ times the scene's image size.

The entire projection, again incorporating scaling and shearing of pixel coordinates, may now be written very simply as a linear mapping:

$$\begin{bmatrix} X \\ Y \end{bmatrix} = \begin{bmatrix} p_{11} & p_{12} & p_{13} & p_{14} \\ p_{21} & p_{22} & p_{23} & p_{24} \end{bmatrix} \begin{bmatrix} x_w \\ y_w \\ z_w \\ 1 \end{bmatrix}. \tag{7.4}$$

The eight coefficients p_{ij} efficiently represent all intrinsic and extrinsic camera parameters [15]. This simple approximation to the projection transformation — the affine camera [11] — will be used as the camera model throughout the chapter. Its advantages will become clear later when it leads to efficient calibration and reduced sensitivity to image measurement error. Note that parallel lines project to parallel lines in the image and ratios of lengths and areas are invariant to the transformation.

7.2.3 Motion of planar objects under weak perspective

There are many situations in computer vision where an object must be *tracked* as it moves across a view. Here we consider the simple, but not uncommon, case where the object is small and has planar faces.

We can define a coordinate system centred about the object face itself so that it lies within the xy plane. If the object is small compared to the camera distance, we again have weak perspective, and a special case of (7.4):

$$\begin{bmatrix} X \\ Y \end{bmatrix} = \begin{bmatrix} a_{11} & a_{12} & a_{13} \\ a_{21} & a_{22} & a_{23} \end{bmatrix} \begin{bmatrix} x \\ y \\ 1 \end{bmatrix}. \qquad (7.5)$$

We see that the transformation from a plane in the world to the image plane is a 2D *affine* translation. As the camera moves relative to the object, parameters a_{ij} will change and the image will undergo translation, rotation, change in scale (divergence) and deformation, but remain *affine-invariant* [8, 2] (Fig. 7.1).

This is a powerful constraint that can be exploited when tracking a planar object. It tells us that the shape of the image will deform only affinely as the object moves, and that there will exist an affine transformation between any two views of the same plane.

Figure 7.1
The gripper being tracked as it translates and rotates under *weak perspective*. The origin and sampling points of the tracker are shown in white. The front of the gripper is approximately planar, and its image shape distorts affinely as it moves under weak perspective.

7.2.4   The affine stereo formulation

In stereo vision two calibrated views of a scene from known viewpoints allow the Euclidean reconstruction of the scene. In the following two uncalibrated views under weak perspective projection are used to recover relative 3D positions and surface orientations.

Recovery of relative position from image disparity

We assume that the cameras do not move relative to the scene during each period of use. Combining information from a pair of images, we have four image coordinates (X, Y, X', Y') for each point, all linear functions of the three world coordinates (x_w, y_w, z_w):

$$
\begin{bmatrix} X \\ Y \\ X' \\ Y' \end{bmatrix} = \mathbf{Q} \begin{bmatrix} x_w \\ y_w \\ z_w \\ 1 \end{bmatrix}, \tag{7.6}
$$

where $\mathbf{Q}$ is a 4×4 matrix formed from the p_{ij} coefficients of (7.4) for the two cameras. To calibrate the system it is necessary to observe a minimum of four non-coplanar *reference points*, yielding sixteen simultaneous linear equations from which $\mathbf{Q}$ may be found. With noisy image data, greater accuracy may be obtained by observing more than four points.

Once the coefficients are known, world coordinates can be obtained by inverting (7.6), using a least-squares method to resolve the redundant information. Errors in calibration will manifest themselves as a linear distortion of the perceived coordinate frame.

Note:

1. It is *not* essential to calibrate a stereo vision system to obtain useful 3-D information about the world. Instead, four of the points observed may be given arbitrary world coordinates (such as $(0, 0, 0)$, $(0, 0, 1)$, $(0, 1, 0)$ and $(1, 0, 0)$). The appropriate solution for $\mathbf{Q}$ will define a coordinate frame that is an arbitrary 3-D affine transformation of the 'true' Cartesian frame, preserving affine shape properties such as ratios of lengths and areas, collinearity and coplanarity. This is in accordance with Koenderink and van Doorn's *Affine Structure-from-Motion Theorem* [9].

2. In hand–eye applications, it might instead be convenient to calibrate the vision system in the coordinate space in which the manipulator is controlled (assuming this maps approximately linearly to Cartesian coordinates). This can be done by getting the robot manipulator to move to four points in its workspace.

3. The integration of information from more than two cameras to help avoid problems due to occlusion is easily accommodated in this framework. Each view generates two additional linear equations in eq. 7.6 that can be optimally combined.

Recovery of surface orientation from disparity gradients

Under weak perspective any two views of the same planar surface will be related by an affine transformation that maps one image to the other. This consists of a pure 2D translation encoding the displacement of the centroid and a 2D tensor – the disparity gradient tensor – which represents the distortion in image shape. This transformation can be used to recover surface orientation [2]. Surface orientation in space is most conveniently represented by a surface normal vector **n**. We can obtain it by the vector product of two non-collinear vectors in the plane which can of course be obtained from three pairs of image points. There is, however, no redundancy in the data and this method would be sensitive to image measurement error. A better approach is to exploit all the information in available in the affine transform (disparity field).

Consider the standard unit vectors $\hat{\mathbf{X}}$ and $\hat{\mathbf{Y}}$ in one image and suppose they were the projections of some vectors on the object surface. If the linear mapping between images is represented by a 2×3 matrix **A**, then the first two columns of **A** itself will be the corresponding vectors in the other image. As the centroid of the plane will map to both image centroids, we can easily use it and the above pairs of vectors to find three points in space on the plane (by inverting (eq. 7.6)) and hence the surface orientation.

7.3   Tracking using affine active contours

An *active contour* (or *'snake'*) [7] is a curve defined in the image plane that moves and deforms according to various 'forces'. These include *external forces*, which depend on local image properties and are used to guide the active contour towards the image features, and *internal forces* that depend on the contour shape and are used to enforce smoothness. Typically, a snake will be attracted to maxima of image intensity gradient, and used to track the edges of a moving object.

7.3.1   Anatomy

Our model-based trackers are a novel form of active contour. They resemble B-spline snakes [3] but consist of (in the order of 100) discrete sampling points, rather than a smooth curve [6]. We use them to track planar surfaces bounded by contours, on the robot gripper and the object to be grasped. Pairs of trackers operate independently in the two stereo views. The trackers can deform only affinely, to track planes viewed under weak perspective [1]. This constraint leads to a more efficient and reliable tracker than a B-spline snake, that is less easily confused by background contours or partial occlusion.

Each tracker is a 2D model of the image shape it is tracking, with sampling points at regular intervals around the edge. At each sampling point there is a *local edge-finder* that measures the offset between modelled and actual edge positions in the image, by searching for the maximum of gradient along a short line segment [5]. Due to the so-called *aperture problem* [18], only the normal component of this offset can be recovered at any point (Fig. 7.2).

The positions of the sampling points are expressed in affine coordinates, and their image positions depend upon the tracker's *local origin* and two *basis vectors*. These are described by six parameters, which change over time as the object is tracked. The contour tangent directions at each point are also described in terms of the basis vectors.

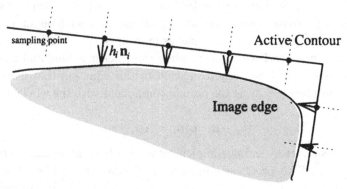

Figure 7.2
An active contour: The image is sampled in segments normal to the predicted contour (dotted lines) to search for the maximal gradient. The offsets between predicted and actual edges (arrows) are combined globally to guide the active contour towards the image edge.

7.3.2 Algorithm

At each time-step the tracker moves and deforms to minimise the sum of squares of offsets between model and image edges (h_i). In our implementation this is done in two stages. First the optimal translation is found, then the deformation, rotation, scale (divergence) components are calculated. Splitting the task into these two stages was found to increase stability, as fewer parameters were being estimated at once. To find the optimal translation $\mathbf{u}$ to account for normal offset h_i at each sampling point whose image normal direction is $\mathbf{n}_i$, we solve the following equation:

$$h_i = \mathbf{n}_i \cdot \mathbf{u} + \epsilon_i. \tag{7.7}$$

ϵ_i is the error term, and we solve the whole system of equations using a least-squares method to minimise $\sum \epsilon_i^2$.

Once the translation has been calculated, the other components are estimated. It is assumed that the distortion is centred about the tracker's local origin (normally its centroid, to decouple it optimally from translation). The effects of translation $(\mathbf{n}_i \cdot \mathbf{u})$ are subtracted from each normal offset, leaving a residual offset. We can then find the matrix $\mathbf{A}$ that maps image coordinates to displacement:

$$(h_i - \mathbf{n}_i \cdot \mathbf{u}) = \mathbf{n}_i \cdot (\mathbf{A}\mathbf{p}_i) + \epsilon_i', \qquad (7.8)$$

where $\mathbf{p}_i$ is the sampling point's position relative to the local origin and ϵ_i' is again the error term to be minimised.

In practice this formulation can lead to problems when the tracked surface moves whilst partially obscured (often, a tracker will catch on an occluding edge and become 'squashed' as it passes in front of the surface). It can also be unstable and sensitive to noise when the tracker is long and thin. We therefore use a simplified approximation to this equation that ignores the aperture problem (equating the normal component with the whole displacement):

$$(h_i - \mathbf{n}_i \cdot \mathbf{u})\mathbf{n}_i = \mathbf{A}\mathbf{p}_i + \mathbf{e}_i. \qquad (7.9)$$

$\mathbf{e}_i$ is an error vector, and our implementation solves the equations to minimise $\sum |\mathbf{e}_i|^2$. This produces a more stable tracker that, although sluggish to deform, is well suited to those practical tracking tasks where motion is dominated by the translation component. The tracker positions are updated from $\mathbf{u}$ and $\mathbf{A}$ using a real time first-order predictive filter. This enhances performance when tracking fast-moving objects.

7.4   Visual feedback for hand–eye coordination

Affine stereo is a simplified stereo vision formulation that is very easily calibrated. Conversely, it is of rather low accuracy. Nevertheless, it gives reliable *qualitative* information about the relative positions of points and can, of course, indicate when they are in precisely the same place. We therefore use a feedback control mechanism to help to guide the gripper to the target, using affine stereo to compute the relative position and orientation of their respective tracked surfaces.

Since the reference points used to self-calibrate are specified in the *controller's* coordinate space, linear errors in the kinematic model are effectively bypassed. The system must still cope with any nonlinearities in control, as well as those caused by strong perspective effects.

We take an iterative approach, based upon *relative* positions. The manipulator moves in discrete steps; each motion is proportional to the difference between the gripper's perceived position and orientation, and those of the target plane. This is equivalent to an *integral* control architecture, in which the error term is summed at each time step (see Fig. 7.3).

The gain is set below unity to prevent instability, even when the vision system is miscalibrated. The process repeats until the perceived coordinates of the gripper coincide with those of the target. Alternatively, to implement a particular grasping strategy, an offset can be introduced into the control loop to specify the final pose of the gripper relative to the target plane. Irrespective of the accuracy of stereo and hand-eye calibration visual feedback will ensure that target and gripper are aligned.

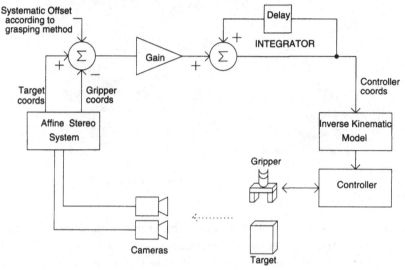

Figure 7.3
The control structure of the system, showing the use of visual feedback.

7.5   Implementation and experiments

7.5.1   Equipment

The system was implemented on a Sun SPARCstation 10 with a Data Cell S2200 frame grabber. The manipulator is a Scorbot ER-7 robot arm, which has 5 degrees of freedom and a parallel-jawed gripper. The robot has its own 68000-based controller that implements the low-level control loop and provides a Cartesian kinematic model. Images are obtained from two inexpensive CCD cameras placed 1m–3m from the robot's workspace. The angle between the cameras is in the range of 15–30 degrees (Fig. 7.4).

7.5.2   Implementation

When the system is started up, it begins by opening and closing the jaws of the gripper. By observing the image difference, it is able to locate the gripper and set up a pair of affine trackers as instances of a hand-made 2D

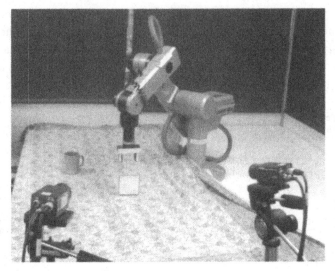

Figure 7.4
The experimental setup. Uncalibrated stereo cameras viewing a robot gripper and
target object.

template. The trackers will then follow the gripper's movements continuously. Stereo tracking can be implemented on the Sun at over 10 Hz. The robot moves to four preset points to calibrate the system in terms of the controller's coordinate space.

A target object is found by similar means — observing the image changes when it is placed in the manipulator's workspace. Alternatively it may be selected from a monitor screen using the mouse. There is no pre-defined model of the target shape, so a pair of 'expanding' B-spline snakes [2] are used to locate the contours delimiting the target surface in each of the images. The snakes are then converted to a pair of affine trackers. The target surface is then tracked, to compensate for unexpected motions of either the target or the two cameras.

By introducing modifications and offsets to the feedback mechanism (which would otherwise try to superimpose the gripper and the target), two 'behaviours' have been implemented. The *tracking behaviour* causes it to follow the target continuously, hovering a few centimetres above it (Fig. 7.5). The *grasping behaviour* causes the gripper to approach the target from above (to avoid collisions) with the gripper turned through an angle of 90 degrees, to grasp it normal to its visible surface (Fig. 7.6).

7.5.3   Results

Without feedback control, the robot locates its target only approximately (typically to within 5cm in a 50cm workspace) reflecting the approximate

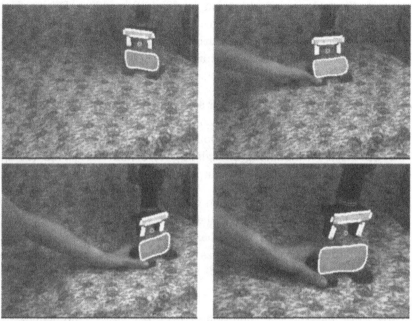

Figure 7.5
The robot is tracking its quarry, guided by the position and orientation of the target contour (view through left camera). On the target surface is an *affine snake* — an affine tracker obtained by 'expanding' a B-spline snake from the centre of the object. A slight offset has been introduced into the control loop to cause the gripper to hover above it. Last frame: one of the cameras has been rotated and zoomed, but the system continues to operate successfully with visual feedback.

Figure 7.6
Affine stereo and visual feedback used to grasp a planar face.

nature of affine stereo and calibration from only four points. With a feed-back gain of 0.75 the gripper converges on its target in three or four control iterations. If the system is not disturbed it will take a straight-line path. The system has so far demonstrated its robustness by continuing to track and grasp objects despite:

Kinematic errors. Linear offsets or scalings of the controller's coordinate system are absorbed by the self-calibration process with complete trans-parency. Slight nonlinear distortions to the kinematics are corrected for by the visual feedback loop, though large errors introduce a risk of ring-ing and instability unless the gain is reduced.

Camera disturbances. The system continues to function when its cam-eras are subjected to small translations (e.g. 20cm), rotations (e.g. 30 degrees) and zooms (e.g. 200% change in focal length), even after it has self-calibrated. Large disturbances to camera geometry cause the grip-per to take a curved path towards the target, and require more control iterations to get there.

Strong perspective. The condition of weak perspective throughout the robot's workspace does not seem to be essential for image-based control and the system can function when the cameras are as close as 1.5 metres (the robot's reach is a little under 1 metre). However the feedback gain must be reduced or the system will overshoot on motions towards the cameras.

Fig. 7.5 shows four frames from a tracking sequence (all taken through the same camera). The cameras are about two metres from the workspace. Tracking of position and orientation is maintained even when one of the cameras is rotated about its optical axis and zoomed (Fig. 7.5, bottom right).

7.6   Future developments

The current system is based upon matching the positions and orientations of two *planes* – the gripper and target. Since the gripper and target planes must be visible in both images at all times, neither can rotate through more than about 120 degrees. We intend to develop the system to track the gripper using a three-dimensional rigid model [6], drawing information from both images simultaneously. We also aim to identify and track more than one of the surfaces of the object to be grasped, both for 3-D tracking and also for analysis of its 3D shape.

We plan to equip such a system with a grasp planner that uses the relative positions, sizes and orientations of the visible surfaces on the object, to direct the robot to grasp unmodelled objects in a suitable way.

7.7   Conclusion

An important component of the system presented in this chapter has been affine stereo. The appendix contains a quantitative comparison with perspective stereo. Affine stereo provides a simple and robust interpretation of image position and disparity that degrades gracefully when cameras are disturbed. Calibration is not only easier (fewer parameters and amenable to linear techniques) but also less sensitive to small perspective effects. It is suitable for uncalibrated and self-calibrating systems and therefore the preferred stereo method for our visual servoing application.

By defining the working coordinate system in terms of the robot's abilities, linear errors in its kinematics are bypassed. The remaining nonlinearities can be handled using image-based control and feedback. We have shown that this can be achieved cheaply and effectively using a novel form of active contour to track planar features on the gripper and target.

Such a system has been implemented and found to be highly robust, without unduly sacrificing performance (in terms of speed to converge on the target).

Appendix: Comparison of full-perspective and affine stereo

Correspondence and the epipolar constraint

In the affine stereo formulation it was assumed that two sets of image coordinates were available for each world point. The task of identifying pairs of image features which correspond to the same point in space is known as the *correspondence problem*.

The image coordinates of a world feature in two images are not independent, but related by an *epipolar constraint*. Consider the family of planes passing through the optical centre of each camera. These project to a family of *epipolar lines* in each image. If a feature lies upon a particular line in the left image, the corresponding feature must lie upon the line in the right image, which is the projection of the same plane. The constraint reflects the redundancy inherent in deriving four image coordinates from points in a three-dimensional world. Most correspondence algorithms exploit this constraint, which reduces the search for matching features to a single dimension, and identifying it is an important aspect of any calibration scheme.

In affine stereo, the epipolar planes are considered to be parallel, and the constraint takes the form of a single linear relation among the four image coordinates. With the full perspective model, the lines need not be parallel, and converge to a point called the *epipole* (the projection of one camera centre on the other camera's image plane). The constraint may be obtained from calibration data, for instance by rearranging the model to predict one image coordinate as a function of the other three.

Fig. 7.7 compares the epipolar line structure predicted by both affine and full perspective stereo models (after calibration using linear least squares). In this setup, in which the camera distance is about 2 metres, both models give similar epipolar accuracy. Furthermore, the affine model can predict epipolar lines using just four reference points; perspective stereo requires a minimum of six.

Accuracy of reconstruction

To compare affine and full perspective stereo, we performed a series of numerical simulations, measuring their ability to estimate the relative positions of points within a workspace, viewed by a pair of pinhole cameras.[1]

Under ideal conditions: Without noise or other disturbances, perspective stereo estimates absolute and relative positions with complete accuracy. At close range affine stereo performs poorly, but the error decreases in inverse proportion to camera distance (Fig. 7.8).

Accuracy is also somewhat dependent on the number and configuration of the reference points used in calibration, and there is a limited improvement as the unit cube is sampled more regularly.

With noisy calibration data: Adding 1% Gaussian noise to the image coordinates of the reference points causes both systems to lose accuracy. Perspective stereo is more sensitive to noise because of its nonlinearlity and greater degrees of freedom, and is *less* accurate than the affine stereo approximation at large viewing distances (Fig. 7.9). (viewing a larger number of reference points reduces the effects of noise and restores the accuracy of perspective stereo).

Camera movements after calibration: In a laboratory or industrial environment it is possible for cameras to be disturbed from time to time and subject to small rotations and translations. If this happens after

---

[1] Reference and test points are confined to a unit cube centred about the origin. There are 6 reference points within the unit cube. Test points are distributed uniformly within the cube. The cameras face the origin from a distance of 3–24 units, angled 20° apart (their focal length is proportional to distance, to normalize image size).

Figure 7.7

Estimation of epipolar lines. (a,b) Two views of 8 reference points defined by the robot. (c,d) Selected points in the left image, and epipolar lines estimated by the perspective camera model after calibration with 8 points. (e,f) Epipolar lines estimated by affine camera model after calibration with 8 points and with 4 points. Although it considers the epipolar lines to be parallel, the affine camera model (e) is almost as accurate as perspective in this experiment (RMS perpendicular error 4.1 pixels). Even with only 4 reference points, it produces a reasonable solution (f) from which stereo correspondence could be performed (RMS error 6.2 pixels).

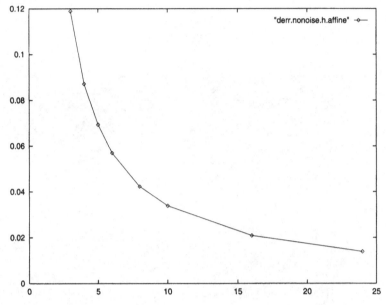

Figure 7.8
RMS relative positioning error (for random point pairs in the unit cube) as a
function of camera distance. The error is due to the approximate nature of the
affine stereo model and drops as camera distance increases.

calibration, it will give rise to a corresponding error in stereo reconstruction.

Table 1 shows the average change in perceived relative position when
one camera is rotated or translated a small distance around/along each
principle axis. The two systems degrade comparably with small movements, the worst of which is rotation about the optical axis. Perspective
stereo is more sensitive to larger movements, and to rotations and translations in the epipolar plane (in which a small error can induce large
changes of perceived depth), because it distorts nonlinearly.

With noisy image coordinates: When gaussian noise is added to the
image coordinates of the points whose relative position is to be estimated (after accurate calibration), the effect is comparable on both
systems, and their performance converges at large camera distance (Fig.
7.10).

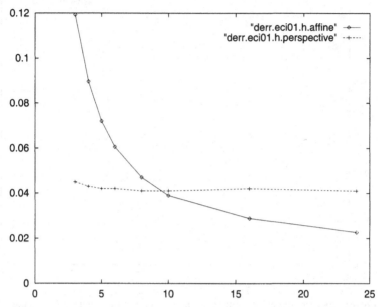

Figure 7.9
RMS positioning error as a function of camera distance, after calibration with noisy
reference point images (standard deviation 1% of image size). The error suffered by
the perspective model (dotted) is comparable in magnitude to the affine stereo
systematic error.

Disturbance	Change (Affine)	Change(Perspective)
xy (cyclic) rotation 1°	.0214	.0214
xz (epipolar) rotation 1°	.0007	.0468
yz (vertical) rotation 1°	.0006	.0049
xy (cyclic) rotation 5°	.1069	.1068
xz (epipolar) rotation 5°	.0095	.1867
yz (vertical) rotation 5°	.0056	.0769
x (epipolar) translation 0.1	.0119	.0207
y (vertical) translation 0.1	.0020	.0007
z (distance) translation 0.1	.0119	.0119
x (epipolar) translation 0.5	.0596	.1168
y (vertical) translation 0.5	.0102	.0139
z (distance) translation 0.5	.0574	.0572

Table 7.1
RMS *change* to relative position estimates of world points, caused by disturbing
one of the cameras after calibration

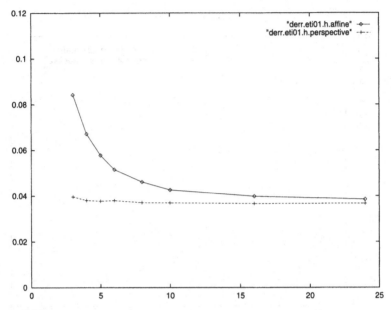

Figure 7.10
RMS relative positioning error from noisy images (standard deviation 1% image
size) of world points after *accurate* calibration with 27 reference points. The two
models converge for camera distances above ~ 10 units.

References

[1] A. Blake, R. Curwen, and A. Zisserman. Affine-invariant contour track-
    ing with automatic control of spatiotemporal scale. In *Proc. 4th Int.
    Conf. on Computer Vision*, pages 66–75, 1993.

[2] R. Cipolla and A. Blake. Surface orientation and time to contact from
    image divergence and deformation. In G. Sandini, editor, *Proc. 2nd
    European Conference on Computer Vision*, pages 187–202. Springer–
    Verlag, 1992.

[3] R. Cipolla and A. Blake. Surface shape from the deformation of ap-
    parent contours. *Int. Journal of Computer Vision*, 9(2):83–112, 1992.

[4] R. Cipolla, Y. Okamoto, and Y. Kuno. Robust structure from motion
    using motion parallax. In *Proc. 4th Int. Conf. on Computer Vision*,
    pages 374–382, 1993.

[5] R. Curwen and A. Blake. Dynamic contours: real-time active splines.
    In A. Blake and A. Yuille, editors, *Active Vision*, pages 39–58. MIT
    Press, 1992.

[6] C. Harris. Tracking with rigid models. In A. Blake and A. Yuille, editors, *Active Vision*, pages 59–74. MIT Press, 1992.

[7] M. Kass, A. Witkin, and D. Terzopoulos. Snakes: active contour models. In *Proc. 1st Int. Conf. on Computer Vision*, pages 259–268, 1987.

[8] J.J. Koenderink. Optic flow. *Vision Research*, 26(1):161–179, 1986.

[9] J.J. Koenderink and A.J. van Doorn. Affine structure from motion. *J. Opt. Soc. America*, pages 377–385, 1991.

[10] B.W. Mel. *Connectionist Robot Motion Planning*. Academic Press, San Diego, 1990.

[11] J.L. Mundy and A.Zissermann editors. *Geometric Invariance in Computer Vision*. MIT Press, 1992.

[12] G.F. Poggio and T. Poggio. The analysis of stereopsis. *Annual review of neuroscience*, vol. 7, pages 379–412, 1984.

[13] L.G. Roberts. Machine perception of three-dimensional solids. In J.T. Tippet, editor, *Optical and Electro-optical Information Processing*. MIT Press, 1965.

[14] M. Rygol, S. Pollard, and C. Brown. A multiprocessor 3D vision system for pick-and-place. In *Proc. British Machine Vision Conf.*, BMVC90 pages 169–174, 1990.

[15] R.Y. Tsai. A versatile camera calibration technique for high-accuracy 3D machine vision metrology using off-the-shelf TV cameras and lenses In *IEEE Journal of Robotics and Automation*, RA-3(4) pages 323–344, 1987.

[16] R.Y. Tsai and R.K. Lenz. A new technique for fully autonomous and efficient 3D robotics hand-eye calibration. In *4th International Symposium on Robotics Research*, volume 4, pages 287–297, 1987.

[17] R.Y. Tsai and R.K. Lenz. Techniques for calibration of the scale factor and image center for high accuracy 3D machine vision metrology. *IEEE Trans. Pattern Analysis and Machine Intell.*, 10(5):713–720, 1988.

[18] S. Ullman. *The interpretation of visual motion*. MIT Press, Cambridge,USA, 1979.

[19] S.W. Wijesoma, D.F.H. Wolfe and R.J. Richards. Eye-to-hand coordination for vision-guided robot control applications. In *Int. J. Robotics Research*, 12(1) pages 65–78, 1993.

8 Control of Visually Guided Behaviors

Jana Košecká, Ruzena Bajcsy, and Max Mintz

8.1 Introduction

8.2 Motivation

This chapter aims at the systematic analysis and design of behaviors of artificial agents. Later we shall concentrate on a specific class of cooperative behaviors. What is a behavior? A general definition is a connection of perception to action. We shall first justify why are we considering behaviors of agents rather than just perception/action systems. The issue here is what is a primitive or elementary unit, i.e. a building block useful and desirable for designing an intelligent autonomous system.

In the traditional approach to building autonomous mobile agents the task is decomposed into separate functional units, such that the information flow is strictly horizontal (the output of one functional unit is the input for another) and the external feedback loop is closed through the environment. Functional units included sensing, mapping the sensory readings into the world representation, planning, task execution and motor control. Motivated by evolution and biology, R. Brooks, proposes a different decomposition of the system in his subsumption architecture [5]. In his approach, the primitives or modules are selected along the lines of behaviors rather than along the special processing functionalities. The primitives in Brooks' design are simple reactive behaviors, very much like those of insects: avoiding danger, attraction to light, and the like. The main idea is that higher-level behaviors subsume (hence the subsumption architecture) the lower-level behaviors, yet when for some reason the higher-level behavior is deactivated the system does not stop but continues to function with the lower or simpler behaviors. Behaviors are modeled as augmented finite state machines (AFSM) interacting with each other in a subsumption like manner. The criticism of Brook's proposal is that it is difficult to generalize and it remains questionable how this approach can scale up to more complicated agents and tasks.

In our work, we have accepted the principle that behavior is a primitive of the system. Further, we attempt to formalize this concept so that a coherent theory of complex behaviors evolves. By definition, an entity is a primitive either when it cannot be further subdivided or it is undesirable to do so. Hence, we shall have primitive behaviors that will connect simple perceptual events to appropriate actions (e.g. obstacle avoidance and tracking behaviors). Perceptual events in our case can arise from visual, contact or other noncontact sensors; actions involve a change of the physical state of the agent (while in motion), or augmenting the information state of participating processes (sending or receiving a message being an example of the latter). As a formalism for modeling behaviors we have selected the Supervisory Control Theory of Discrete Event System (DES) [15] introduced in Section 3. We have identified two open problems with this behavior-based approach:

- The perception to action connection is more complex when visual sensors are used.

- There is a lack of methodology for composing elementary behaviors while taking into account uncertainty introduced by the system and the environment.

8.2.1   Visual perception and action connection

The issue here is that visual perception is far more complex than any other modality; thus its connection to action is nontrivial. The need for integration of different visual modules, utilizing different cues at various levels, has been realized for quite some time. One type of integration stemming from efforts to obtain a 3D description of the world proposes how different vision modules should contribute to the description [3]. For the domain of mobile agents, where vision serves to accomplish a particular action-task, the purposive solution turns out to be appropriate[1]. The purposive approach considers vision as a collection of dedicated vision processes and focuses on extraction of qualitative information needed to accomplish the task. Even though this approach relates the task and the perceptual capabilities needed to accomplish it, the issue of control have thus far been overlooked. The early ties between perception and action were established in the area of active vision, primarily addressing control of intrinsic and extrinsic camera parameters [4, 7, 9].

In more complex tasks involving navigation control has been successfully accomplished using various behavior-based methods [5, 2]. The success of reactive behaviors was mostly due to the fact that the coupling between sensors and actuators was very tight and the sampling rate was very high. This was possible because the sensors used to demonstrate the approach were very simple (e.g. infrared, ultrasound); therefore, there was no need for selecting a specific data acquisition strategy. The combination of sensory readings and generation of commands to the actuators was fairly straightforward. This is not the case for visual sensory data. Due to the large

---

[1] Extensive discussion of this topic can be found in [16]

amount of information inherent in the visual data, we need to select acquisition and processing strategies to obtain the qualitative and quantitative information needed to control the actuators of a given system. One attempt to follow the 'classical behavioralism' can be found in [11], where the constraints of the environment (ground plane, color of the carpet, etc.) were used to extract some primitives from the images that were directly coupled to the actuators. The agent successfully moved around and was able to track arbitrary moving objects (visitors) upon request.

In the long run, we would like to address more complicated behaviors or tasks, such as occur in the cooperation between two or more mobile agents, following one another or following a given path while avoiding unexpected obstacles. Here, the qualitative information and choice of control strategy are more task dependent and are affected by some risk and cost function measures that affect the behavior of the agent. We will argue that the idea of having multiple parallel perception to action processes is feasible, but in the case of systems with multiple degrees of freedom and a larger variety of tasks, there is a need for supervisory process that will guarantee the constraints imposed by the task.

In this chapter we concentrate on the description of the architecture of a single mobile agent with multiple degrees of freedom whose behavior is modeled as a composition of multiple motor and perceptual processes running in parallel. We will demonstrate our approach by describing in detail the interactions between obstacle avoidance, tracking and path following behaviors. The main contribution of this chapter is a systematic framework for modeling behaviors of autonomous agents and their interactions. We propose how to combine different components of the system modeled by continuous control theory techniques or reactive behaviors[2] while taking into account asynchronous interactions with the environment or other system components. Specifically, in Section 3 we introduce the notion of a **hybrid system**,[3] outline its DES model, follow with an overview of Supervisory Control Theory of Discrete Event Systems [15]. The description of the experimental platform used to justify our approach and experimental results is given in Section 4. There we also present the DES models of motor and perceptual processes, address the control issues at the discrete event level and design a supervisor for the overall system. In Section 5 we conclude with a discussion of possible extensions of the system.

---

[2] Reactive behaviors can be viewed as "heuristic" control theory techniques where the control law is derived experimentally without having an explicit model of the plant.

[3] The definition of a hybrid system is slightly modified from the one introduced in [1]

8.3   Why DES?

Intelligent systems are typically too complex to be able to describe them by one behavior. Hence, the question we wish to answer is: what are the interactions and interconnections between multiple behaviors, either within a single agent or amongst several independent agents?

The extraction of appropriate qualitative information from sensory data allows us to develop some simple obstacle detection and avoidance and target detection and tracking strategies. Most of these control strategies control the actuators in the *continuous mode*, but this mode may change to *point-to-point* or *reactive control* as a response to external environmental stimuli or the task at hand. The behaviors activated in order to achieve a given task may have conflicting effects on the actuators of the system. In the case of navigation, one possible solution is to compute a "blend" (weighted average) of all preferable steering directions suggested by participating processes [8] and choose the resulting command by optimizing the blend. This approach works well when both the number of participating processes and the degrees of freedom of the system are small. As soon as the number of degrees of freedom increases or their coupling is task dependent this approach may no longer be suitable. Further, this solution requires the assumption that control is uniformly continuous (i.e. the control rule does not change over time). However, environmental stimuli are not necessarily continuous. As the stimuli change they may require different control for carrying out the action. This fact necessitates a consideration of discrete events and states.

In order to encapsulate both discrete and continuous aspects of system behavior and achieve its compact description we have chosen the theory of Discrete Event Systems developed by Ramadge and Wonham [15]. The DES formalism models systems in terms of finite state machines (FSM). In our domain the observations — the qualitative information extracted from sensory and encoder data — are represented in terms of **events**. With the **states** we associate particular observation and control strategies. Introducing a notion of **hybrid system** we propose a way to obtain a DES model of a system described by differential equations. The DES framework is suitable for investigating control-theoretic properties of the system such as **controllability** and **observability**, which can be conveniently predicted. Moreover, various visually guided behaviors can be combined in a modular and hierarchical fashion such that the resulting behavior will be *guaranteed* to be controllable.

In the following section we will introduce a more formal notion of a hybrid system and provide a framework for obtaining a DES model of such system.

8.4   Hybrid systems and the DES framework

The traditional definition of the hybrid system [1] is a combination of a
continuous plant and the discrete state system controller, which has finite
number of control inputs. The plant is typically modeled by difference or
differential equations. The controller and the plant communicate through an
interface where the plant translates the plant output $\mathbf{z}$ to event $\tilde{\mathbf{z}}$ (the output
signal is represented by a piecewise-continuous vector-valued variable). The
controller, in contrast to the model proposed by [1], outputs discretized
command signals r for the plant input (see Fig. 8.1). The controller is
essentially a finite state machine that has a particular control law associated
with each state, where the input and the state of the system are related in
the following way:

$$\dot{\mathbf{x}} = f(\mathbf{r}, \mathbf{x})$$

$$\mathbf{z} = g(\mathbf{x})$$

where $\mathbf{x} \in \Re^n$, $r \in \Re^m$ and $\mathbf{z} \in \Re^p$ are state, input and output vectors
respectively. $f : \Re^n \times \Re^m \to \Re^n$ and $g : \Re^n \to \Re^p$.

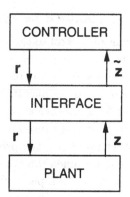

Figure 8.1
Model of a Hybrid System.

In our case the output variables are the same as state variables, i.e. $\mathbf{z} = \mathbf{x}$.
To model the plant and the controller as a discrete event system we must
identify a set of operating regions of the continuous state space and control
laws that are applicable within a region. Subsequently, these regions will
form equivalence classes of a mapping α:

$$\tilde{\mathbf{z}} = \alpha(\mathbf{x})$$

that maps the continuous observations to the set of events. An event is
generated by the interface (Fig. 8.1) when the plant state $\mathbf{x}$ crosses the

boundary between two regions of the state space.[4] This mapping abstracts
the behavior of the plant and the controller to the discrete event level. In
our case only the observations are discrete, while preserving the control
signal continuously. Later, we will refer to this hybrid model of plant and
controller as the DES plant.

Let Σ denote the set of events. Then event trajectories can be thought
of as strings over this fixed alphabet Σ. Let the subset $L \subseteq \Sigma^*$ represent
all event trajectories that are physically possible for the system and fully
characterize its behavior. In the case when **language** L is regular there
exists some finite automaton $\mathcal{G}$, such that L is generated or accepted by $\mathcal{G}$.

Let this automaton $\mathcal{G}$ be a 5-tuple

$$\mathcal{G} = (Q, \Sigma, \delta, q_0, Q_m)$$

where

Q - is the set of all possible states,

Σ - is the set of all possible events

δ - is the transition function $\delta : \Sigma \times Q \to Q$

q_0 - is the initial state,

Q_m - is the subset of states called marker states, $Q_m \subset Q$

In order to adjoin the means of control to the system at the discrete event
level, events are classified into two categories: **uncontrollable events** Σ_u
that can be observed but cannot be prevented from occurring (e.g. ob-
stacle_detected, target_detected), and **controllable events** Σ_c that can be
prevented from occurring or forced to occur (e.g. path_computed), where
$\Sigma = \Sigma_u \cup \Sigma_c$. For the types of events caused by asynchronous interaction
with the environment or other processes, the proper classification into one
of the two categories can be determined directly. Let us recall the type of
event that corresponds to a crossing of a particular region boundary in the
state space of the system, where each region of the state space has associated some control law. Such an event is said to be controllable when the
control law associated with the region of the state space is applicable to the
new state. This essentially means that if two neighboring regions have the
same control law associated with them (abstracted to the particular discrete
state of the DES model) the events corresponding to crossing boundaries
between them are controllable. This type of controllable event originates
and ends in the same state of the DES model of the plant. In the case
when the control laws are different, an event is said to be uncontrollable

---

[4] There is no general recipe for deriving the mapping α. Mapping reflects the granularity
of description we want to achieve at the discrete event level and depends on the task we
want to accomplish.

and causes a transition to a different state. Uncontrollable events correspond to the abrupt changes in the observations of the controller where in order to preserve continuity of the output we need to change the control law (i.e. the state of the DES model). This will be clearly demonstrated in the examples in the system description section. The controllable events will be denoted throughout the figures by with '$:c$'.

8.4.1   Supervisory control

A supervisor can be thought of as a state machine in which each state has associated some control pattern determining which controllable events are enabled and which are disabled. The existence of a supervisor for a given DES plant[5], i.e. the existence of an appropriate feedback control, is closely related to the concept of **controllability**. A system is said to be **controllable** if, given any initial state, there is a control law by which we can reach any desired state of the system. If the desired behavior of the plant is controllable the existence of a supervisor is guaranteed [14]. The control issues addressed by the DES framework differ from those in classical continuous control theory. The control at the discrete event level models the changes between different strategies triggered by abrupt observations (events) or driven by different tasks. The overall behavior of the system can be changed by changing the supervisor.

8.4.2   A risk-driven cost model for cooperative behavior

So far we have considered dynamic systems that have no uncertainty, and the criteria for discretization of events and the subsequent switching of their control strategies is rigid. In designing and operating purposeful realistic dynamic systems it is necessary to select control strategies that achieve the stated operational goals with proper regard to both efficiency and safety. The problem of control strategy selection can be modeled by a family of dynamic decision problems. These models must include adequate representations of the underlying uncertainties in the dynamic systems, sensors, and environments. The necessity to contend with such uncertainties is what makes this problem challenging.

There are two basic costs associated with the operation of these dynamic systems in the presence of uncertainty: (i) the nominal cost of a feasible solution based on its efficiency, e.g. time requirements and energy requirements; and (ii) the risk cost associated with failure modes, e.g., the cost of a collision between a mobile robot and an obstacle.

A proper system design must account for both types of costs since both

---

[5] The DES plant model is the model of the plant and the controller as introduced in the previous section.

efficiency and safety are important design criteria. Here, we do not necessarily require that the resulting control selection be globally optimal but merely that it suffice in that it meets the stated design objectives.

We consider two approaches to formulating these decision problems. In the first (P1), we set a priori a maximum allowable value for the risk cost and then minimize the nominal cost (or seek a near-minimum) subject to the risk-cost constraint. In the second (P2), we set a priori a maximum allowable value for the nominal cost and then minimize the risk cost (or seek a near-minimum) subject to the nominal-cost constraint. This class of constrained optimization problems is frequently encountered in other areas, for example, in two-class hypothesis testing, where the probability of a type I error is constrained to be no more than a given value, and the probability of a type II error is minimized subject to this constraint. The selection of P1 versus P2 depends on the values the user places on constraining each of the two costs.

8.5   System description

In this section we describe the experimental platform used to demonstrate our approach. The mobile agent in our experiments consists of a camera pan platform mounted on a TRC Labmate mobile base with two independent driving wheels. The axis of rotation of the camera pan platform (the camera in the center of Fig. 8.2 and the mobile base are identical. An additional stereo pair of cameras having a fixed tilt angle with respect to the horizontal plane is positioned on the sides of the mobile base (see Fig. 8.2). Each physical component of this system is characterized by its actuators, sensors and encoders. Adopting the control terminology, each such component or their composition form a plant — the subject of our control.

In order to achieve higher autonomy and accomplish more complicated tasks, the notion of the plant is extended to include additional sensing capabilities. We will concentrate on the visual sensing and its specifics, but our approach can be applied to other types of sensors as well. For the components at hand we propose a systematic way to partition the state space, choose the set of events and subsequently determine the DES model of the given component. The system is described in more detail below.

8.5.1   Pan platform and target tracking

The platform has a dual stepper motor system that operates in two possible movement modes: *continuous* motion, where the platform moves at a set velocity, or *step count* motion (point-to-point motion), where the motor uses the step count to move to a given position. The state of the system is

Figure 8.2
Mobile agent.

described at each instance of time by $(\omega, \dot{\omega})$, where ω is a current orientation of the pan platform while moving at a given velocity $\dot{\omega}$. The camera mounted on the pan platform is used for tracking a target. The choice of suitable features to track and thereby uniquely describe the motion of the target has been addressed by several researchers [6, 10]. For the time being we track an easily detectable "bright spot," where at each instance of time we can detect the centroid of the target (see Fig. 8.4). In our present implementation, the distance to the target is obtained artificially.

The pan platform and the camera form one module of the system that can operate in two different modes — *exploratory mode* (State 0 in Fig. 8.5) and *tracking mode* (State 1 in Fig. 8.5). The exploration strategy associated with the first mode pans the camera around until the target is detected. Once the target is detected the tracking mode is initiated to keep the target in the center of the field of view (FOV). The control strategy applied in this case is depicted in Fig. 8.3 where

$$\dot{\omega} = K_v.(\dot{x}_{ref} - \dot{x}_m) + K_p.(x_{ref} - x_m)$$

If the target is lost (the measurement x_m exceeds the bounds in order to be used for the control law in Fig. 8.3) we switch back to the *exploration mode*. The state space of the tracking behavior can be partitioned into three regions: when the target is outside the FOV, in the middle of the FOV (with some tolerance), and outside the center of the FOV (see Fig. 8.4).

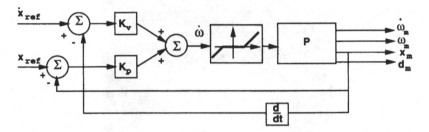

Figure 8.3
Pan control for target tracking: d_m is the distance from the target, $\dot{\omega}$ is the turning velocity of the pan platform, ω_m and $\dot{\omega}_m$ are the current position and velocity estimates of the pan platform, K_p and K_v are position and velocity gain factors and x_{ref} and $\dot{x}_{ref}$ are desired relative position and velocity, which are 0.

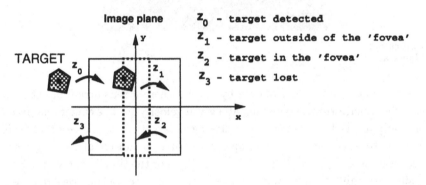

Figure 8.4
Tracking Events. Fovea is referred to the region in the center of the FOV throughout our examples.

The change of control strategies is then driven by events, which correspond to the crossings of the boundaries between different regions of the state space. Note also that the direction of boundary crossing is important, introducing therefore some temporal (dynamic) aspect to the DES description (e.g. event z_0 and z_3 are different). The finite state machine describing the behavior of this module is shown in Fig. 8.5. State 0 corresponds to the *exploration mode* and State 1 to the *tracking mode* with the control strategy in Fig. 8.3.

8.5.2 Mobile base

The mobile base has rotational and translational degrees of freedom and operates in two basic modes: *point-to-point* mode and *go* mode. The *point-to-point* mode uses a trapezoidal velocity control profile to perform turns and straight line moves of a specified distance. The *go* mode moves the Labmate

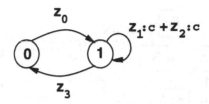

Figure 8.5
DES model for tracking. Controllable events are denoted by :c.

in a straight line at the current velocity setting. In this mode a continuous turn rate $\dot{\theta}$ can be superimposed on the existing forward velocity. The state of the system is fully determined by $(xpos, ypos, \theta, vel, tvel, mode)$, where $(xpos, ypos, \theta)$ is the current position and heading of the mobile base, and vel and $tvel$ are its current linear and turning velocity settings. In both the mobile base and pan platform the point-to-point mode uses position encoders (odometry) and corresponds to a simple *feedforward* control strategy, while motion in continuous mode corresponds to a *feedback* control strategy servoing on an external measurement determined by perceptual processes. One example of such servoing is the case of tracking behavior where the mobile base servos on the "neck of the system" (pan platform) ω_m and the distance of the target d_m. The description of different modes (control strategies) in which the platform can operate follows.

The goal of the control strategy while tracking a target is to align with the neck of the system and at the same time keep the distance to the target constant. This is accomplished by the following control rule:

$$
\dot{\theta} = K_v.(\dot{\omega}_{ref} - \dot{\omega}_m) + K_p.(\omega_{ref} - \omega_m)
$$
$$
v = K_d.(d_{ref} - d_m)
$$

where the block diagram is in Fig. 8.6.

Within this mode we can distinguish two types of events that correspond to the crossing of the boundary of the desired operating region (see Fig. 8.7).

So far the transitions between states have been caused by crossing the boundary of the state space of a particular module of the system. The control strategy, however, may also be changed by the external asynchronous events generated by other participating processes. In our case there is a human operator who is a part of the system and can at any instant direct the mobile base to follow a given path. This would correspond to an event that can bring the mobile base module to another mode — "path following". In State 0 (the DES model of this motor process is shown in Fig. 8.8) the mobile base is servoing on the neck of the system (the control diagram

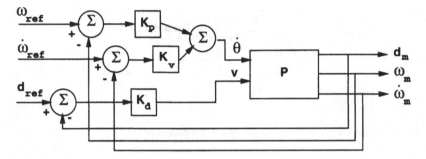

Figure 8.6
Servoing the neck: ω and $\dot{\omega}$ are the current position and velocity of the pan platform, v and $\dot{\theta}$ are the linear velocity and turning rate of the base and d_m is the current estimate of the target velocity.

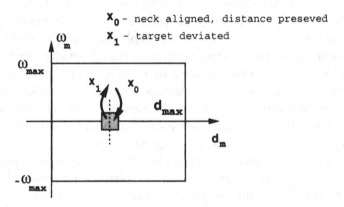

Figure 8.7
Events for neck servoing: ω_{max} is the maximal orientation of the pan platform with respect to the mobile base; d_{max} is the maximal distance of the target.

in Fig. 8.6) and in State 1 the base is following a given path. Event x_2 represents an asynchronous interrupt from the human operator (or the path planner) that the path has been computed. Event x_3 is an attempt for the deviation from an intermediate goal of the plan, and events x_4 and x_5 are asserted upon path completion or path interruption.

8.5.3 Obstacle detection and avoidance

The third module of our system is the obstacle avoidance module. Obstacles are detected through the difference between a pair of stereo images after applying the proper inverse perspective mapping proposed by [13]. Differences in perspective between left and right views are used to determine the presence of an obstacle and its approximate location. The subsequently

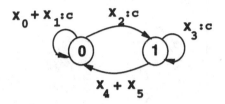

Figure 8.8
DES model of the robot process. Event x_2 is asserted when the path is computed, events x_4 and x_5 correspond to the path completion or interruption respectively, events x_0 and x_1 relate to the neck servoing control strategy and event x_3 is attempts to correct a deviation from a given path in case the goal is still ahead. Controllable events are denoted by :c.

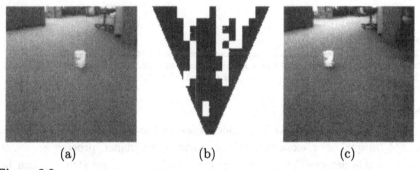

Figure 8.9
(a) Left Image; (b) Map of the free space in lower resolution (obstacles in white);
(c) Right Image.

computed map of the free space in the common field of view of both cameras [12] is used for obstacle avoidance maneuvers (see Fig. 8.9). We chose to accomplish the avoidance maneuver in a purely reactive way. Based on the *distance* to the obstacle and the *clearance* by which we want to avoid the closest obstacle (see Fig. 8.10) in the vehicle's path, we compute the appropriate turning rate $\dot{\theta}$ in the following way:

$$\gamma = atan\left(\frac{-clearance}{distance}\right) \tag{8.1}$$

$$\dot{\theta} = K_t \frac{\gamma.vel}{distance - safety} \tag{8.2}$$

The *safety* term parameterizes how close we want to come to the obstacle.

The initial control strategy of the obstacle avoidance process is to monitor the free space ahead (State 0). When an obstacle is encountered the module switches to State 1 and applies the reactive *steer away* control strategy until the path is again free (event d_3) or the obstacle becomes too close to steer safely away from (event d_2). Event partitioning for obstacle avoidance

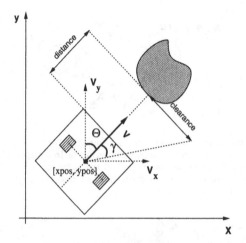

Figure 8.10
Steering away maneuver. $(x_{pos}, y_{pos}, \theta)$ is the current position and absolute
heading of the mobile base in the world coordinate system. γ is the angle by which
the heading needs to be changed in order to avoid the obstacle.

behavior is shown in Fig. 8.11.

The choice of particular DES models, as well as the semantics of events,
is not unique. For example, in the obstacle avoidance process an event
d_0 "obstacle detected" that triggers the avoidance control strategy can be
asserted when the obstacle is 3m, 4m, etc. away. One can then think about
the boundaries between different regions of the state space "sliding", where
the position of the boundary is driven by some risk and cost functions
determined by the task.

8.5.4   Composite behaviors

The activation of different behaviors is closely related to the task to be
accomplished. Composite behaviors are a combination of the elementary
behaviors described in the previous section. Elementary behaviors in our
case are controllable (in the discrete event sense) because either there is
only one possible controllable event that can take place in each state (e.g.
d_1 in the obstacle avoidance process, x_1 in robot process), or the event that
is suggested by the plant and enabled in a particular state is determined by
the task and control strategy for that state (e.g. event x_2 path_computed).
However, this might not be the case for the combination of more than one
behavior. Such situations can occur when the task of the agent is to follow
a given target. This task requires an activation of "motor" behavior P_1
(Fig. 8.8), target detection and tracking P_2 (Fig. 8.5), and obstacle detection
and avoidance behavior P_3 (Fig. 8.12). Parallel execution of these behaviors

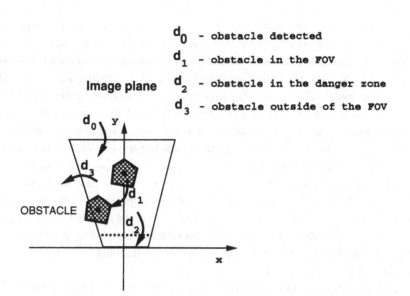

d_0 - obstacle detected

d_1 - obstacle in the FOV

d_2 - obstacle in the danger zone

d_3 - obstacle outside of the FOV

Figure 8.11
Events for obstacle avoidance. x and y coordinates span the common field of view of the stereo pair.

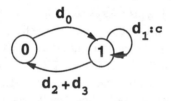

Figure 8.12
DES model of the obstacle avoidance process. Controllable events are denoted by :c.

may lead to possible conflicts. For example we can envision a situation when the tracking process is in State 1, following the target when the obstacle is detected. Suddenly the tracking behavior that assures that the mobile base is aligned with the camera pan platform has a goal conflicting with the obstacle avoidance process. To prevent this type of unwanted interaction some supervisory control is needed.

Parallel execution of the component behaviors is modeled in an interleaving fashion, so the resulting behavior represents all possible sequences of events. The composition of n behaviors $P_1, ..., P_n$ results in a new behavior, P, which is obtained as a **synchronous product** [14]

$$P = P_1 \| P_2 \| ... \| P_n$$

of the component behaviors. Constraints on the composite behavior of the system can be expressed in terms of another finite state machine (see Fig. 8.13. In our case the constraint is very simple — expressing the fact that once the obstacle is detected the obstacle avoidance behavior takes over the control of the mobile platform until the event d_3 "clear_path" or d_2 "obstacle too close" is asserted. By applying this constraint to the composite behavior of the system we can synthesize the resulting supervisor, guaranteeing satisfaction of the constraint. For this particular scenario with four component processes the resulting supervisor has 8 states and 48 transitions but only 4 of these states have associated the control pattern disabling the events controlling the mobile base (i.e. x_0, x_1, x_3) in case an obstacle is detected. The resulting behavior obtained by applying this discrete event control strategy is that in the absence of obstacles the mobile base is coupled with the pan platform; when avoiding obstacles this coupling is violated and the base steers away from the obstacle while the tracking system is still able to keep track of the target.

This selection process of different paths subject to a risk and cost function can also be described as *cooperation between processes*. Thus, *cooperative behavior* in this context denotes the establishment and management of relationships between perception-action pairs. Consider the following example of cooperation between a tracking process and an obstacle-avoidance process. We select the tracking process as the nominal process that is essentially risk free when obstacles are not present. We define the nominal cost to be the path-traversal time from the current position to the target. We define the risk cost to be $1/distance_{min}$, where $distance_{min}$ denotes the distance of closest approach to the obstacle. We assume that the endpoint p_f of the nominal path is obstacle free. Thus, the decision problem P1 becomes: Minimize the path-traversal time from the vehicle's present position to p_f, subject to the constraint that the vehicle maintains a minimum distance of closest approach $distance_0$ to the obstacle.

Similarly we have cooperation between obstacle avoidance and path following behavior, where upon observing the event 'obstacle detected' the obstacle avoidance behavior steers the mobile base away from the obstacle until the path ahead is again clear. When the system asserts a free-path, the vehicle switches behavior and follows a recomputed obstacle-free path that minimizes the traversal time to reach p_f from its current position.

In both previous examples of cooperative behaviors the switch between different behaviors occurs upon observing a certain event. (This switching process can be also driven by some additional measures, which are in essence going to effect the assertion of an event.) We may ask why do we need supervisory control in these seemingly simple cases? Why not use just a simple interrupt routine? We hope that the reader will see that this methodology

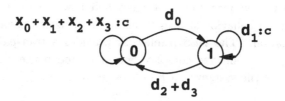

Figure 8.13
Composition constraint. Controllable events are denoted by :c.

allows us to scale up easily to situations that need some additional (possibly task dependent) constraints. For example, when the agent is following a path we want to prevent gaze shifts or when the path is interrupted we want to reinvoke a path planner.

8.6   Conclusions and future work

In this chapter we have posed the problem of systematic analysis and design of behaviors of artificial agents. To this end, a formalism of Discrete Event Systems has been selected as a suitable modeling tool for our purposes. In our investigations we have identified some primitive behaviors from which more complex behaviors can be composed, and have dealt with the issue of continuous control, as well as with discrete events and states. However, while the formalism of DES offers a systematic way of composing complex behaviors from primitive ones, additional constraints have to be added. The reason for this is that the visual sensors through which these agents perceive the world, and act upon it given the mobility task, add an extra degree of complexity to the system and necessitate the selection of an acquisition and processing strategy to obtain the qualitative and quantitative information needed to control the actuators of the system. The type of constraint we have imposed is a mutual exclusion constraint, which prevents the fact that different processes from generating commands to the same actuator.

In real situations the mobile agent has several ways to accomplish its task, *i.e.* it must be able to select its path. In order to make this decision systematic, we have introduced the concepts of efficiency and safety of the agent. The efficiency is measured by the nominal cost (in our case, the traversal time); the safety is measured by the risk cost (in our case, the inverse of the distance between the agent and an obstacle).

The main advantage of employing the DES framework is that it enables us to synthesize the supervisor based on the task, including the cost functions. This methodology affords scaling up in the task space and environments. Thus far we have theoretically and experimentally investigated the control of composite behaviors within one agent and now are in the process of extending this to behavior of two, three and four agents navigating while keeping formation. The DES framework provides a transparent schema for the designer to analyze complex behaviors and hence guarantee the controllability of the system that produces them.

Acknowledgements

Navy Grant N00014-92-J-1647, AFOSR Grant 88-0296; Army/DAAL 03-89-C-0031PRI; NSF Grants CISE/CDA 88-22719, IRI 89-06770, and ASC 91 0813; Du Pont Corporation.

References

[1] P. J. Antsaklis, M. D. Lemmon, and J. A. Stiver. Learning to be autonomous: Intelligent supervisory control. Technical Report ISIS-93-003, Department of Electrical Engineering,University of Notre Dame, Notre Dame, IN 45656, 1993.

[2] R. C. Arkin. Motor schema based navigation for a mobile robot. In *Proceedings Intl. Conf. on Robotics and Automation*, 1987.

[3] J. Aloimonos and D. Shulman. *Integration of Visual Modules*. Academic Press, Inc, 1989.

[4] D. H. Ballard. Animate vision. *Artificial Intelligence*, 48(1):57–86, February 1991.

[5] R. A. Brooks. A robust layered control system for a mobile robot. *IEEE Journal of Robotics and Automation*, RA - 2.(1):14 – 23, March 1986.

[6] B. Bhanu, P. Symosek, J. Ming, W. Burger, H. Nasrand, and J. Kim. Qualitative target motion detection and tracking. In *DARPA Image Understanding Workshop*, 1989.

[7] D. J. Coombs and C. M. Brown. Cooperative gaze holding in binocular vision. *IEEE Control Systems Magazine*, 11(4):24–33, June 1991.

[8] M. Fossa, E. Grosso, G. Sandini, M. Zapendouski, F.Ferrari, and M. Magrassi. A visually guided mobile robot acting in indoor environments. In *Proceedings of IEEE Workshop on Applications of Computer Vision*, Palm Springs, CA, 1992.

[9] C. Fennema, A. Hanson, E. Riseman, J.R. Beveridge, and R. Kumar. Model-directed mobile robot navigation. Technical Report COINS TR

90-42, University of Massachusetts, Computer and Information Science, June 1990.

[10] X. Hu and N. Ahuja. Model-based motion estimation from long monocular image sequences. *University of Illinois at Urbana-Champaign*, 1991.

[11] I. Horswill. A simple, cheap, and robust visual navigation system. In *Proceedings: From Animals to Animats II : Second International Conference on Simulation of Adaptive Behavior*. MIT Press 1993, 1993.

[12] J. Kosecka and R. Bajcsy. Cooperation of visually guided behaviors. In *Proceedings ICCV 93*, Berlin, Germany, May 1993.

[13] H.A. Mallot, H.H. Bulthoff, J.J. Little, and S. Bohrer. Inverse perspective mapping simplifies optical flow computation and obstacle detection. *Biological Cybernetics*, 64:177–185, 1991.

[14] P.J. Ramadge and W.M. Wonham. Supervisory control of a class of discrete event processes. *SIAM J. Contr. Optimization*, 25(1):206–230, 1987.

[15] P. J. Ramadge and W. M. Wonham. The control of discerete event systems. *Proceedings of the IEEE*, 77(1):81–97, January 1989.

[16] M. Tarr and M. Black et al. Panel discussion. In *Proceedings IJCAI'93*, pages 1991–1666, Chambery, France, August 1993. Morgan Kaufman.

9 Hybrid Problems Need Hybrid Solutions? Tracking and Controlling Toy Cars

John Hallam

9.1 Introduction

One of the major unsolved problems in modern robotics is that of designing an appropriate collection of interacting competences to achieve some task in a given environment. For a reasonably large class of problems, there is an obvious (though not necessarily correct) way to proceed, however, in that the problem can naturally be split into a symbolic component and a non-symbolic component. The splitting criterion is a mixture of naturalness and simplicity—things that can naturally and easily be dealt with at a symbolic reasoning level (search, plan construction, and the like) are *assumed* to be appropriately done that way; things that are difficult to deal with symbolically for reasons of representational or intellectual tractability (for example, much of the uncertainty present in a dynamic world) are dealt with outwith the symbolic level and are concealed from it.

This principle of division of labour between symbolic and non-symbolic levels in a hybrid system, though merely an assumption, is interesting since it potentially addresses a usefully large class of problems and, more significantly, it suggests ways of solving these problems that appear easier to design and engineer than approaches that eschew one or other component of the hybrid.

Note that the argument in favour of this approach is an engineering one— it appears to make sense both in terms of economy of design effort and of performance achieved. This is not to say that the approach represents a correct one in general to the design of autonomous robotic systems; merely that it is an interesting conjecture worth exploring a little further.

9.2 The SOMASS system

To illustrate this conjecture we consider an example of a successful system, SOMASS, that encapsulates this particular approach to system decomposition. Its domain of operation is assembly, and it is one of the few complete robotic assembly systems in the world—complete in the sense that its input consists of a description of the shapes of the pieces and final assembly and a set of approximate positions for the pieces in the robot's workspace, while its output is a finished object on the robot's worktable. The first implementation of the system used no sensors (apart from those used to control the robot's joint positions) and required only six man-months to design and build. The interested reader should consult [8, 10] for a full description of the system.

In order to permit the construction of a complete system—of critical importance in robotic work [11]—the problem of shape representation was simplified by restricting the assembly domain to the SOMA world [3, 4, 1]. SOMA parts comprise collections of cubes glued together face-to-face so that each part has at least one concavity. The simplest set of parts, the SOMA4 set, consists of seven parts that can be assembled into a large cube of side three basic units (*cubits*) in 240 different ways (ignoring symmetries) as well as into a rich variety of other shapes. The SOMA domain was chosen as a research model because it retains the crucial assembly property of shape-dependent part mating (unlike the popular 'blocks world', for example), while providing a rich world of things to build.

SOMASS is a hybrid system: it incorporates both conventional symbolic reasoning, and tacit knowledge in the form of skills or behaviours providing a non-trivial agent for the planner to instruct. The planner reasons about the disposition of SOMA parts in the finished assembly, determines whether there exists a sequence of intermediate partial assemblies that are gravitationally stable (the robot has only one hand) and permit the necessary finger clearances for successful construction, and sorts out any regrasping needed. The executive agent (and not the planner) knows the physical size of a cubit and the approximate initial disposition of the parts. It comprises a collection of hand-crafted behaviours that reliably acquire a part (given an approximate location for it), reorient it, and place it in a specified position and orientation. The planner plans *part* grasps and rotations; the executive agent fills in the necessary translations, and interprets part motions into *robot* motions at run time.

This separation of knowledge between planner and agent is not accidental. The planner is kept ignorant of all the detail of the uncertainty in the parts (being real parts made of wood and plastic in various sizes, they are not especially precise in side, shape or internal alignment) and even of the basic unit of size. This considerably simplifies its construction without depriving it of any of the information needed to play its part in the system. In particular, the planner never needs to reason about whether an assembly might fail because of part tolerance, physical characteristics such as friction or stiction and the like: the hand-crafted executive agent guarantees that failure will not occur for these reasons.

The interesting point about SOMASS, for our purposes, is that it exemplifies the somewhat unusual approach to the activity orchestration problem that is demanded by our conjecture. The conventional view in assembly robotics has tended to be that the planning component of the system should anticipate and deal with the various possible reasons for assembly failure; this has, in practice, proved computationally and intellectually intractable. SOMASS, on the other hand, takes the position that the planner should concentrate on those aspects of the problem that can tractably be expressed in symbolic form, leaving the execution agent to cope with the specifically manipulative difficulties of the assembly problem. Since the agent is hand-crafted, most of the consequences of the uncertainties in the parts and their manipulation are dealt with by the human programmer who has years of experience of object manipulation to call on when diagnosing and repairing failures in the tacit skills of the executive agent. The reliability of the complete system when faced with previously untested assemblies (about 2% failure in 45 hours of testing on some 4000 lines of previously untried automatically generated robot program [9]) and the relatively small amount of effort required to design and build it (about six man-months) can be attributed to the separation between planner and agent and the choice of the virtual assembly machine – part rather than robot motions – at the interface between them.

9.3   A real-time hybrid system

The SOMASS system demonstrates the plausibility of our conjecture that

a hybrid system, comprising symbolic and non-symbolic components interfaced by carefully chosen virtual machines, which appropriately conceal problem complexity from the symbolic levels, constitutes an efficient solution to a problem apparently involving both reasoning and manipulative skill.

However, though a considerable success, SOMASS addresses a somewhat restricted problem. Aside from the obvious simplification of shape representation which, as argued above, is an abstraction that retains the salient features of the target domain, SOMASS is also not a real-time system in the sense that it does not matter (except for the spectator's patience) if it takes a long time to run. If the agent must wait a long time for the planner the performance of the system is unimpressive, but not incorrect. It would therefore be interesting to discover whether the same architectural strategy can be applied to a problem in which time is of the essence. The hope is that the same property of easy disposition of knowledge, which makes the system engineering tractable, will also facilitate timely application of that knowledge in a real-time problem. The remainder of this chapter describes the start of an attempt to test our conjecture on such a problem.

The demonstrator problem chosen for this investigation is that of controlling a number of model cars in a model town. Models are used for reasons of safety, convenience and cost. However, the use of real models (radio-controlled $\frac{1}{24}$ scale Porsche 962C toy cars) lends reality to the problem—the models are quite complicated dynamical systems that must be controlled continuously in real time. Within the model world it is natural to describe the desired behaviour of the vehicles in terms of intentions, plans and goals (for example, a driver may start from home, need to visit the shops and the garage, and ought to be parked by 10:45 so that colleagues do not steal the parking space). Temporal constraints, sequencing and multiple agent interaction all arise in the problem domain and can be modelled in real life with the toy cars.

This is clearly a hybrid problem. A mixture of conventional symbolic reasoning and conventional control theoretic techniques constitute the most plausible path to an autonomous control system for the traffic scenaria contemplated here, so it fits the description of the space of problems to which our conjecture relates. Of course, the assumption that the plausible solution is the natural one, in the sense of requiring least engineering effort for performance achieved, is just that—an assumption. The (partial) testing of this assumption by the construction of a hybrid solution to the problem is the scientific motivation[1] of the exercise.

In this chapter, then, we describe the first steps in the construction of a complete integrated solution to this car control problem and present a motivational argument that the system can be completed in the spirit in which it was begun by describing the virtual interface between the lowest (continuous control) layer and the higher layers and suggesting the nature of the content and interfacing of those higher layers. While it is still early days for the CARS system the interested reader should be able to judge the realism of the implicit claim that such a real-time hybrid system can successfully be constructed.

9.4   System architecture

The scope of the CARS system, and thus the details of its architecture, is determined by the twin aims of testing the architectural conjecture of the previous section and of building, in a reasonable time, a system that is as easily extensible as possible. With these criteria in view, the system should provide facilities to

- observe the current position and velocity of each car;

---

[1] Two other motivations are: a successful car control system opens up all sorts of possibilities for investigating the interaction of independent agents with goals, plans and behaviour—in effect, a test-bed for distributed AI is realised; and it is fun, probably a significant motivation in most research!

- regulate the car's behaviour so that it follows its reference trajectory closely;

- detect potential collision situations or malfunctions in the low level control of the cars, and deal with them;

- construct and coordinate reference trajectories from individual statements of intention and constraint for the vehicles involved;

- modify the reference trajectories in the light of the behaviour of other vehicles;

- provide suitable command and display facilities for the system users.

The architecture of the CARS system is dictated in part by the functionality required and in part by the constraints imposed by the computational resources available. The system will have at least three computational layers: the topmost layer, where vehicle intention and constraint statements can be made and analysed; the bottom layer, where the continuous regulator drives the cars along the appropriate reference trajectories; and the intermediate layer, where routing, timing and coordination are managed. Computation of vehicle position and velocity is handled at the lowest level, since this information is required by the continuous regulator as well as by the vehicle behaviour interpretation processes at the intermediate and high levels.

The three architectural layers are shown schematically[2] in Fig. 9.1, the lowest level being at the top. The detail in the layers reflects the extent of their implementation—the lowest layer is almost complete; the design of the higher layers is rather more speculative.

The lowest architectural layer comprises a tracker, which is the principal source of information in the system of the actual behaviour of the cars, and the micro-controller that is responsible for generating commanded reference trajectories and regulating the paths of cars under computer control. There is one tracker instance and one micro-controller instance per vehicle. These components are implemented as a continuous (though sampled) system together with a little 'glue' in the form of a finite state machine to keep track of initialisation and errors.

The middle layer, handling the coordination and scheduling responsibilities of the system, is not yet implemented. However, the kind of techniques needed in constructing it are reasonably obvious. The lowest level implements a 'road-following' virtual machine that is almost finite state[3]; the

---

[2] The method of indicating the dataflow paths for both continuous and discrete data follows a convention suggested by Erik Sandewall during various conversations.

[3] Although the road network is a finite graph, each state of the 'finite' state machine is in fact a continuous manifold of possible trajectories because the car dynamics is continuously parameterisable.

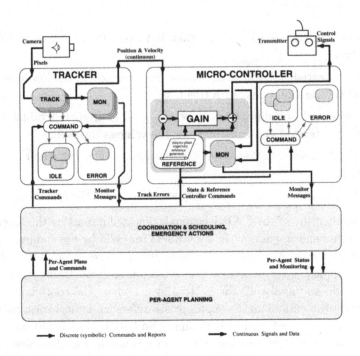

Figure 9.1
CARS System Computational Architecture.

next layer, therefore, can be built with a pure graph model of the road network and a simple discrete model of time, given a set of design rules for default parameterisation of actual trajectories.

The highest layer—planning car activity on the basis of stated intentions and constraints—has not yet been considered in detail. No doubt the relative wealth of literature on knowledge-based planning and on distributed multiple agent systems will afford useful insight into the organisation and implementation of this layer. The tightest constraints will, however, be imposed by whatever virtual machine it proves possible to synthesize as the upper interface of the coordination layer. Ideally, it would be nice to be able to hide almost all the details of the timings and coordination of the interactions between vehicles, but this may prove too difficult.

9.5   Components in the lowest level

In the following sections we shall consider in some detail the principal components of the lowest level of the CARS system—the tracker, and the micro-controller. The interested reader is referred to the CARS system design document [6] for further details and discussion of the design and implementation of these components.

9.5.1 First attempts at tracking the cars

The vision problem faced by the tracker is that of measuring in real time the position and velocity of several moving targets within the field of view. In most experiments, this will be the only source of information about actual vehicle behaviour in the system: it is impractical to instrument the model cars to return information about what they are actually doing, and the system may have to deal with cars not under computer control (important for testing and for system generality). The tracker is thus designed to be as knowledge free as possible. In particular, it makes no assumptions about the motion and dynamics of the targets being tracked other than that their velocity is locally constant (which corresponds to a limit on the *acceleration* of a successfully tracked target).

The camera is mounted on the ceiling about 2.5m above the workspace on the floor. It is roughly centred with respect to the workspace and is approximately aligned with the room axes. The lenses used in our system give a useable workspace of about 3.5m by 4.5m and a resolution of around a centimetre per pixel. The camera alignment is not set accurately.

Within this general context, two distinct implementations of the tracker component have been built. The original tracker, built by the author while in Linköping, is described first. The deficiencies of this implementation are discused, and a newer implementation built over the course of several student projects at Edinburgh is described.

9.5.1.1 The original tracker

The original tracker can track four independently moving targets with a cycle rate of $10Hz$ on a *SUN Microsystems 386i* workstation (chosen because its expansion bus is convenient for adding vision and digital-to-analogue conversion hardware) with a *Matrox PIP-1024B* framestore. The targets may move at up to about $1.5ms^{-1}$ and the tracker acceleration limit is around $1g$ in practice.

The tracking problem is compounded by two pragmatic considerations: the actual vision hardware available and the amount of processing power provided by the machine that hosts it. The following further assumptions were made by the original tracker system to make the problem fit the available resources.

1. Each target carries a bright light mounted roughly at its centre of mass. This greatly simplifies the tracking problem, since now points rather than cars are to be tracked. The light is sufficiently bright to saturate the camera so a high threshold can be used to eliminate distracting detail from the image.

2. The placement of the light at the car's centre of mass reduces the possibility of high acceleration of the tracked point—for example, during skid turns. We therefore assume that the tracked point moves with constant velocity between samples and further that the acceleration is locally small, *i.e.* the velocity does not change much over a short time period.

3. Since the target's velocity is known, we assume at each moment that the target will be found in a small window of the captured image whose position is predicted on the basis of the track to date. This allows us to circumvent the bandwidth limitations of the communication between vision hardware and the processor as well as limiting the amount of image that needs to be processed. Of course, it complicates track initiation.

Note that these assumptions are made for engineering rather than scientific reasons: an implementation with more specialist vision hardware and more powerful processors at its disposal could do things quite differently.

The target window used was 24 pixels (X) by 32 pixels (Y), the different dimensions being chosen with regard to the *CCIR* standard aspect ratio to give a square search area (about $20cm$ on a side) on the floor. It is possible for two cars to fit in this area simultaneously and confuse the tracking system—however, this eventuality is easily detected by monitoring the total pixel brightness within each window.

The tracker operates by recursively estimating the position and velocity of each target once in every sample time interval (in our case $100ms$). The estimates are derived from a measurement of the target position and are used to predict the target position at the next sample time. The position estimate for each target is obtained by computing the first moment of the brightness distribution within its associated image window using fixed point arithmetic with four bits after the point. Windows are assigned initial positions when targets are commended by the user to the tracker for attention, and their position is updated ready for each subsequent cycle using a prediction of the target's motion based on the simple dynamical model below (equation 9.1).

Once we have a position estimate for the target, we update a fixed gain α-β tracking filter, similar to those used in the early radar literature (*e.g.* [7]), to generate the new position and velocity estimates. The filter we used is derived like this. Assume that we have a sequence $\{x_k\}$ of position estimates that we believe are generated by a dynamic model

$$\mathbf{x}_k = \mathbf{x}_0 + k\mathbf{v}_0 \qquad (9.1)$$

in which $\mathbf{x}_0$ and $\mathbf{v}_0$ are constant parameters. $\mathbf{x}_0$ is the target initial position, while $\mathbf{v}_0$ is the constant velocity[4]. We now construct a least-squares esti-

---

[4] Although we shall call this a velocity it is, of course, the displacement that occurs in a single sampling interval.

mator for the two parameters given the sample sequence: we choose $\hat{\mathbf{x}}(0|n)$ and $\hat{\mathbf{v}}(0|n)$ to minimise the total error criterion, equation 9.2.

$$E = \sum_{k=1}^{k=n} \left(\mathbf{x}_k - \hat{\mathbf{x}}(0|n) - k\hat{\mathbf{v}}(0|n)\right)^2 \tag{9.2}$$

The estimates we are really interested in for tracking are $\hat{\mathbf{x}}(n+1|n)$ and $\hat{\mathbf{v}}(n|n)$, *i.e.* the predicted next position and the estimated current velocity, which, after a little straightforward manipulation, can be shown to be given by

$$\begin{pmatrix} \hat{\mathbf{x}}(n+1|n) \\ \hat{\mathbf{v}}(n|n) \end{pmatrix} = \begin{pmatrix} \hat{\mathbf{x}}(n|n-1)+\hat{\mathbf{v}}(n-1|n-1) \\ \hat{\mathbf{v}}(n-1|n-1) \end{pmatrix} + (\mathbf{x}_n - \hat{\mathbf{x}}(n|n-1)) \begin{pmatrix} \frac{4}{n} \\ \frac{6}{n(n+1)} \end{pmatrix}.$$
$$\tag{9.3}$$

We now take a suitable choice for n, and obtain the fixed gain α-β filter used in the tracker. A value of four for n gives good results in practice; one might expect that taking a larger n would improve the tracker's noise rejection, but the improvement would be at the expense of the acceleration limit since the value of n determines the window within which the fixed velocity assumption implicit in equation 9.1 is applied.

With the machinery of equation 9.3, tracking proceeds as follows. At each sample instant the target-specific windows of the current image are scanned and the estimates of target position within a window are computed. If the target is not in the window—the total pixel brightness vanishes—an error is signalled and tracking (and control) stops. Otherwise, the filter equation 9.3 is applied and the target-specific window positions are adjusted in an attempt to maintain the invariant that *the target is always at the centre of its window.*

The least-squares estimate of the target's current position $\hat{\mathbf{x}}(n|n)$ is constructed and transformed from pixel into world coordinates for use by the micro-controller. A third-order polynomial transformation from image coordinates to world coodinates was used for this purpose, the actual transformation being determined by imaging a light at points on a grid on the floor (marked out with string and marker pens to about $5mm$ accuracy) and taking a least-squares fit for the transformation matrix.

The micro-controller also requires an estimate of the target velocity for comparison with the reference trajectory the car should be following. Two methods of providing this were tested: the first, taking the tracker's estimate of target velocity and applying the Jacobean of the world coordinate transformation was found to give estimates of velocity that were too noisy to be effective for control; the second alternative, and the one finally adopted, was to construct an estimate of target velocity by filtering the sequence of position estimates using a low-pass differentiating filter. The low-pass action of the filter allowed suppression of high-frequency noise at the expense of some phase lag in the velocity estimates.

9.5.1.2   The edinburgh version of the tracker

In terms of its original design objectives, the tracker was a success: it was able to track four independently moving points of light at the full $10Hz$ rate with tracking noise in its position estimates of the order of $\pm 5mm$. However, in interaction with the controller it became obvious that a more sophisticated tracker was required. The problem (discussed rather more fully below) was essentially that the original tracker is unable to determine unambigously the car's direction of travel: although the velocity of the car is known, it might be travelling forward or backward and the controller needs to know which to determine the sign of steering corrections to apply.

New design criteria for the tracking component of the system were thus established:

- Each car would carry three lights, one at the centre of mass (as before) and two at the tail of the car. This allows unambiguous determination of the orientation of the vehicle.

- The tracker should run at full frame rate ($25Hz$) rather than the $10Hz$ of the original tracker, the latter figure being largely a consequence of bus-bandwidth constraints rather than choice. Using full frame rate was expected to improve the performance of the tracker (and also the controller) by improving the accuracy of the approximations built into them.

- The small window method of tracking is retained, though with adjustments made for the presence of two light sources on a single car. In particular we keep the constant velocity assumption used in the original tracker.

- A more sophisticated track initiation scheme in which the tracker itself identifies targets to track and assigns tracker windows to them is required.

A tracking system embodying these new assumptions has been built at Edinburgh over the course of a number of student projects[5] and is based on transputer hardware. The system runs on three transputers hosted by a standard PC-AT computer. Its organisation is shown in Fig. 9.2. The functions of the original tracker, which was constructed as a single process,

---

[5] Andrew Milligan built a basic three-light tracker in 1991; his contemporary, Martin Reilly, looked at tracking the image appearance of the car rather than using lights, though this strategy was eventually rejected since it required too much computation. Stephen McCoy revised and extended the three-light tracker in 1992. The work described here builds on McCoy's implementation and is being carried out by John Elliot.

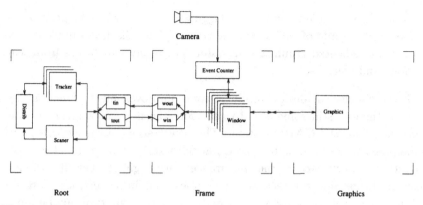

Figure 9.2
The Edinburgh Car Tracker

are now distributed amongst a collection of transputer processes allocated
to the three transputers:

- Image capture and analysis is handled by the dedicated frame grabber
  module (a Transtech TTG/F) which supports a memory-mapped frame
  store and digitisation unit. The event counter process controls synchroni-
  sation with the camera video signal while the window processes (one per
  light source being tracked) compute moments of their designated pieces
  of frame buffer. The windows used (16 by 24) are smaller than those of
  the original tracker to prevent both of the light sources on a single car
  appearing in a single window.

- The windows are positioned by corresponding tracker processes, running
  on the root transputer module (which also hosts standard input, output
  and file management facilities for the system) and report back moments
  to their controlling tracker.

- Each tracker implementes the constant velocity $\alpha - \beta$ tracking filter
  described above. In addition to controlling a pair of windows (one for
  the front light and one for the rear lights of a single car) the tracker
  process contains heuristics to deal with loss of target in one but not both
  windows.

- Between windows and tracker is the distributor process, which runs on
  the root module and deals with track initiation and loss of target. A
  scan window the full width of the frame buffer and 16 pixels high is
  swept across the buffer cyclically and any unaccounted-for lights found
  are assigned by the distributor to tracker processes for tracking; each
  tracker process validates data passed to it by the distributor and ignores
  data that is inconsistent with the state of the light source it is tracking.

- A graphics module provides a debugging display showing the positions of the windows and of each car being tracked. This display is implemented using a dedicated graphics transputer that receives messages from windows and trackers.

These changes in design result in some improvement in functionality, though there is still some way to go before the new tracker can be coupled back into the CARS system. The new tracker can track three cars simultaneously (*i.e.* six light sources) at full frame rate and simultaneously monitor the workspace for the appearance of new light sources. If a window loses its target and the recapture heuristics built into the tracker process fail to relocate the window appropriately, the target will typically be found by the scanning window in about 1.3 seconds.

9.5.2 The continuous controller

The second major component of the lowest level of the architecture is the continuous controller. This takes specifications of vehicle trajectories and attempts to ensure in real time that the model cars follow the desired trajectories. It comprises a continuous regulator and a small amount of 'glue' for connecting the regulator, tracker and command interface. Here, we shall just describe the regulator in detail, and comment briefly on the other aspects of the controller.

(Note that the controller described in this section is the one that complements the original tracker. A new controller to suit the newer tracker is under construction.)

In designing the regulator there are two main concerns: how are the reference trajectories[6] for the vehicles to be defined; and what regulator structure is appropriate for the job of keeping the actual vehicle close to the reference?

9.5.2.1 Parameterising the trajectories

The answers to both the questions above are strongly influenced by the way we parameterise the continuous behaviour of the cars. To some extent the parameterisation is dictated by the global Cartesian geometry imposed by the camera; however, a reasonable compromise between this imposed reference frame and the "natural" parameterisation of the system is to use the Cartesian position and the polar velocity as the representation of the

---

[6] We tend to use the term "trajectory" to mean the relationship between a vehicle's position in space and the time elapsed since the beginning of the motion; we will use the term "path" to refer to the geometric locus of points occupied by the car during its travel.

vehicle state. In fact, we need only the polar velocity since the position, in any reference frame, is just the integral over time of the former. We therefore use a simple dynamical system[7] whose state comprises the current position (x, y) of the car in world (floor) coordinates, its heading ϕ, and its speed v, the latter pair of values being the polar velocity.

The car is controlled by two inputs – accelerator/brake and steering. These are modelled by a speed demand input β and a rate-of-turn demand input α. In terms of the geometry α corresponds directly to the curvature of the path followed by the car and is proportional to the front wheel steering angle. Since this control is servoed in the model cars we assume that steering takes place instantaneously compared to the dominant time constant of the vehicle.

Speed demand, on the other hand, is assumed to be the input to a first-order lag system whose output is car speed. This is physically plausible if the speed demand control is actually interpreted by the car as a motor current signal, and in any case appears to be an adequate model of the car's behaviour. The time constant of the lag, while not known precisely, is approximately $2.5s$; it will be denoted here by τ.

With the foregoing model assumptions we can write the continuous time plant dynamics of the toy car as equation 9.4.

$$\frac{d}{dt} \begin{pmatrix} x \\ y \\ \phi \\ v \end{pmatrix} = \begin{pmatrix} v \cos \phi \\ v \sin \phi \\ v\alpha \\ (\beta - v)/\tau \end{pmatrix} \tag{9.4}$$

For the purpose of both representation and control we need to integrate these equations: we must be able to parameterise the reference trajectories for the vehicle in an economical and natural way; and we need to know the relationship between control signals and the underlying path geometry in order to provide reference information to the regulator. To facilitate the integration we assume that *the curvature demand signal is piecewise constant*, changing only at the discrete time sample points at which the regulator is computed. This assumption implies that the paths followed by the cars consist of straight lines and circular arcs.

We can now integrate the continuous plant model over an inter-sample interval to give the discrete plant model of equation 9.5. The equation defines

---

[7] This parameterisation was also used by Johan Kullstam who (in a student project at ISY, Linköping University) built a system able to track and control a single car given a complete predefined trajectory.

the dynamics of a circular arc trajectory: the linear trajectory dynamics
can be obtained by allowing the curvature α to tend to zero.

$$
\begin{pmatrix} x_{k+1} \\ y_{k+1} \\ \phi_{k+1} \\ v_{k+1} \end{pmatrix} = \begin{pmatrix} x_k - \frac{1}{\alpha_k} \sin \phi_k + \frac{1}{\alpha_k} \sin (\phi_k + \alpha_k s_k) \\ y_k + \frac{1}{\alpha_k} \cos \phi_k - \frac{1}{\alpha_k} \cos (\phi_k + \alpha_k s_k) \\ \phi_k + \alpha_k s_k \\ \tau_1 v + (1 - \tau_1) \beta_k \end{pmatrix} \tag{9.5}
$$

In the above,

$$
\tau_1 = e^{-\frac{\Delta t}{\tau}}
$$

and

$$
s_k = \beta_k \Delta t + \tau(1 - \tau_1)(v_k - \beta_k)
$$

with Δt being the inter-sample interval. The mean velocity during the
sampling interval[8] is given by $s_k/\Delta t$.

The discrete plant model, equation 9.5, comprises three qualitatively different sorts of parameter given the assumption of piecewise constant α.
These are: the geometric parameters, which determine the path followed by
the car (the curvature α and the initial position and orientation of the vehicle); the dynamic parameters, which determine the timing of the motion as
the car follows the path (the initial speed and the speed demand values β);
and the model parameters of the plant dynamics (in this case, just τ). We
can use this distinction to simplify the specification of reference trajectories
by separating the path geometry, which is a property of the underlying road
segment, from the trajectory dynamics.

This leaves the problem of specifying the trajectory dynamics. To do this,
we define intrinsic coordinates that depend on the geometry of a segment
– the coordinates used are arc length s and transverse displacement d with
respect to the central axis of the segment. For an arc, these coordinates are
curvilinear. The trajectory timing is then expressed in terms of these intrinsic coordinates by means of a simple constant acceleration point dynamic
process defined as follows.

Let $\mathbf{p}(t)$ represent the current position of the vehicle in the intrinsic
coordinate system (*i.e.* $[s, d]$), $\dot{\mathbf{p}}(t)$ its intrinsic velocity, and $\ddot{\mathbf{p}}(t)$ the intrinsic acceleration. The intrinsic position and velocity of the car at some
time t is determined by the initial quantities $\mathbf{p}_0$, $\dot{\mathbf{p}}_0$ and $\ddot{\mathbf{p}}_0$ by the following
equations

---

[8] Note that we have assumed, for the integration, that β is also piecewise constant. This
is not necessary as long as we define s_k to be the true arc distance travelled by the vehicle
during an inter-sample interval, *i.e.* the integral of the speed with respect to time, and
the velocity component of the plant equation changes in accordance with β.

$$\ddot{\mathbf{p}}(t) = \ddot{\mathbf{p}}_0$$
$$\dot{\mathbf{p}}(t) = \dot{\mathbf{p}}_0 + \ddot{\mathbf{p}}_0 t \qquad (9.6)$$
$$\mathbf{p}(t) = \mathbf{p}_0 + \dot{\mathbf{p}}_0 t + \frac{1}{2}\ddot{\mathbf{p}}_0 t^2.$$

These *intrinsic trajectory dynamics* are transformed from the curvilinear intrinsic coordinates into Cartesian world coordinates, and the appropriate control demands α and β are computed, when the reference trajectory is being generated for the regulator. Each reference trajectory (or piece thereof) is thus commanded in terms of the geometry of a road segment (*i.e.* its initial point, orientation and curvature) and the six initial parameters of the intrinsic dynamics.

9.5.2.2   Regulating the cars' behaviour

The objective of the regulator is to ensure that the car follows a certain trajectory in state space. To ease the notational burden in this section we shall represent the car state by $\mathbf{z}$ and rewrite equation 9.4 as

$$\frac{d}{dt}\mathbf{z} = f(\mathbf{z}, \mathbf{u}) \qquad (9.7)$$

where $\mathbf{u}$ is the vector of control variables $[\alpha \ \beta]^T$ and $f(\cdot, \cdot)$ represents the system dynamics. The desired trajectory of the car, $\{\bar{\mathbf{z}}(t)|t \in [t_i, t_f]\}$ should of course be a solution of equation 9.7 for some initial state $\bar{\mathbf{z}}_i$ and control sequence $\{\bar{\mathbf{u}}(t)|t \in [t_i, t_f]\}$. As we have seen, such trajectories can be parameterised using the integrated vehicle dynamics when we make the simplifying assumption of piecewise constant control $\bar{\mathbf{u}}$.

The regulator is realised through linearisation about some nominal trajectory $\bar{\mathbf{z}}$ and the use of a feedback control law applied to the difference system. If we define $\tilde{\mathbf{z}}$ to be the error between actual car state and the reference signal, we can write

$$\frac{d}{dt}\tilde{\mathbf{z}} = \frac{d}{dt}(\mathbf{z} - \bar{\mathbf{z}}) \qquad (9.8)$$
$$= f(\mathbf{z}, \mathbf{u}) - f(\bar{\mathbf{z}}, \bar{\mathbf{u}})$$
$$= f_z(\bar{\mathbf{z}}, \bar{\mathbf{u}})(\mathbf{z} - \bar{\mathbf{z}}) + f_u(\bar{\mathbf{z}}, \bar{\mathbf{u}})(\mathbf{u} - \bar{\mathbf{u}}) + \cdots$$
$$\approx A(\bar{\mathbf{z}}, \bar{\mathbf{u}})\tilde{\mathbf{z}} + B(\bar{\mathbf{z}}, \bar{\mathbf{u}})\tilde{\mathbf{u}} \qquad (9.9)$$

where $\tilde{\mathbf{u}}$ is the difference between actual control and reference (nominal) control and $A = f_z$ and $B = f_u$ are the partial derivatives of f by its first and second arguments respectively. We have assumed that the nominal trajectory is a solution of the plant dynamic equation. This is a time-varying linear system and our objective is to keep $\|\tilde{\mathbf{z}}\|$ small.

The approach taken in this design[9] is to construct a regulator gain $K(\bar{z}, \bar{u})$ so that the eigenvalues of $A(\bar{z}, \bar{u}) - B(\bar{z}, \bar{u})K(\bar{z}, \bar{u})$ are appropriate for the control task. Our goal is to construct an analytic expression for the gain in terms of the reference state and control values. The resulting time-varying feedback regulator will be easily computable and depend only on the parametrised reference trajectory chosen for the vehicle.

The feedback gain matrix $K(\bar{z}, \bar{u})$ has eight components[10], while the characteristic polynomial of $A - BK$ is of fourth order; eigenvalue placement will yield only four constraints on K. This gives some degrees of freedom for computational economy.

To determine K we first transform the coordinate system to a block controllability form by setting $\tilde{z} = Tw$ for a suitable choice of T. We can then rewrite equation 9.9 in the new coordinates as

$$\frac{d}{dt}w = T^{-1}ATw + T^{-1}B\tilde{u} \tag{9.10}$$

and, for a suitable choice of T, we have the following.

$$T^{-1}AT = \begin{bmatrix} 0 & 0 & 0 & 0 \\ 1 & 0 & 0 & \frac{\alpha}{\tau v} \\ 0 & 0 & 0 & 0 \\ 0 & 0 & 1 & -\frac{1}{\tau} \end{bmatrix}$$

$$T^{-1}B = \begin{bmatrix} 1 & 0 \\ 0 & 0 \\ 0 & 1 \\ 0 & 0 \end{bmatrix}$$

Now, if we choose the gain matrix in the new coordinates to be of the form

$$KT = \begin{bmatrix} \bar{k}_{11} & \bar{k}_{12} & 0 & 0 \\ 0 & 0 & \bar{k}_{23} & \bar{k}_{24} \end{bmatrix} \tag{9.11}$$

then we can compute the characteristic polynomial of the transformed regulator (which is of course the same as that of the original) as

$$\Xi_{A-BK}(s) = \left(s^2 + \bar{k}_{11}s + \bar{k}_{12}\right)\left(s^2 + (\frac{1}{\tau} + \bar{k}_{23})s + (\frac{\bar{k}_{23}}{\tau} + \bar{k}_{24})\right) \tag{9.12}$$

and we can now choose the $\bar{k}$ values to place the eigenvalues as we wish. The implemented controller is then obtained by transforming back to the original coordinate system.

---

[9] The *design* of the regulator was done by Råger Germundsson of ISY, Linköping University. It was implemented by the author.

[10] We suppress the state and control arguments from now on.

The choice of eigenvalue placement is a matter of heuristics. The eigenvalues should have negative real part and be at a distance from the origin that is both greater than $\frac{1}{\tau}$ (so that the regulator is faster than the car dynamics) and less than $\frac{\pi}{T_s}$ (*i.e.* the regulator should not act faster than we are sampling). These constraints, with our estimated system time constant of $2.5s$ and the $100ms$ sampling time, give $d \in (0.4, 10)Hz$. We chose $d = 5Hz$ for this regulator, with the eigenvalues λ on the lines $\mathcal{R}(\lambda) = \pm\mathcal{I}(\lambda)$, since this placement gives good results in simulation.

9.5.2.3   Discussion of the regulator

The regulator was tested extensively in simulation with a variety of trajectories and with both perfect and noisy position and velocity data. In all of these tests it performed adequately. However, in implementing the real system there were certain unforseen problems.

The most significant problem arose because, it turns out, the controller needs to know which way the car is driving (*i.e.* forwards or in reverse). This is obvious with hindsight: as any driver knows, the direction of the control actions taken depends on whether one is driving forward or reversing. The problem turns up most seriously when the regulator is commanded to keep the car stationary—an important special case not tested at simulation time!

The root problem in our system is that it is impossible, given a single light for tracking, to tell the orientation of a stationary target or the unambiguous velocity of a moving car. Errors in the velocity sense result in the regulator applying positive rather than negative feedback, and losing control of the car either completely or for a short period.

The solution to the problem is complicated, and comprises two parts.

- First, during initialisation, the controller probes the target, commanding it to move forward. When the car has moved about $10cm$ the controller commands it to stop. This both tests the existence of the control loop through the model car and the tracker (it's always possible to find good reasons for doing something, in hindsight) and allows the controller to calculate the orientation and sense of the car (because it has moved).

- Second, the controller pays attention to the estimates of the car velocity delivered by the tracker. When the car is moving 'fast' (more than about $5cms^{-1}$) these reliably indicate the direction of motion; the sense of motion is inferred by checking to see whether the car's motion has recently reversed and whether it has recently been commanded to do so. If the car is moving slowly, the tracker heading is not so reliable, and the motion sense deduction is based both on commanded motion and on the sense and direction of motion last time the car moved 'fast', if this is sufficiently recent to be credible.

This solution to the problem is fairly complex, and illustrates a point made at greater length in [5]: there are, in robotics, various different ways of tackling the same problem, and it is difficult to forsee the consequences of any particular approach. In this case, the hardware constraints necessitated single light tracking and forced a software solution to the problem thus raised; in practice the simplest solution is to attach three lights to each car and infer the full motion from their tracks as the new tracker implementation aims to do.

A second problem also arose in testing the regulator on the real cars. The transformation above allowing us to construct a time-varying linear system incorporates the fact that the rate of turning of the car is the product of its forward speed and the curvature demand. The effect of the linearisation, not obvious at the time, is to require the regulated car to have a steering time-constant *independent of speed*—this is what the choice of a fixed steering regulator eigenvalue implies. Unfortunately, this makes the curvature demand for a fixed size angular error rise as the speed of the car falls; the practical effect is that when the regulator is attempting to maintain the car stationary the front wheels flick from side to side at random driven by the fluctuations in the position estimates from the tracker.

The third point to make here is that the regulator does not stand alone: it must interface with the tracker and with the processes that command reference trajectories. It is thus embedded in a finite state machine incorporating states for active and suspended driving, probing activity, and an error state to catch tracking or control failures. The full details of the states can be found in [6].

The interface between the intermediate level and the low level takes the form of commands to execute reference trajectory segments—each command consists of a geometry specification (the name of the road segment), the initial parameters of the intrinsic dynamics, a start time and a life time for the segment. Each such segment denotes a *micro-behaviour*, so called because it is the smallest unit in the system worth a symbolic description, and the controller for each car supports a small sequential collection of micro-behaviours, called the *micro-plan*, which describe the next few segments of reference trajectory.

The key point about this interface, for our purposes, is that it allows a simple conceptual model of the low level of the system to be defined: the micro-controller (which controls the execution of the micro-plan) appears to be a transition process operating on the graph of road segments, *i.e.* it is a finite state automaton. Of course, the process is not really *finite* state, since the intrinsic dynamics is parameterised by real numbers (making each 'state' a manifold of space-time trajectories); this is one of the interesting theoretical lines of development opened by the CARS system. However, it could be made into a finite state automaton by specifying suitable 'design rules' to choose intrinsic dynamics on the basis of segment geometry and, in any case, the finite state machine *abstraction* is a reasonable one.

This brings us full circle, to consider again the architectural conjecture presented above. The CARS lowest level, embodying the non-symbolic continuously-regulated driving skills of the system, has been made to appear in familiar, straightforward, symbolic terms in a way that permits information hiding. In view of the naturalness of the construction so far, and the familiarity of the interface, it is plausible that the remainder of the system can also be constructed.

9.6 Conclusion

A conjecture about the appropriate architecture for systems that address hybrid problems —those which appear to fall naturally into both symbolic and non-symbolic components—has been proposed and discussed with reference to the Edinburgh SOMASS system and to the problem of controlling a collection of toy cars in real time. The success of the CARS system to date, despite its only being a partial system, suggests strongly that the complete hybrid system can in fact be constructed and the real-time control of a number of independent cars achieved. Furthermore, the economy of effort required to design and build the lowest level suggests that the conjecture is worth further study. Future work will show how these tentative conclusions fare.

A second point emerging from the study is that, as others have found [2], it is not easy to predict in advance where the difficulties will occur in building a robotic system. In this case, the simplifying assumption of using a single light—necessary to make the real-time tracking of the cars possible with the original hardware—causes considerable complication in the interfacing of the regulator. The natural solution for this problem, with hindsight, is a hardware one: cars should carry three lights, and more powerful vision hardware should be used. The newer version of the tracker sketched here incorporates this hardware solution.

Acknowledgements

The bulk of the work done in constructing the original CARS system was done while the author was a guest researcher at the University of Linköping in Sweden, visiting Lennart Ljung and Mille Millnert in Institutionen för Systemteknik there. Thanks go to them for encouragement, assistance, and fruitful discussions of the project; thanks also go to the members of the PROMETHEUS group in Institutionen för Datavetenskap, especially to Erik Sandewall, for stimulating the thoughts that led to this chapter.

The SOMASS project, directed by Chris Malcolm in the Department of Artificial Intelligence at the University of Edinburgh, was funded by the ACME Directorate of the SERC under grant no. GR/E/6807.5.

The newer implementation of the tracker is built on the results of final year undergraduate project work by Andrew Milligan and Martin Reilly, and Masters project work by Stephen McCoy; the design reported here is being tested in project work by John Elliot.

Computing and other facilities were provided by the Universities of Edinburgh and Linköping; the author was funded during his visit to Sweden by a Western European Fellowship from the Royal Society of Great Britain (through Kungliga Vetenskapsakadamien in Sweden), by the University of Linköping, and by Försvarets Forskningsanstalt 3 in Linköping.

References

[1] G. S. Carson. Soma cubes. *Mathematics Teacher*, 583–592, November 1973.

[2] A. M. Flynn and R. A. Brooks. Battling reality. MIT AI Lab. AI Memo 1148, October 1989.

[3] M. Gardner. *More Mathematical Puzzles and Diversions*. Penguin, 1966 edition, 1961.

[4] M. Gardner. Pleasurable problems with polycubes. *Scientific American*, September 1972.

[5] J. Hallam. *Autonomous Robots: from Dream to Reality*. Research Report 526, Department of Artificial Intelligence, University of Edinburgh, April 1991.

[6] J. Hallam. CARS: an experiment in autonomous real-time control. 1991. Research Report LiTH-ISY-I-1236, Institutionen för Systemteknik, University of Linköping, 1991.

[7] J. E. Holmes. The development of algorithms for the formation and updating of tracks. In *Proceedings of RADAR-77 IEE International Conference*, pages 81–85, London, 1977.

[8] C. Malcolm. *Planning and Performing the Robotic Assembly of Soma Cube Constructions*. Master's thesis, University of Edinburgh, 1987. (Shared Rank Xerox Best Dissertation Prize).

[9] C. Malcolm and T. Smithers. Programming assembly robots in terms of task achieving behavioural modules: first experimental results. In *International Advanced Robotics Programme: Second Workshop on Manipulators, Sensors, and Steps towards Mobility*, pages 15.1–15.16, Manchester, UK, October 1988.

[10] C. Malcolm and T. Smithers. Symbol grounding via a hybrid architecture in an autonomous assembly system. *Robotics and Autonomous Systems*, 6:123–144, 1990.

[11] C. Malcolm, T. Smithers, and J. Hallam. An emerging paradigm in robot architecture. In T. Kanade, F.C.O. Groen, and L.O. Hertzberger, editors, *Intelligent Autonomous Systems 2*, Stichting International Conference of Intelligent Autonomous Systems, Amsterdam, 1989.

Contributors

R. Bajcsy
GRASP Laboratory, Department of Computer and Information Science, University of Pennsylvania, 3401 Walnut Street, Philadelphia, PA 19104, USA.

A. Blake
Robotics Research Group, Department of Engineering Science, University of Oxford, Parks Road, Oxford OX1 3PJ, UK.

K. Bradshaw
Robotics Research Group, Department of Engineering Science, University of Oxford, Parks Road, Oxford OX1 3PJ, UK.

M. Brady
Robotics Research Group, Department of Engineering Science, University of Oxford, Parks Road, Oxford OX1 3PJ, UK.

C. Brown
Computer Science Department, University of Rochester, Rochester, NY 14727-0226 USA.

R. Cipolla
Department of Engineering, University of Cambridge, Cambridge CB2 1PZ, UK.

I. Craw
Department of Mathematical Sciences, University of Aberdeen, Aberdeen AB9 2TY, Scotland.

R. Curwen
Robotics Research Group, Department of Engineering Science, University of Oxford, Parks Road, Oxford OX1 3PJ, UK.

S. Fairley
Robotics Research Group, Department of Engineering Science, University of Oxford, Parks Road, Oxford OX1 3PJ, UK.

J. Hallam
Department of Artificial Intelligence, University of Edinburgh, 5 Forrest Hill, Edinburgh EH1 2QL, Scotland.

N. Hollinghurst
Department of Engineering, University of Cambridge, Cambridge CB2 1PZ, UK.

J. Košecká
GRASP Laboratory, Department of Computer and Information Science, University of Pennsylvania, 3401 Walnut Street, Philadelphia, PA 19104, USA.

P. McLauchlan
Robotics Research Group, Department of Engineering Science, University of Oxford, Parks Road, Oxford OX1 3PJ, UK.

M. Mintz
GRASP Laboratory, Department of Computer and Information Science, University of Pennsylvania, 3401 Walnut Street, Philadelphia, PA 19104, USA.

D. Murray
Robotics Research Group, Department of Engineering Science, University of Oxford, Parks Road, Oxford OX1 3PJ, UK.

I. Reid
Robotics Research Group, Department of Engineering Science, University of Oxford, Parks Road, Oxford OX1 3PJ, UK.

L. Shapiro
Robotics Research Group, Department of Engineering Science, University of Oxford, Parks Road, Oxford OX1 3PJ, UK.

P. Sharkey
Department of Cybernetics, University of Reading, Reading RG6 2AZ, UK.

G. Sullivan
Intelligent Systems Group, Department of Computer Science, University of Reading, Reading RG6 2AZ, UK.

R. Szeliski
Digital Equipment Corporation, Cambridge Research Lab, One Kendall Square, Bldg. 700, Cambridge, MA 02139 USA.

D. Terzopoulos
Canadian Institute for Advanced Research and Department of Computer Science, University of Toronto, 10 King's College Road, Toronto, ON, M5S 1A4, Canada.

D. Tock
Department of Mathematical Sciences, University of Aberdeen, Aberdeen AB9 2TY, Scotland.

R. Weiss
Computer and Information Science Department, University of Massachusetts at Amherst, Amherst, MA 01003, USA.

A. Zisserman
Robotics Research Group, Department of Engineering Science, University of Oxford, Parks Road, Oxford OX1 3PJ, UK.

Printed in the United States
By Bookmasters